Critical Concepts™ Series . . .

Walleye
Fundamentals

Foundations For Sustained Fishing Success

D0899711

Critical Concepts™ Series . . .

Walleye Fundamentals

Foundations For Sustained Fishing Success

Expert Advice from North America's
Leading Authority on Freshwater Fishing

THE IN-FISHERMAN STAFF

In·Fisherman

Critical Concepts™ Series . . .
Walleye Fundamentals—Foundations For Sustained Fishing Success

Publisher *Stuart Legaard*
Editor In Chief *Doug Stange*
Editors *Dave Csanda, Steve Quinn, Matt Straw, Steve Hoffman*
Contributing Staff Members *Dan Sura, Jim Lindner, Joann Phipps*
Director *Al Lindner*
Publisher Emeritus *Ron Lindner*
Project Coordinator *Scott Lawrence*
Copy Editor *J.Z. Grover*
Cover *Nelson Graphic Design*
Layout & Design *Scott Lawrence with Jan Finger and Jim Pfaff*

Acknowledgments

Phil Bettoli *Sauger discussion, Chapter 11*
Bruce M. Carlson *Ciscoe discussion, Chapter 5*
Eileen Firkus *Data gathering, Chapter 9*
Elmer Heyob *Saugeye discussion, Chapter 11*
Ralph Manns *Color vision chart, Chapter 1; Co-author, Chapter 8;*
                Author, Lunar influence, Chapter 10
Cory Schmidt *Data compilation, Chapter 9*
Joe Tomelleri *Fish illustration, Cover, Chapter 1, Chapter 5, Chapter 7*

Walleye Fundamentals—Foundations For Sustained Fishing Success

10 9 8 7 6 5 4 3 2

First Edition

Library of Congress Cataloging-in-Publication Data
ISBN: 0-929384-92X

Dedication

To Al and Ron Lindner, the founders of In-Fisherman, whose entrepreneurial spirit has changed freshwater fishing by helping anglers have more fun while catching more fish.

In Pursuit Of Walleyes

Each time walleye graces the menu at our house, I'm reminded of why we fish for them with a passion that reaches beyond common sense. They are the essence of what a freshwater fish can be at the table, served so easily in a dozen different ways. And are they not even better—more memorable—as the focus of a traditional shore lunch? Thank God for each one of those rendezvous in the wilderness. And I include here, as an essential prayer for all of us before this season begins, a plea for yet another year rich with the company of friends sitting near such a cooking fire, a morning of sweet pursuit just past, an afternoon and evening of fulfillment yet to come.

Yes, yes, other reasons call for the pursuit of this fine fish. Aspects of the pursuit can become an integral part of one's life, even life-changing, or, at least in some sense, life-defining. I am who I am in small part because for so many of my most formative years in fishing, I spent 30 nights each season shuffling around in waders at the mouths of currents, casting for those walleye monsters that moved silently through the shallows in search of baitfish.

Yes, other reasons call for the pursuit of this fine fish.

I stood there hoping and scheming—so much alone with so many thoughts—until I began to find a way to make the catching happen. Drinking countless cups of coffee by the light of a quarter moon. Some nights, rain, sleet, and snow pelting my back. Standing, too, on those perfect nights, those still nights, the smell of smoldering leaves in the air, a harvest moon rising in the east. Doctoring plugs to make them run just so. And in other ways, defining and redefining the process—the rod, the reel, the line, the lures, the spots, the time of year—until that process became a fine science.

Soon enough, too, having spent the time, paid enough dirty dues, I began to work my system so well—my senses so finely tuned in the darkness, so abruptly interrupted by a "walleye pause" in the midst of a slow, dead retrieve. And then kneeling there, one of those monsters at net, flashlight beam reflecting the life in those marble eyes. In early years, a fish for the wall. Soon enough, those fish released, the satisfaction in a photo instead. These days, no more than a smile and a salute send the big ones on their way. Smaller fish, though, as I have said, still fare well on my table. Even two smaller fish, the focus of a fine meal.

Those midnight trips to wade for walleyes are much less frequent today. Still, I feel each full moon rising in these bones. I still lie sleepless many nights, wondering how busywork can interrupt such essence in anyone's life. My grandpa taught me, though, that we also fish if only for a moment and at some distance, when we have hard-won experiences to remember and the hope of more to come.

Soon enough, too, began the season-long sessions of discovering the secrets of livebait rigging with crawlers, leeches, chubs, and waterdogs—those trips interspersed with journeys from my home in Iowa to explore the new reservoirs in the Dakotas, first drifting plugs in the boiling tailwaters in May, and then in June drifting or trolling over those huge reservoir flats with early day spinner rigs and crawlers.

Later in the season, when the fishing turned difficult on natural lakes, I twitched surface baits at twilight to scratch a walleye or two holding tight in heavy weed-cover. Even today, this remains a technique not fully explored, and certainly seldom written about. We also used Buck Perry methods, trolling Spoonplugs, Mudbugs, or Hellbenders at speeds that puzzle minds of anglers today. Such techniques seem to have been lost in time.

Of course, it was shorecasting and longlining again in fall. Then, to finish the open water season, at least a week of pushing a duck boat across an iced-up bay to reach open water and cast and swim Cap's Rock-A-Roo jigs over a rock bar—which, by the way, was just where those old walleyes were when first-ice finally put an end to open water. Then, what else was there to do each weekend of winter than to have a morning and evening affair with walleyes on ice? And finally, late winter in the air, the yearly cycle began again.

You see, a good portion of my life has revolved around walleyes. Looking back, I would not have had it any other way. And it is hopeless to expect change now.

Last night was another of those nights. Arriving home at midnight, a couple strips of bacon hit the pan. Bacon finished, a little butter added to season the bacon fat, then the fillets dusted in flour and cornmeal, plus salt, cayenne, and black pepper. After three minutes, turn those fillets and add a couple eggs to fry alongside the fillets. Won't be long now, so pour that glass of wine, tear off a hunk of bread. Relive the night past, and toast days of pursuit to come.

Good fishing to you this season and beyond from a staff of hardcore fishheads who consider you our best friends.

Doug Stange
Editor in Chief

From The Editors—
A Word About This Book

Successful walleye fishing can be learned. The basic process is quantifiable and predictable—even relatively simple, although it does take time. But the basis for sustained walleye fishing success usually gets overlooked today, overshadowed by the same old factors that have always made fishing success difficult.

Too many anglers seek shortcuts to success—a magic lure, a secret bait, a new color, just the right jigging motion. Meanwhile, the winner of the most recent tournament stands on stage pronouncing that a special lure keyed his success, while a television fishing show focuses briefly on a hot new lure or definitive pattern that works like magic on at least one body of water during one season. Temptations, all of these. Temptations, urging us to believe such things are the essence of successful fishing.

Magic lures. Hot baits. Even sturdy, reliable fishing patterns—these are all, at best, small pieces of the overall puzzle. The foundation for solving *any* puzzle in walleye fishing, the *real* foundation for learning how to catch walleyes consistently, lies in the first five chapters of this book. These basic, vital chapters are in turn supported by the concepts and practices found in the last seven chapters.

Old files among you will recognize in the initial chapters the heart of the In-Fisherman teaching system as it was introduced over 20 years ago. A generation of exceptional anglers has learned the necessity of understanding the walleye's basic nature (Chapter 1). You've also learned that walleyes move through seasonal periods of response and that understanding these Calendar Periods, as they are called, is the basis for patterning walleyes and for finding them consistently during different yearly periods (Chapter 2).

To apply this information about walleyes to particular bodies of water all across North America, you also need to recognize different lake, river, and reservoir types (Chapter 3). Fortunately, those thousands of bodies of water fall neatly into little more than a dozen patterns that with practice become easy to recognize. What you've learned on one body of water is readily transferable to similar bodies of water.

Finally, no angler can progress past the most basic stages of fishing without understanding the effect that edges and structure have on walleyes (Chapter 4). And it's vital to calculate how the habits of preyfish influence when and how walleyes use those edges and structure (Chapter 5).

Admittedly, laying a solid foundation is trenchwork compared to offering a lively discussion of the hottest baits on the walleye scene. Yet there's never been a top walleye angler who hasn't had to learn and apply the foundation material contained in this book.

So, alas, no quick cures. We learn a little or a lot about one fishing principle or another, move forward trip by trip, season by season, often progressing by fits and spurts, and pretty much loving it all. Because after all—it's fishing, even though we're often frustrated by the outcome of some of our experiments. Soon enough, though, it begins to happen: the theory and practice come together, the science and poetry mesh. Thousands of exceptional walleye anglers are testament to the success of the process we present here. You can be, too.

Contents

The World Of Walleyes

ALL ABOUT THIS
FAVORITE FISH

The number of walleye anglers in the United States and Canada has increased over the last 20 years from 5.2 million in 1980, to 5.8 million in 1990, to over 6 million in 1996. Anglers rate walleyes as the most popular gamefish in three states, the second in four, and the third in four more, indicating its broad geographical appeal. In areas where bass, crappies, catfish, and stripers have had top billing since the first survey takers rapped on doors, walleyes are moving up the charts as anglers on the fringe of its range discover the walleye's combination of large size, challenging behavior, and unsurpassed table excellence.

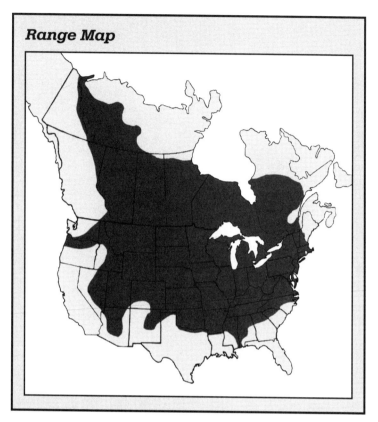

Range Map

Ichthyologists believe the ancestors of walleyes originated in Eurasia, moving across the Bering Sea land bridge to colonize North America, apparently during the Pliocene Epoch (5 to 1.8 million years ago). The earliest fossils of walleyelike fish in North America date back to the late Pleistocene, less than a million years ago. Present distribution of walleyes and their closest cousin, the sauger, was established during the glacial retreat less than 10,000 years ago.

Ichthyologists originally noted two subspecies of walleye: the usual form, *Stizostedion vitreum vitreum*, and the blue pike, *Stizostedion vitreum glaucum*. Most researchers believe the blue pike is extinct, due to overfishing and habitat alteration, or that it has been absorbed into the walleye's gene pool.

DISTRIBUTION

The native range of walleye *(Stizostedion vitreum)* extended on the north from Great Bear Lake to James Bay and the Gulf of St. Lawrence, and south along the Allegheny Mountains to Georgia and into the Gulf Coast drainages of Alabama and Mississippi. Its western limit originally extended along a line from Arkansas north through the Dakotas. Stocking programs have extended the walleye's range to Atlantic Coast drainages from Vermont to South Carolina, and west throughout all western states except California, as well as into British Columbia.

Within these boundaries, naturally reproducing populations of walleyes commonly occur in large lakes of moderate fertility (mesotrophic) and in large rivers. In the Upper Midwest and Canada, natural populations also inhabit smaller streams within the drainages of major walleye rivers. Populations of walleyes sustained by stocking thrive in smaller lakes and impoundments in both their natural and expanded ranges.

SPAWNING

The Spawning Period begins the walleye year. In natural populations, success of the spawn affects fishing in future years. And walleye behavior in spring determines fishing patterns from ice-out until early summer.

When water temperatures rise into the upper 30°F, walleyes leave their deep overwintering areas and move toward spawning sites. In lakes and reservoirs, they may migrate into tributaries while ice remains. In rivers, they spawn over rocky shoals or gravel bars, or migrate up tributaries to find suitable substrates and currents. In either case, this prespawn movement is called the walleye "run."

Timing of the spawning run varies with latitude and local weather. Spawning as early as January has been reported in the Pearl River in Mississippi and as late as July in the Yukon and Northwest Territories. Male walleyes move to spawning grounds first and remain longer than females because males spawn with several females over a period of a week or two, while females generally release all their eggs in one night.

Southern walleye populations spawn at somewhat higher temperatures and over longer periods than northern fish. At the southern edge of the walleye range, biologists note that spawning reaches its peak at water temperatures of around 50°F, and lasts up to six weeks. In Minnesota, runs peak at water temperatures of 42°F to 45°F and last about two weeks.

From 50,000 to over 600,000 eggs are produced by a fish in the 12-pound class. Eggs hatch in 12 to 18 days at usual postspawn water temperatures if environmental conditions are favorable. Studies of walleye recruitment (annual production of young fish) often show 10- to 50-fold annual fluctuations. Strong year classes can support a walleye fishery for several years, but when several weak year classes follow, catch rates dip dramatically once older fish are harvested or die of natural causes.

Factors that affect hatching success and survival of young walleyes include water quality, river flows, wave action, turbulence, siltation, spring water temperatures, availability of zooplankton and small fish to feed young walleyes, abundance of predators on young walleyes (including cannibalism), and competition for food. Studies suggest that the number of adult spawners has little effect on success of a year class compared to the many environmental factors.

In most bodies of water, as prespawn walleyes approach the Spawn Period, they move shallow after dark onto rock-rubble bars or into rubble-bottomed feeder creeks.

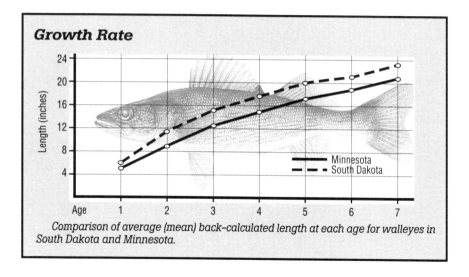

Growth Rate

Comparison of average (mean) back-calculated length at each age for walleyes in South Dakota and Minnesota.

GROWTH AND ABUNDANCE

Walleyes grow fast for the first 3 or 4 years of life, with average size reflecting the length of growing season or latitude, productivity of water, and abundance of forage. Females live longer than males and grow faster, particularly after they reach maturity.

Within a body of water, growth rates of year classes may vary considerably because of climatic conditions and abundance of prey. Walleyes in southeastern reservoirs grow fastest, with some young fish approaching 12 inches at age 1. The average for Minnesota walleyes, however, is 12 inches at age 3, while in South Dakota, they average 15 inches at that age.

In infertile northern waters, older walleyes may grow negligibly from year to year, so even a 20-year-old fish may not be huge. In Montana's Frenchman Reservoir, old walleyes may actually shrink from year to year, apparently because of limited forage.

Walleye density also varies greatly among lakes and reservoirs. Stable populations in northern waters may contain from 5 to 10 pounds of adult walleyes per acre. Highest recorded abundance was reported at Storm Lake, Iowa, where biologists in the 1940s estimated a biomass of 33 pounds of walleyes per acre. Walleyes thrive in mesotrophic waters whose productivity at all levels of the food web is lower than in eutrophic (fertile) waters.

PREY

Walleyes are opportunistic predators, consuming whatever fish and invertebrates are locally abundant, reasonably nutritious, and catchable. During mayfly hatches, walleyes seem to subsist on these small insects until they have flown away to mate and die. On many Minnesota lakes, success in fishing for walleyes may be more closely related to the abundance of yellow perch than to the abundance of walleyes: when small perch are dense, walleyes focus so closely on them that anglers' minnows, leeches, crawlers, and crankbaits receive little attention.

In Lake Erie and other Great Lakes, walleyes take advantage of seasonal and annual peaks in young gizzard shad, alewives, spottail and emerald shiners, white perch, and rainbow smelt. Research studies on the walleye's prey preference suggest that walleyes prefer slender-bodied, spineless prey but can thrive on far spinier meals. In prairie lakes of the Midwest, walleyes rely on warmwater gamefish like bluegills, crappies, and bullheads.

Walleyes browse along weededges, sometimes suspending in the water column to feed on schools of small panfish. During lower light levels at dawn, dusk, and after dark, walleyes move onto shallow flats where they feed heavily. In all waters, peak walleye feeding occurs at dawn and dusk, a pattern termed crepuscular.

This feeding cycle enables walleyes to feed when their sensory systems offer them an advantage over their prey species. Even at air temperatures of -30°F, in the dimly lit waters of lakes covered by two feet of ice and a layer of snow, evenings often bring a flurry of feeding.

In many lakes in the north-central and northeastern portions of the walleye range, yellow perch are the dominant prey once walleyes switch from invertebrates to a fish diet in their first year. Studies on Oneida Lake in New York indicate that perch are important prey because when young perch are abundant, walleyes selectively feed on them. When perch year classes are weak, walleyes cannibalize each other, reducing the strength of their year classes.

Various members of the minnow family are also important prey species. Commonly called shiners, they form huge schools, lack spines, speed, and other defenses, and inhabit almost every lake, river, and reservoir containing walleyes. The two most important shiner species are spottail shiners, which range from Georgia northwest into Saskatchewan, and emerald shiners, whose range overlaps that of the spottail but is absent from the Atlantic coast.

Walleyes key on shiners, particularly in May and June, when these species

Walleye Shape

With their gas bladders, walleyes can make themselves neutrally or negatively buoyant in order to expend as little energy as possible while suspending or holding on bottom. But because the density of water is much greater than the density of air, swimming fish encounter water's resistance and must be optimally shaped to move forward through it efficiently. The streamlined or cigar shape is hydrodynamically best. But hydrodynamics is a compromise between speed, method of propulsion, maneuverability, protection from predators, and other factors.

Walleyes are one of many predators that propel themselves forward with lateral body thrusts of their caudal fins. Walleyes face river currents and the need to snatch forage

fish from among rocks or weedstalks. Their shape is a compromise between the cigar and the disc, with a widening toward the belly to help them stay near bottom in currents.

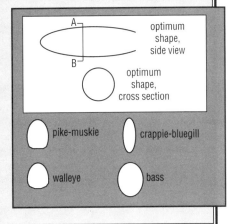

Age Determination

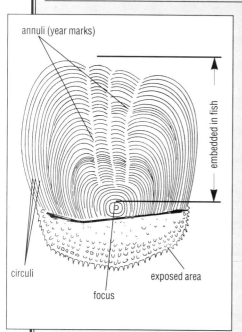

annuli (year marks)

embedded in fish

circuli

focus

exposed area

Scale reading has been the traditional method for determining the age of fish and the average growth rate of populations. The assumption is that scales grow proportionately to fish length. And this relationship usually holds true.

During periods of slow or no growth, as in winter, rings (called circuli) are narrowly spaced. Fast growth brings widely spaced circuli. Year marks (annuli) show rather clearly under magnification, and measurements from the central focus to succeeding annuli provide the fish's growth history.

Scales of slow-growing fish or fish from consistently warm climates may not reveal true age. For these fish, otoliths (ear bones) are more accurate. But these must be removed from the skull and usually sectioned, a more difficult process than scale reading.

spawn on gravel shoals and near the mouths of feeder creeks. At this time of year, other prey aren't so abundant in shallow, hard bottom areas.

In northern lakes of moderate or low fertility, walleyes prey heavily on ciscoes, small members of the whitefish family. Ciscoes (also called lake herring and tullibees) range from the upper Mississippi drainage and the Great Lakes basins north to Labrador and northwest to the Mackenzie River drainage. Ciscoes are coolwater fish, preferring temperatures below 60°F.

Ciscoes school in open water, rising toward the surface at dusk to eat zooplankton and invertebrates. Walleyes near main lake structure or suspended in the main basin approach these schools and feed heavily during the night. Anglers keying on this pattern make great catches from tough lakes by trolling after dark. In late fall, when ciscoes spawn on reefs, walleyes again focus on them, producing great fishing for anglers seeking trophy-size fish in frigid conditions.

Since the early 1900s, when smelt entered the Great Lakes, walleyes as well as introduced trout and salmon have preyed on them. The success of this coldwater preyfish led to stocking it in other important walleye waters like lakes Oahe and Sakakawea. In these waters, the best walleye fishing in late spring and early summer is in spots where deep structure intercepts the preferred coolwater habitat of smelt.

In Lake Erie and many reservoirs in the southern portion of the walleye's range, gizzard shad are the principal prey from early summer until fall. In most waters, schools of shad suspend in open water or graze along shallow flats, grazing on bottom plankton and detritus. Shad schools move with their food source, along with wind and current, and walleyes follow.

Successful fishing in shad-laden waters depends on using sonar to locate prey and predators, and then longline trolling to place baits at the correct depth. Key on points, windblown flats, and other spots where walleyes may try to intercept shad schools.

WATER QUALITY
Walleyes tolerate a range of environmental conditions, as indicated by their broad distribution and variety of habitat. They're generally most abundant in medium-to-large lakes and river systems with cool temperatures, shallow to intermediate depths, extensive shorelines, slight turbidity, large expanses of clean rocky bottom, and medium fertility.

Walleyes survive and grow in water from crystal clear to murky, but become most abundant in moderately turbid conditions. Peak feeding conditions occur in water with a surface visibility (Secchi disc) of 3 to 6 feet. Activity decreases when visibility is less than 3 feet or more than 16 feet.

Walleye fry seek light until they're 1 to 1.5 inches long, at which size they gradually become photonegative and seek dim light during bright periods. During the brightest parts of the day, adult walleyes often hold in cover and in deeper water. They frequently move inshore at night, feeding most during low-light hours.

The pH of prime walleye waters ranges from 6.0 to 8.0. Walleyes seem to display no behavioral changes at pH levels within that range. Below 6.0, walleye spawning and recruitment often fail, while pH levels over 9.0 are unsuitable to most freshwater fish, including walleyes.

Adult walleyes often inhabit areas with current except during winter, when they tend to avoid all but the slightest current. Walleyes can swim for only about

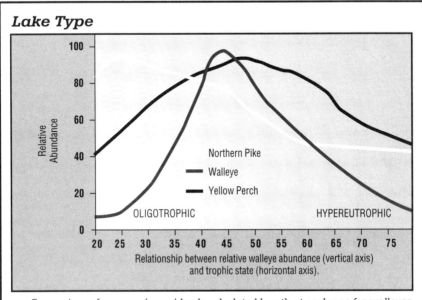

Comparison of average (mean) back-calculated length at each age for walleyes in South Dakota and Minnesota.

10 minutes in water flowing at 2.5 cubic feet per second. They seek current breaks to conserve energy while remaining in range of potential prey.

Walleye embryos that hatch in rivers rely on water currents to transport them downstream toward plankton-rich waters before their yolk sacs are absorbed (3 to 5 days). If current is absent, they starve. Fry don't begin to feed, however, until water temperatures reach the upper 50°F.

Lab tests have shown that walleyes grow fastest at temperatures between 68°F and 75°F, avoiding water over 75°F. Growth of adults apparently stops below 53°F, while temperatures between 84°F and 95°F have proven fatal. Like most other freshwater fish, walleyes thrive in water containing at least 5 parts per million (ppm) of dissolved oxygen. Adult fish can tolerate 2 ppm for short periods, while fry require 5 ppm.

SENSES

Walleyes learn about their environment using the five senses we're most familiar with (smell, taste, feel, hearing, and vision), as well as a lateral line that senses low-frequency underwater vibrations. Sensory lobes compose a large portion of a walleye's brain. Survival, growth, and reproduction depend on the function of these lobes.

Smell and Taste: The senses of smell and taste are linked in humans, making it difficult for us to distinguish a bite of apple from a bite of potato without first smelling both of them. For fish, these senses are linked more closely because they must detect molecules of substances dissolved in water. Whether walleyes respond to smell or to taste is therefore difficult for researchers to determine.

A fish's chemoreception (including both smell and taste) is critical for finding prey, avoiding predators, locating fish of the same species, coordinating spawning time, and homing to residence areas or spawning sites. For most fish, sense of smell (olfaction) is primarily important for detecting distant substances, while taste (gustation) determines the palatability of a substance once it's taken into the mouth.

Walleyes have paired nares (nostrils) located along the top of the head toward the upper jaw; these are used to sense molecules dissolved in water. While fish swim or remain still in moving water, molecules pass through their nares and contact their olfactory organs, which include their olfactory lobes. The nares contain tiny, hairlike cilia that move water through the nares, even when walleyes are still.

The olfactory organ contains folds that are thought to enhance the sense of smell, for its surface contains receptor cells that increase with the surface area of the olfactory organ. Walleyes have about 29 folds in their nares, a number partway between channel catfish (142 folds) and members of the sunfish family (about 10 folds).

The most sensitive sniffer belongs to the eel, which is capable of detecting amino acids in the range of a few parts per quadrillion. Although we know of no studies on the olfactory acuity of walleyes, it seems they can probably detect amino acids in a dilution of several parts per 10 million. That's acute—one part per million is the equivalent of about one ounce of a pure substance dissolved in enough water to fill 1,000 railroad tank cars.

In hatchery tests, researchers have lured young walleyes up one side of a y-shaped maze by dripping solutions of amino acids, including betaine, into one side. Salt solutions also proved attractive to them. Other amino acids, fish mucus, and essences of walleye body parts, on the other hand, repelled the fish.

It's no surprise that walleyes smell well, for livebait is often the only answer to a tough bite and inactive fish. Sometimes the addition of a bit of crawler or a minnow head provokes a strike that we surmise is due primarily to olfaction.

For walleyes, taste spurs the decision to spit a bait or to swallow it. Here again, a jig tipped with a minnow passes the taste test more often than one tipped with a twistertail. Researchers at Berkley, Classic Manufacturing, Kodiak, and other companies that produce plastics impregnated with attractants hope to eventually synthesize a formula that appeals to walleyes and other species more than natural prey. Certainly, plastics flavored with attractive amino acids, preyfish essences, and salt cause fish to hold them in their mouths and sometimes to attempt swallowing them.

Vision: Nighttime walleye fishing is a summertime tradition, but night's also one of the best times to catch walleyes in winter, spring, and fall, particularly in clear lakes and reservoirs. Walleyes often feed nocturnally because they see better at night than the prey they pursue. The only freshwater fish with better night vision is the walleye's cousin, the sauger.

The walleye's eye is large, allowing the pupil—the light gathering part of the eye—to gather as much light as possible. No creature can see in complete darkness, but starlight provides enough light for walleyes and other nocturnal animals. The principal adaptation for night vision in nocturnal animals is the *tapetum lucidum*, a reflective layer on the retina that concentrates light after it enters the

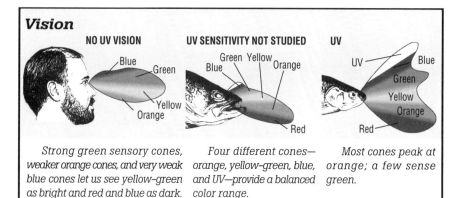

Vision

NO UV VISION — Blue, Green, Yellow, Orange

UV SENSITIVITY NOT STUDIED — Green, Yellow, Orange, Blue, Red

UV — UV, Blue, Green, Yellow, Orange, Red

Strong green sensory cones, weaker orange cones, and very weak blue cones let us see yellow–green as bright and red and blue as dark.

Four different cones— orange, yellow–green, blue, and UV—provide a balanced color range.

Most cones peak at orange; a few sense green.

eye. Cats, raccoons, skunks, deer, and some other fish have structures similar to those of walleyes and sauger.

Vision begins when light passes from the pupil opening through the cornea and then to the lens, which focuses the image as a camera lens does. Light then reaches two types of light-sensitive cells in the retina—rods and cones. Cone cells detect color when exposed to daylight. Rod cells distinguish shades of gray and allow vision when sunlight isn't present. Walleye and sauger eyes contain a larger proportion of rods than the eyes of perch, shiners, and other fish that are most active in daytime.

The *tapetum lucidum* is a layer of guanine crystals located in the lower portion of the retina's deepest layer. This physiology suggests that walleyes see lures and baits moving above them more clearly than those moving slightly below their level. And fishing experiences suggest that for the best response, lures should be set to run slightly above sonar images of fish. Luminous paint or strips of tape applied to a crankbait belly catch the fish's eye.

Underwater sound waves pass through a fish's body with little effect because a fish's density is nearly the same as water's.

Walleyes also possess color vision, based on analysis of the structure of their light-sensitive cones. Scientists indicate that walleyes should see red, orange, and yellow best, followed by green. Jigs and crankbaits in those colors often are top producers, along with those in colors that imitate natural prey. Theory suggests that walleyes see blue and violet less well; these colors may even appear black.

Hearing: Sound waves in water and air are produced by particles rebounding after compression, imparting directional energy to neighboring particles. Because molecules in water are closer together than in air, directional energy is transferred from molecule to molecule almost 5 times faster underwater. Walleyes lack external and middle ears, but their inner ears are similar in structure and function to human ones.

Underwater sound waves pass through a fish's body with little effect because a fish's density is nearly the same as water's. Sound waves do, however, cause vibrations in the calcium carbonate otoliths (earbones) of fish, which are located on either side of the skull. Fish recognize familiar patterns of frequencies as sounds, just as we hear airborne sound waves.

Walleyes hear well underwater, though not so well as fish equipped with Weberian ossicles, like catfish and minnows. These small bones transmit vibrations from the gas bladder to the inner ear, increasing the threshold and range of hearing manyfold.

Research suggests that walleyes hear underwater sound waves in the range of 100 to 2,000 Hertz (cycles per second). For a walleye, important sounds indicate the presence of prey or predators, including humans. Their hearing range includes most sounds produced by rattling crankbaits and other noisy lures.

High-pitched rattles are new in the underwater world. They may arouse curiosity in fish that haven't been exposed to them. Fish test for identity and check for edibility by biting. When they do this, alert anglers stick another fish.

Lateral Line Sense: Underwater lures produce vibrations that walleyes detect through their lateral lines. Even lures that don't seem to vibrate, like jigs or flat spoons, send out pressure waves that trigger neuromast organs in the lateral line that runs down the fish's side.

The lateral line detects low-frequency sound waves in the range of about 1 to

When Sound Becomes Feeling

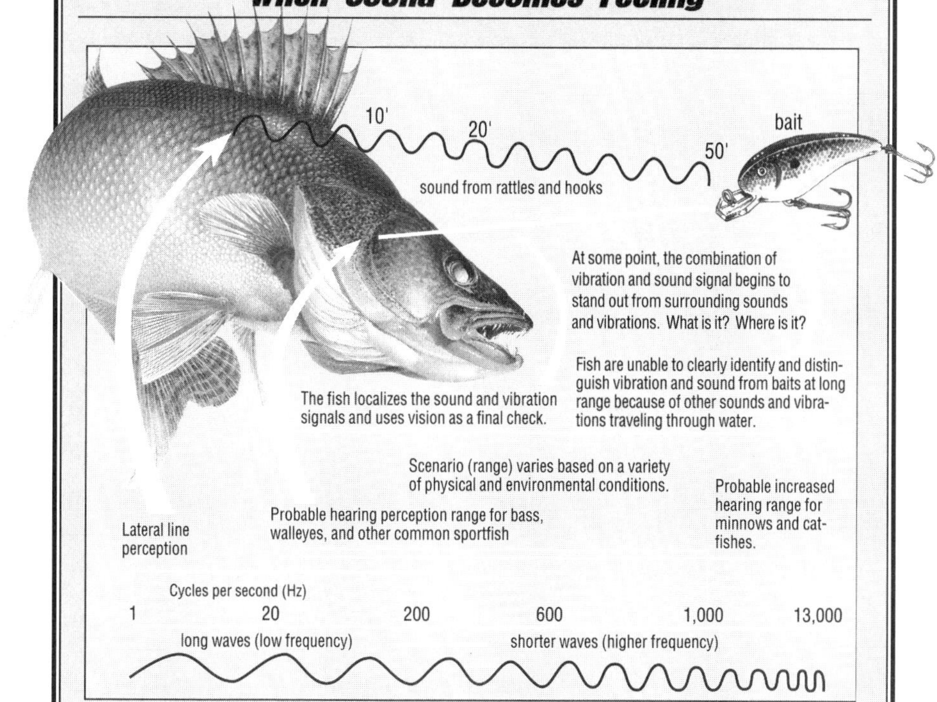

10'

20'

50'

bait

sound from rattles and hooks

At some point, the combination of vibration and sound signal begins to stand out from surrounding sounds and vibrations. What is it? Where is it?

Fish are unable to clearly identify and distinguish vibration and sound from baits at long range because of other sounds and vibrations traveling through water.

The fish localizes the sound and vibration signals and uses vision as a final check.

Scenario (range) varies based on a variety of physical and environmental conditions.

Lateral line perception

Probable hearing perception range for bass, walleyes, and other common sportfish

Probable increased hearing range for minnows and catfishes.

Cycles per second (Hz)

| 1 | 20 | 200 | 600 | 1,000 | 13,000 |

long waves (low frequency)

shorter waves (higher frequency)

Some vibrations can only be felt (lower pitches or frequencies within about the 1 to 200 cycle per second [Hz] range), while other vibrations can only be heard (higher pitches within the 20 to 600 and 3,000 to 13,000 Hz ranges, depending on the fish species). There apparently is an area of overlap in which a fish can hear and feel vibrations (about 20 to 200 Hz).

A lure moves toward a fish. At 50 feet, higher-frequency sound waves from rattling shot and hooks tinkling on the body of the bait reach the fish's inner ear, and low-frequency sound waves from rattling shot and hooks tinkling on the body of the bait reach the fish's inner ear, while low-

frequency vibrations from the plug's wobble reach its lateral line. Something's out there, but to the fish the sound is probably insignificant, given the myriad other vibrations and sounds reaching the fish.

As the lure comes closer, however, the vibration and sound from the bait begin to stand out from the surrounding drone. What is it? Where is it?

Using vision in combination with hearing and feeling, the fish tries to locate where and what the thing (lure) is. The closer the sound comes, the more distinguishable it becomes. Successful fishing involves persuading the fish that the lure's edible before it is rejected as a fake.

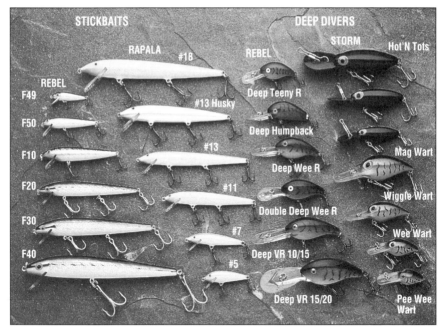

One approach to determine the vibrations walleyes prefer is to choose from among a spectrum of baits—one type of bait from one manufacturer. Become familiar with each model and the slight variations in vibration that result from size. Expand your versatility by adding new lines of baits. You'll need a well organized tackle box.

200 Hertz. (Note the range of overlap with hearing.) Hair cells located inside the many tiny neuromasts of the lateral line detect water movement and send messages to the brain. To help walleyes and other species locate what's producing the vibrations and where it's located, some sensory cells are oriented in one direction, others in the opposite direction.

A crankbait bill causes the lure to wobble and produce vibrations that a walleye may sense more than several boat lengths away. Certainly, in murky water or at night, fish feel the presence of lures before they see them. Some vibrations may startle walleyes; others attract them; most are probably ignored.

Each crankbait has a set of vibration characteristics determined by its shape, size, and bill and body material. Minor differences exist even among lures of the same model. "Magic" baits that outproduce other apparently identical models probably produce slightly different vibrations that are more appealing to fish. And preferred vibration patterns may vary among lakes and times of the year.

Once you've found fish, success depends on choosing a lure that triggers an aggressive response, then running it at the right speed to produce the most attractive vibration to complement the lure's appeal to a walleye's other senses.

Year of the Walleye

**SECRETS TO
SEASONAL PERIODS
OF RESPONSE**

No creature is less physically affected by seasonal changes in the environment than humans. We feel cheerful on a warm spring day or down after a week of rain; we dress light when it's sultry and cover up when it's cold, but in every case our metabolism remains about constant. We eat three meals a day, go to work, raise the kids, walk the dog, and sleep on a similar schedule year round.

Scientists call us homeotherms—creatures with stable body temperatures, regardless of the outside environment. Other mammals and birds also are homeothermic (often called warm-blooded), although many of those species are more likely to migrate or hibernate, eat less, or grow extra fur during cold seasons. Most animals also mate, give birth, and raise young only during certain seasons that allow adults to eat heavily and feed their young while forage is most abundant. We don't feel those constraints.

Seasonal and even daily changes in weather and water temperature affect fish like walleyes far more than they affect birds and mammals. The feeding activity, digestion, metabolism, and growth rate of walleyes are influenced by season and water temperature in accordance with the fishes' genetic makeup. Angling success, therefore, depends in large part upon understanding the changing seasonal activities of walleyes.

In-Fisherman founders Al and Ron Lindner developed the concept of Calendar Periods before publishing the first issue of *In-Fisherman* magazine. They used this concept in their early days of guiding and promoting fishing tackle. It worked like magic. Indeed, they termed their traveling fishing show, which often produced fish (usually walleyes) on waters where local anglers weren't catching any, their "magic act."

This is practical information that has revolutionized walleye fishing.

So it was that Al and Ron, who learned to fish in natural lakes in the northern United States, became particularly interested in how seasonal changes affect fish behavior and determine successful angling techniques. The seasonal changes we note here are most dramatic in the North, where water temperatures range from around 80°F in the heat of summer to 32°F for several months of winter. Yet the more subtle and gradual changes that occur in southern waters, even those in the tropics, also profoundly affect fish behavior.

The In-Fisherman Calendar includes 10 periods in an annual cycle. Dividing the annual continuum into 10 periods is arbitrary; indeed, the periods sometimes overlap. The 10 time frames, however, focus on subtleties in changing water conditions and in fish response. The In-Fisherman Calendar Periods don't follow the 12-month Gregorian calendar, since fish like walleyes have no regard for such artificial schemes.

Even though the Lindners based the original In-Fisherman Calendar of Fish Activity on the behavior of fish in lakes and reservoirs, the same seasonal trends occur in rivers (with the exceptions of the Turnover Period and, sometimes, the Frozen Water Period). Other periods, like Summer Peak and Postsummer, occur in rivers, though their timing may differ from the same periods in nearby lakes. The reactions of walleyes to running waters are different, too; walleyes in rivers often migrate much farther after spawning and before winter than lake fish.

Practical Application—Understanding the In-Fisherman Calendar of Fish Activity is one basis for learning the patterns of walleyes and developing the skill to find them. The calendar serves as a reference. Understanding that fish progress through distinct periods of activity that vary only in their length from year to year, based on changes in weather, allows anglers to note similarities and differences in fish behavior from one activity period to the next.

One overriding factor in discussion among anglers, therefore, is the Calendar Period under (or surrounding) which the discussion takes place. It does little good for walleye anglers to discuss the productivity of minnow-imitating baits like the Rapala Minnow for walleyes without first noting the Calendar Period in question. Rapala Minnows are classic bait for walleyes during Coldwater Periods in Spring and Fall. They may also be a prime option for walleyes during Postspawn, Presummer, and at night during the Summer Peak. This varies, though, depending on the water classification involved, the subject of the next chapter.

Some of this information may at first seem like a return to high-school science class. In a sense, we suppose it is. But applied as In-Fisherman applies it, this is

---

Year of the Walleye

1 Prespawn	4 Presummer	7 Postsummer	10 Winter*
2 Spawn	5 Summer Peak	8 Fall Turnover	
3 Postspawn	6 Summer	9 Coldwater	*Coldest water of the year.

Gregorian Calendar	Jan	Feb	Mar	Apr	May	June	July	Aug	Sept	Oct	Nov	Dec
Northern Range	10			9 1 2 3 4 5		6			7 8	9		10
Mid Range	10		9 1 2 3 4 5			6			7 8	9		10
Southern Range	10	9	1 2 3 4 5			6			7 8	9		10

The 10 Calendar Periods of fish response can vary in length by as much as four weeks from one year to the next. The periods aren't based on the Gregorian calendar, so they don't occur on specific dates each year. Instead, the Calendar periods are based on nature's clock.

The Calendar Periods vary by regions of the country. Southern waters have an extended Summer Period and a brief Winter Period. In contrast, lakes along the US-Canada border have extended Coldwater and Winter periods. Walleyes in Alabama or Texas can be in the Spawning Period while those in Minnesota are still in the Winter Period.

practical information that has revolutionized fishing for millions of anglers, many of whom were certainly puzzled at first about the relevance of this information to their everyday fishing.

COLDWATER PERIOD (SPRING)
Water Temperature: Warming Slightly from Annual Minimum
General Fish Mood: Neutral

In northern parts of the walleye range, prespawn movement may begin at the end of the Frozen Water Period, making the Spring Coldwater Period scarcely distinguishable. A Coldwater Period may occur in years with early ice-out, however. And in more southern walleye waters, the spring Coldwater Period begins with the first rise in the thermometer, accompanied by lengthening days.

This period is one of staging before movement to spawning areas begins or after reaching staging areas. Walleyes move from deep offshore humps to shallower structure, particularly along shorelines with points, rockpiles, and other features that provide cover and attract prey. In reservoirs, walleyes gather in holes at the mouths of tributaries or in deep channel areas in the lower portions of creeks that provide spawning habitat. As the sun warms shallow bays, walleyes also wander in to feed on preyfish that have entered the area to feed on plankton or bottom-dwelling invertebrates.

Groups of shallow, deep, or staging walleyes provide good fishing once they're located on sonar or by fishing likely areas. Fish on deeper structure seem to bite better and can be fished for with vertical presentations. Walleyes in shallow bays often are taken unintentionally by crappie anglers.

Seasons of Change

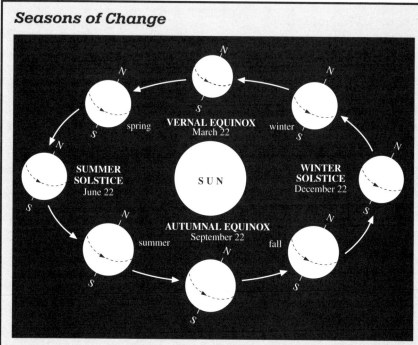

Spring, summer, fall, winter. The pendulum swings between seasons, bringing evident changes on land, but more difficult-to-define changes underwater. Studies show that photoperiod (length of daylight) influences the tempo of the environment, from microorganisms to top-of-the-line predators. The intensity and duration of light in a yearly cycle influences migrations, spawning, and feeding.

Fish Activity Level—
Walleyes in a Natural Lake in Central Minnesota

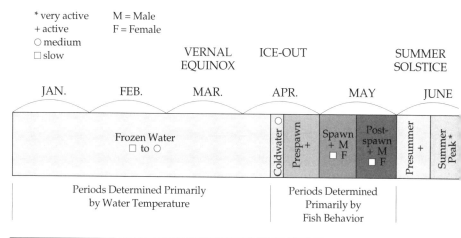

* very active   M = Male
+ active   F = Female
○ medium
□ slow

VERNAL EQUINOX   ICE-OUT   SUMMER SOLSTICE

JAN.   FEB.   MAR.   APR.   MAY   JUNE

Frozen Water □ to ○

Coldwater ○ | Prespawn + | Spawn + M □ F | Post-spawn + M ■ F | Presummer + | Summer Peak *

Periods Determined Primarily by Water Temperature | Periods Determined Primarily by Fish Behavior

PRESPAWN PERIOD

Water Temperature: Upper 30°F to Low 40°F Range
General Fish Mood: Neutral

The Prespawn Period begins as walleyes move from wintering areas toward spawning locations. Such journeys may be short in small lakes or rivers, or extensive in large lakes, large reservoirs, and the Great Lakes. In expansive systems, individuals may swim over 100 miles to reach spawning areas. They often bypass apparently appropriate spawning sites to return to more distant areas where they spawned previously. Some biologists suspect that walleyes return to the area where they hatched, in the manner of salmon, but this hasn't been proven.

In northern waters, the migration begins shortly before or just after ice-out; in southern waters, late winter. Males lead the progression to spawning grounds, which may be shallow, rocky areas in a lake or reservoir, or shoals in a tributary river. When water temperatures are in the 40°F range, shining a powerful light can easily reveal males on spawning grounds at night. Biologists use this method to count spawning populations.

Where spawning migrations are blocked by dams, walleyes concentrate below them prior to spawning. In reservoirs where riprap banks simulate natural spawning areas better than any other features, walleyes congregate along the banks. Offshore humps or rocky deltas at the mouths of feeder creeks also draw fish.

Walleyes feed regularly throughout winter, and warming waters spur that feeding as well as migrating. Consider, however, that anglers must adjust their pace from the highly successful but nearly static approach of ice fishing to fishing open water from a boat.

Slow-moving presentations in key areas spell success, and bank anglers often score if migrating or spawning fish are within range. Walleyes hit crankbaits, spoons, spinners, and livebait. The concentration of fish in the Prespawn Period compensates for less than aggressive feeding.

In some states and provinces, closed seasons prohibit walleye fishing until after the spawn because the sometimes huge aggregations of fish may become vulnerable to overharvesting. In other situations, the season opener is based more on tradition than on biology.

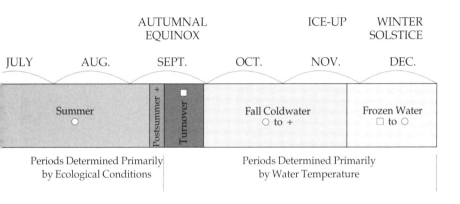

The Top Ten Largest Kept Walleyes In In-Fisherman's Master Angler Contest

Water	Date	Weight	Moon Phase
*1. Greers Ferry, AR	03/14/82	22 lbs. 11 oz.	
2. Greers Ferry, AR	02/10/89	20 lbs. 10 oz.	
3. Columbia River, OR-WA	02/20/90	19 lbs. 15 oz.	
4. Greers Ferry, AR	02/28/81	19 lbs. 2 oz.	
5. Columbia River, OR-WA	04/09/90	18 lbs. 12 oz.	Full-1
6. Greers Ferry, AR	01/11/82	18 lbs. 4 oz.	
7. Greers Ferry, AR	03/13/86	17 lbs. 13 oz.	Dark
8. Greers Ferry, AR	03/02/81	17 lbs. 8 oz.	
9. Greers Ferry, AR	01/11/82	17 lbs. 7 oz.	F+3
10. Greers Ferry, AR	03/01/83	17 lbs. 7 oz.	1/2D

Most of the largest walleyes ever caught were taken during winter or spring, a time frame that encompasses the Cold Water, Prespawn, and Spawn Periods. Walleyes usually are at their heaviest during these periods.

Al Nelson and the present world-record walleye (22 lbs. 11 oz.) from Greers Ferry, AR, March 14, 1982.

SPAWN PERIOD
Water Temperature: 43°F to 52°F
General Fish Mood: Neutral to Negative

Male walleyes precede females onto the spawning grounds, but once both sexes are present, they waste little time. Most spawning activity is nocturnal, with several males chasing a larger female across a shoal. Some females may stage in deeper holes adjacent to spawning areas while their eggs ripen. But they drop all their eggs within a day or two and then begin the journey back to the main lake or reservoir. In rivers, major movements to postspawn locations may not follow spawning as quickly because nearby features offer the fish cover and prey.

Females broadcast from 40,000 to 600,000 eggs, with larger females producing larger clutches. Eggs stick to the rough surfaces of gravel or lodge between larger stones, where current or moderate wave action keep them aerated and free of silt until they hatch one to three weeks later.

Males may run with milt for several weeks. Most remain in spawning areas until females have departed; then they follow the females. Males can be caught on spawning areas since they feed sporadically and strike lures or baits aggressively. Females staging in spawning areas can also be caught, though action is slow, considering the abundance of fish.

POSTSPAWN PERIOD
Water Temperature: Low 50°F Range
General Fish Mood: Neutral to Negative

Female and then most male walleyes evacuate spawning shoals once the ripe eggs have been fertilized. Walleyes provide no parental care, so adults'

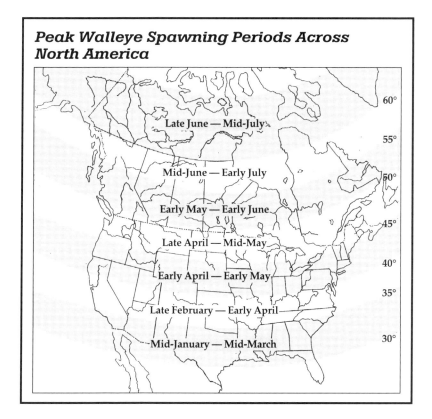

Peak Walleye Spawning Periods Across North America

Late June — Mid-July

Mid-June — Early July

Early May — Early June

Late April — Mid-May

Early April — Early May

Late February — Early April

Mid-January — Mid-March

60°
55°
50°
45°
40°
35°
30°

feeding quickly resumes. Postspawn walleyes are notoriously hard to catch, but at least part of the problem lies in finding groups of fish rather than in their reluctance to bite.

In some lakes and rivers, walleyes gradually move deeper after spawning. Finding them can be simple once you determine where they spawned. Find nearby feeding flats with adjacent deep water, and you'll find walleyes. Typical feeding depth for postspawn walleyes ranges from 6 to 20 feet, depending on water clarity, structural features, and dominant preyfish. Uniformly cool water and high oxygen content offer walleyes and other species the freedom to choose among holding areas for the one providing the most abundant prey.

Where shiners, perch, or other panfish provide forage, walleyes hold shallow, particularly at night. Where shad, alewives, or ciscoes are important prey, walleyes suspend off structure or near schools of baitfish.

Night fishing often provides the best bites shortly after the spawn, but feeding peaks at dusk and dawn soon become typical. Postspawn walleyes in rivers are easy to find because they hold near current breaks.

In systems where walleyes make major migrations, locating postspawn fish is tougher because they may move many miles in one day. Check with regional fishery biologists, who often have conducted tagging or biotelemetry studies to document walleye movements. Such reports provide valuable information even if they're not recent because movement patterns often are specific to the population and vary little from year to year.

PRESUMMER PERIOD
Water Temperature: Mid-50°F Range to Low 60°F Range
General Fish Mood: Neutral to Positive

The Presummer Period continues the trend toward summer fishing patterns that began at the end of the Postspawn Period. Yet because different patterns are developing and groups of fish are moving, fishing success can be sporadic. A hot bite one evening may be followed by only a few stragglers the next day.

The key to success during the Presummer Period lies in checking many areas and depths with a variety of lures and bait. Select shiners, fathead minnows, chubs, leeches, crawlers, and any other locally popular bait, giving them sufficient time in the water to determine what walleyes want.

Trolling, rigging, jigging, or float fishing on shoreline structures and offshore bars or in open water may work best on an individual outing. Monitor sonar closely for suspended fish as well as for how fish are relating to structure. One problem is that other species may be in the same spots as walleyes, so don't waste too much time on fish that refuse to bite. Keep moving.

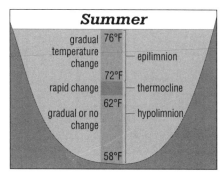

The upper (warmwater) layer may be from 12 to 40 feet thick, while the thermocline may be 2 to 15 feet thick. The lower (coldwater) level usually contains less dissolved oxygen than the upper layer.

SUMMER PEAK PERIOD
Water Temperature: Mid-60°F Range to Low 70°F Range
General Fish Mood: Positive

The Summer Peak is a short period lasting perhaps one to two weeks, in which a lake or reservoir suddenly blooms with life. Spawning is over for most fish, and tiny fry teem in the shallows and over open water. Predators probably can't tell them apart any better than we can and probably don't care.

Young perch, shad, shiners, crappie, bluegills, carp, and other species are prey. Active walleyes may roam in water from two feet (usually at night) down to 30 feet or more until thermal stratification develops and restricts them to the layers above the thermocline.

The Summer Peak is most obvious in lakes and reservoirs, but it also occurs in rivers, where high production of young fish and increased metabolisms due to quickly warming waters spur fast fishing. Blooming aquatic plants that typify this period in lakes may not be present in rivers, and increased production of plankton also isn't as pronounced.

Fishing on all types of waters typically is good, though high fishing pressure increases competition for key spots and gradually increases the spookiness of walleyes. Time to explore new patterns or styles of fishing, or to look for "secret" lakes.

SUMMER PERIOD
Water Temperature: Annual Maximum for an Extended Period
General Fish Mood: Variable—Negative to Positive

The Summer Period may begin in late spring in southern waters and not until late July in the far North. In the South, it's the longest period, second only to the Winter Period in the North.

Walleyes have established feeding patterns that remain stable for weeks or even longer. Their degree of activity, however, varies according to weather patterns and preyfish behavior. During summer, a cloudy, windy day with a dropping barometer is the time to go fishing. Such conditions often produce the hottest bites of the year.

On clear, cool, and breezy days, go to work. On sunny, hot, calm days, take the kids waterskiing. Walleyes can be found, but they rarely bite well. Dawn, dusk, and several hours after dark offer the best fishing. Darker waters typically produce better daytime bites.

River fishing often is good because currents and murkier waters seem to keep walleyes more willing to bite predictably. Holding areas also are more easily defined in all weather conditions on rivers.

POSTSUMMER

Water Temperature: Cooling Substantially from Annual Peak
General Fish Mood: Neutral to Positive

The Postsummer Period is a reversal of the warming Presummer Period. Warm days yield to increasingly cooler nights as daylight shortens and the intensity of the sun's rays lessens in the northern hemisphere. This period is a winding down of the summer feeding time for warmwater and coolwater fish, but fishing patterns may remain fairly intact until this period ends with the Fall Turnover.

Walleyes tend to occupy more vertical structure than during the Summer Period. Steep shoreline breaks and pinnaclelike humps hold an increasing number of walleyes, though their precise location and typical holding depth must be determined by fishing. And walleye location may change from day to day or during a day or night.

Walleyes that have spent the summer on flats in thick beds of aquatic vegetation may shift to rock structure or to beds of coontail, bladderwort, and other hardier plants when species like cabbage (broadleaf pondweed) turn brown. Again, fish shift to spots with easy access to deep water.

Once you find walleyes, however, they may bite readily even during daylight. Windy days spur the bite in shallow cover, while fish holding deeper may bite in bright sun at midday. Still, true to their basic nature, most walleye continue to feed most heartily and consistently during twilight periods.

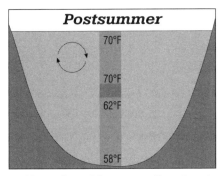

Postsummer

70°F
70°F
62°F
58°F

The surface of the water radiates heat to the atmosphere at night as water above the thermocline gradually cools. The thermocline remains intact but becomes closer in temperature to the layer above. Oxygen-poor water remains trapped below the thermocline.

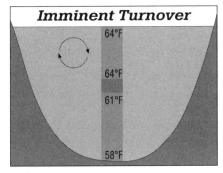

Imminent Turnover

64°F
64°F
61°F
58°F

The thermocline shrinks as it approaches the same temperature as the uniform mass of water above.

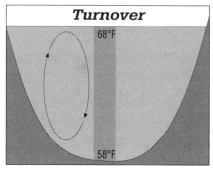

Turnover

68°F

58°F

The thermocline disintegrates, and water mixes from surface to bottom. The water continues to cool as it circulates, aided by wind. The oxygen level of the water drops for a short time as the oxygen-depleted hypolimnion mixes with the water above.

TURNOVER PERIOD

Water Temperature: Upper 50°F Range to Low 50°F Range

General Fish Mood: Neutral to Negative

Turnover is the most dramatic change that occurs in a lake or reservoir. The three layers of water that for several months have been characterized by different temperatures, oxygen concentrations, and other water quality parameters suddenly mix.

In some situations, the thermocline may slowly erode as the warm surface layer cools and wind pushes it down toward the upper part of the thermocline. In some lakes, the turnover is dramatic, with water color changing as particles of debris dislodged from the bottom float to the surface or suspend in midwater. In eutrophic systems, hydrogen sulfide gas arising from the depths may give the lake a sulfurous odor for a day or two.

Walleyes and other fish are affected by Turnover, and fishing invariably slows. Fish may be upset by sudden changes in their environment, like aquarium fish when a new filter is added or the water is changed. More likely, though, fish quickly shift locations in response to changing temperature, oxygen, and water color.

Walleyes may eat less as they adjust. For whatever reason, Turnover slows fishing, so relocate to a river, a lake still enjoying the Postsummer Period, or one advanced into the Fall Coldwater Period.

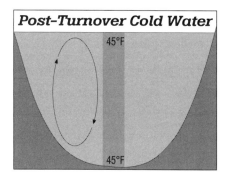

Post-Turnover Cold Water

45°F

45°F

Temperature becomes uniform. Wind action circulates and oxygenates water, which reaches a uniform temperature.

COLDWATER PERIOD (FALL)

Water Temperature: Low 50°F Range to Annual Minimum

General Fish Mood: Neutral to Positive

Effects of Turnover soon vanish as waters clear and all areas again hold sufficient oxygen for fish. Location shifts that were noticeable in the Postsummer Period now become intensified. Walleyes favor fast-breaking structure, but their choice of depth remains varied.

Trolling shallow-running minnow baits after dark seems to work almost everywhere. Yet jigging or livebait rigging along 40-foot-deep structural features can take big fish all day. As ice-up approaches, however, slower presentations dominate.

Vertical jigging with leadheads or spoons in ice-fishing fashion can be deadly in lakes, reservoirs, and rivers. Livebait goes from optional at the start of the Coldwater Period to nearly essential at its close. Few anglers take advantage of this period.

WINTER OR FROZEN WATER PERIOD

Water Temperature: Annual Minimum for an Extended Period
General Fish Mood: Variable—Negative to Positive

Lakes and reservoirs freeze throughout most of the walleye's range but remain open in much of the lower third of the United States. Where waters don't freeze, the Coldwater Period extends throughout winter, since patterns remain similar.

Fishing through the ice presents its own challenges, but often the way walleyes relate to structure and respond to baits remains similar from the end of the Coldwater Period into the Frozen Water Period. Fishing at early-ice often is excellent on offshore humps or along turns and points on steep structure along prominent main lake bars.

Walleyes in deep lakes and reservoirs seem to favor humps and structural features of shoreline breaks in the 20- to 40-foot range. Groups of fish hold near these spots for weeks at a time, so fish them regularly and thoroughly. Walleyes typically feed within a foot of the bottom, so keep baits down unless sonar shows fish hovering higher.

Prime fishing occurs at dawn, dusk, and within two or three hours after dark. Action may be sporadic throughout the day and night.

Rivers that remain ice-free can provide excellent winter fishing for walleyes that have become concentrated in areas of reduced current. Anchor and drift baits through these spots or maneuver through high-percentage areas and vertically jig with leadheads or spoons tipped with minnows.

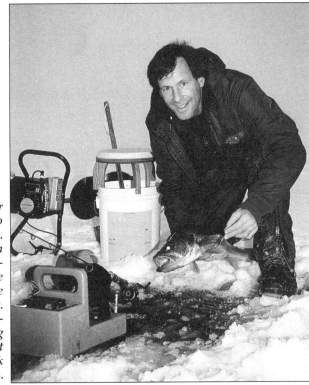

There's no finer time than first-ice to bag a big walleye. Recent advances in ice tackle and paraphernalia make ice fishing a more pleasant affair. For more information about ice fishing for walleyes, consult In-Fisherman's book **Ice Fishing Secrets.**

Chapter 3

Classifying Walleye Water

**CATEGORIZING
LAKE, RIVER, AND
RESERVOIR TYPES**

When In-Fisherman first began publication in the mid-1970s, several overriding principles were offered as part of a learning package that guaranteed anglers they could learn to fish successfully, or their money back. Chapter 2 discussed the Calendar Periods that walleyes move through as the seasons pass. The ability to identify Calendar Periods remains one overriding factor in understanding how walleyes are likely to be affected by their environment—where they may be and how they may react to an angler's choice of presentation.

Calendar Periods also serve as a reference point and therefore as a basis for communication. Anglers who understand the system can discuss fish response and place it in context when, say, one is referencing walleye behavior in a lake in Minnesota and another is referring to walleye behavior in an Arkansas reservoir. If the angler in Arkansas is reacting to walleyes' response to conditions during a Cold Water Period and the Minnesota angler is reacting to the fishes' response during the Summer Peak, they are really talking apples and oranges.

The ability to classify lakes, rivers, and reservoirs is another basic, critical concept In-Fisherman offers for understanding the structural makeup of different bodies of water. Learning to classify waters helps the angler to note similarities and differences in fish behavior and to place these in context. For example, an angler referencing walleye behavior in a canyon reservoir isn't on the same page as an angler noting walleye behavior in a middle-aged natural lake. Surprisingly, the thousands of lakes, rivers, and reservoirs across North America fall somewhat neatly into little more than a dozen divisions that are easy to grasp with a bit of practice.

NATURAL LAKES

Obviously, no two lakes are exactly alike. Broadly, though, all lakes can be classified into one of three environmental age groups: oligotrophic (young), mesotrophic (middle-aged), and eutrophic (old). Factors like the lake's predator-prey relationships, the amounts and types of aquatic vegetation, and many other structural considerations help to determine the basic lake classification, and ultimately help you determine where walleyes should be located within each Calendar Period.

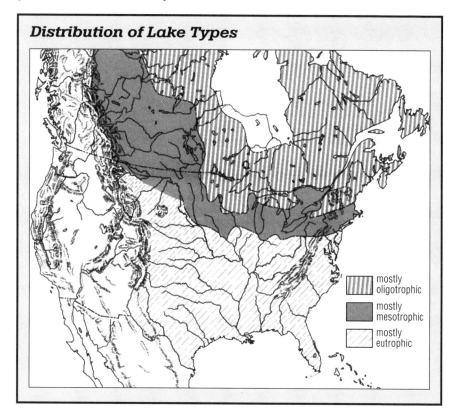

Distribution of Lake Types

mostly oligotrophic
mostly mesotrophic
mostly eutrophic

No matter where your favorite lake is located, it's changing. In some waters, visible change may take centuries. In other waters, change may occur in a few years. This aging process is often called eutrophication, and all lakes pass through it. A lake grows older not only in time but in condition. The initial stages of eutrophication may take thousands of years. The final ones may happen quickly, especially with the addition of manmade factors.

Throughout this process, the lake environment—structural makeup, food chains, vegetation levels, and dominant fish species—changes. Man-caused eutrophication, or aging, is in part due to expanding human population and often to waste disposal. Man may accomplish in a generation what may otherwise take hundreds of years.

Because of the manmade changes on most North American lakes, we classify natural lakes according to their environmental condition rather than their chronological age. Each category is a point of reference. Anglers quickly learn to recognize similarities in bodies of water and can readily transfer what they've learned on one lake to another with similar water. This is one method for patterning walleyes and applying those patterns to bodies of water an angler has never fished before but nevertheless recognizes.

As lakes age, then, their character changes. Environmentally young lakes are deep and clear, while older lakes are shallow and murky. The young lakes are oxygen-rich and support lake trout, whitefish, and some walleyes. Old lakes are weed-choked and oxygen-poor, and these support carp, bullheads, and perhaps some walleyes. Between these two extremes fall most lakes, each one more or less hospitable to certain fish species. Walleyes usually thrive in the middle category (mesotrophic water).

The three basic categories of natural lakes can be regrouped into nine even more specific categories. First, though, consider the three basic categories.

OLIGOTROPHIC LAKES

The youngest, most infertile lakes typically have rock basins and are almost exclusively found in the northern latitudes of North America. They usually have steep sharp drop-offs, few weeds, and conifer-studded shorelines. The nutrient level of the water is usually low and oxygen is available in deep water. These lakes usually support low gamefish populations; a few pounds of gamefish per acre is common. Walleyes may begin to do well in the later stages of this lake classification.

Infertile

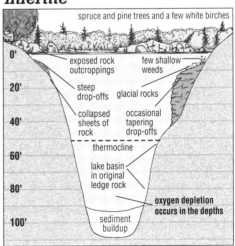

spruce and pine trees and a few white birches

0'
exposed rock outcroppings — few shallow weeds

20'
steep drop-offs — glacial rocks

40'
collapsed sheets of rock — occasional tapering drop-offs

thermocline

60'
lake basin in original ledge rock

80'
oxygen depletion occurs in the depths

100'
sediment buildup

Moderately Fertile

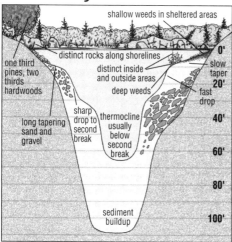

shallow weeds in sheltered areas

one third pines, two thirds hardwoods

distinct rocks along shorelines

distinct inside and outside areas

deep weeds

long tapering sand and gravel

sharp drop to second break

thermocline usually below second break

0'
slow taper
20'
fast drop
40'
60'
80'

sediment buildup

100'

Fertile

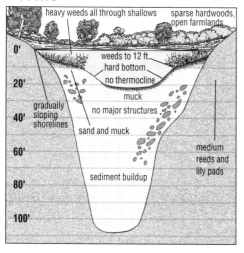

heavy weeds all through shallows

sparse hardwoods, open farmlands

weeds to 12 ft.
hard bottom
no thermocline

0'

20'

gradually sloping shorelines

muck

no major structures

40'

sand and muck

60'

medium reeds and lily pads

sediment buildup

80'

100'

MESOTROPHIC LAKES

In middle-aged lakes, shorelines are less gorgelike and drop-offs less abrupt. Big boulders give way to smaller rocks, and sand and gravel are more apparent. Weedgrowth abounds. Shoreline terrain is more varied and plant life more diverse. The water contains more nutrients. The lake is moderately fertile, the water is cool, and many pounds of fish are present per acre. This is the type of lake in which walleyes thrive.

EUTROPHIC LAKES

The environmentally oldest lakes are warmwater environments. Shallow weedgrowth is thick as long as the water remains somewhat clear. Lake bottoms consist of muck or clay, and shorelines taper gradually to the waterline. Often there are no secondary drop-offs. Marshy areas usually dot adjacent sections of lake. Hardwood trees and flat shorelines are the rule.

Eutrophic lakes often are called "dishpan lakes" because of their overall shallow depth and uniform shape. Typically, these old lakes are fertile and have large fish populations. Walleyes do well at first, but as these lakes continue to age, walleyes give way to species like bullheads and carp. Walleyes may thrive, though, where they are stocked and protected from freeze-outs by aeration systems.

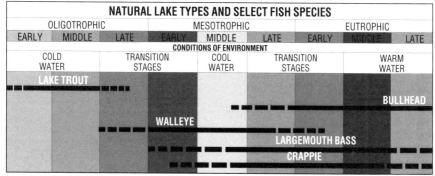

NATURAL LAKE TYPES AND SELECT FISH SPECIES

OLIGOTROPHIC			MESOTROPHIC			EUTROPHIC		
EARLY	MIDDLE	LATE	EARLY	MIDDLE	LATE	EARLY	MIDDLE	LATE
CONDITIONS OF ENVIRONMENT								
COLD WATER		TRANSITION STAGES		COOL WATER		TRANSITION STAGES		WARM WATER

LAKE TROUT

BULLHEAD

WALLEYE

LARGEMOUTH BASS

CRAPPIE

The Lake Aging Process

STABLE, YOUNG, INFERTILE COLDWATER ENVIRONMENTAL PHASES
  1. Early-stage oligotrophic (no walleyes present)
  2. Midstage oligotrophic (perhaps a few walleyes present)

TRANSITION FROM COLD- TO COOLWATER ENVIRONMENTAL PHASES
  3. Late-stage oligotrophic (walleyes become a key species, especially in transition habitats like bays and river inlets and outlets)
  4. Early-stage mesotrophic (walleyes begin to thrive)

STABLE, MIDDLE-AGED, MODERATELY FERTILE COOLWATER ENVIRONMENTAL PHASE
  5. Midstage mesotrophic (walleyes thrive)

TRANSITION FROM COOL- TO WARMWATER ENVIRONMENTAL PHASES
  6. Late-stage mesotrophic (walleyes continue to thrive)
  7. Early-stage eutrophic (walleyes still thrive, although natural reproduction begins to decline)

STABLE, OLD, FERTILE WARMWATER ENVIRONMENTAL PHASE
  8. Midstage eutrophic (walleyes mostly absent)

TRANSITION FROM WARM- TO VERY WARMWATER ENVIRONMENTAL PHASE
  9. Late-stage eutrophic (no walleyes present)

RIVERS

Rivers come in many sizes and provide habitat for many fish species. Different stretches of the same river can have contrasting personalities and different fish species. For example, a young, clear, coldwater river plunges downhill, flowing over and cutting through solid rock. Here, trout and grayling can thrive, but not walleyes. As a river matures, it becomes increasingly fertile, flows more slowly, and begins to meander. A coolwater environment favors walleyes and perhaps smallmouth bass and muskies. Finally, in old age, a river winds through a flood plain. The warmwater environment supports mostly largemouth bass, catfish, gar, and carp.

Middle-aged and old rivers are slow flowing, shallow rivers with broad flood plains. These wide flood plains create complex backwater areas with abundant habitat. The mouths of flooded backwaters, oxbow lakes, and connecting lakes can be excellent areas for walleyes. During spring and early summer, brush, stumps, and timber are common fish attractors.

Channels, meanwhile, provide connections to other prime spots and often attract the majority of walleyes during most yearly periods. Since backwaters can be a mile or more from the main channel, they often function more as reservoirs than as rivers.

RIVER CLASSIFICATION

Streams must be viewed by stretches. A particular stretch can be young, old, or somewhere in between. For instance, a stream may be shallow with only gradual gradient changes for several miles, and possess backwater areas with soft bottom and aquatic weedgrowth. Crappies and largemouth bass find adequate habitat here. Then this stream may break through a rocky, clifflike area, creating a rapids and finally pouring into a boulder-based pool. This stretch may hold walleyes and smallmouth bass.

Rarely is a stream the same from beginning to end because few of them flow through regions that are geographically so consistent. Because of these variations, we use the following method to classify streams. Most river stretches in North America fall within one of seven categories. River stretches, though, often exhibit transitional tendencies, just as a natural lake may have eutrophic bays while its main body is mesotrophic.

Distribution of Species by River Age Category

This chart shows the species present in each river category. Notice how a fish's numbers peak and then gradually decrease as the river evolves. Each aging stage favors certain varieties of cold-, cool-, or warmwater species.

Young, picturesque mountain trout streams may be unpolluted and unaffected by man. These streams are infertile since they run over rock beds and gain few nutrients from the land. Very young and young streams cannot support large fish populations.

Coldwater species disappear in the adult stage. In sections with less gradient, the water flows slower and warms to a temperature that trout cannot survive. This environment favors coolwater fish like smallmouth bass.

In the mature stage, coolwater fish like walleyes, saugers, pike and muskies begin to dominate. Then, as a river gets older, coolwater species begin to fade. Warmwater fish like largemouth bass and catfish become dominant, and fish like carp become common.

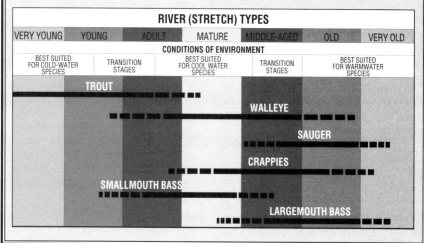

As rivers age slightly and slow, trout give way to coolwater species like small-mouth bass and walleyes.

Young stream sections host trout that thrive as water flows quickly over rock and gravel.

Walleyes thrive in mature river stretches.

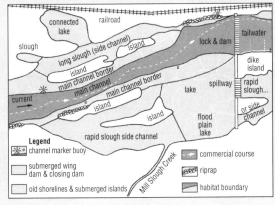

Aging river stretches flow slowly through farm country. Walleyes may be present but catfish are more common.

Habitat In One River Category

connected lake
railroad
slough
tailwater
lock & dam
long slough (side channel)
island
island
dike island
main channel border
main channel
main channel border
lake
spillway
rapid slough...
current
island
or side channel
island
flood plain lake
rapid slough side channel
Mill Slough Creek

Legend
channel marker buoy
submerged wing dam & closing dam
old shorelines & submerged islands
commercial course
riprap
habitat boundary

The river category in question determines available habitat, and available habitat determines the available fish species and their location. This section of the upper Mississippi River shows typical habitat areas in a mature river. High and low water and yearly period dictate the movement of fish from backwaters to the main channel.

RESERVOIRS

A reservoir is a body of water impounded behind a dam. Water floods the landscape—marshes, plains, hills, mountains, plateaus, and canyons—depending on the geographic area. In general, reservoirs in the North, West, and Northwest provide cooler water environments than those in the South, Southwest, and Southeast. Because walleyes are coolwater fish, they are therefore more common in the cooler regions.

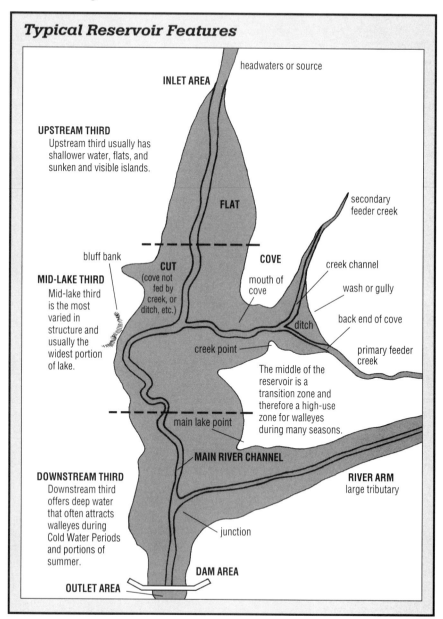

Typical Reservoir Features

headwaters or source

INLET AREA

UPSTREAM THIRD
Upstream third usually has shallower water, flats, and sunken and visible islands.

FLAT

secondary feeder creek

bluff bank

CUT
(cove not fed by creek, or ditch, etc.)

COVE

mouth of cove

creek channel

wash or gully

MID-LAKE THIRD
Mid-lake third is the most varied in structure and usually the widest portion of lake.

back end of cove

ditch

creek point

primary feeder creek

The middle of the reservoir is a transition zone and therefore a high-use zone for walleyes during many seasons.

main lake point

MAIN RIVER CHANNEL

DOWNSTREAM THIRD
Downstream third offers deep water that often attracts walleyes during Cold Water Periods and portions of summer.

RIVER ARM
large tributary

junction

DAM AREA

OUTLET AREA

Taking a cross section of North America, we see that some areas are low, swampy, and flat. These are old flood plain regions. Other places are hilly. Still others have mountains with highland ridges that form foothills. These are usually low mountain ranges like the Boston and Ouachita ranges in Arkansas, the Appalachian chain in the East, the Cumberland highlands of Kentucky and Tennessee, and the low coastal ranges of the West Coast.

Reservoirs lying within each of these landforms have the same basic configuration; that is, they have a similar cross section and shape. Canyon reservoirs, for example, are long and snakelike with towering, sharp, almost vertical walls. Waters impounded in flood plains are wide and offer expanses of shallow flats.

The shape of an impoundment is the key factor in determining its classification. By studying a topographical map, you can usually determine what classification an impoundment falls into. Other facets of a reservoir's personality include (1) annual fluctuation of water level; (2) water clarity; (3) fertility; and (4) temperature.

IMPOUNDMENT CLASSIFICATION

We classify reservoirs into six broad categories: canyon, plateau, highland, hill-land, flatland, and lowland (or wetland). These classes are based on regional and geological aspects of North America's various landforms. Both natural and manmade characteristics determine what class an impoundment fits into. There are, of course, many exceptions: smaller reservoirs are hard to classify exactly, and some reservoirs have portions characteristic of different classes, just as lakes and rivers do.

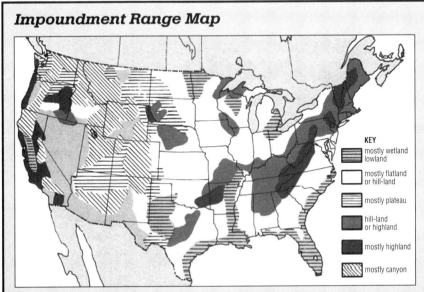

Impoundment Range Map

KEY

mostly wetland lowland

mostly flatland or hill-land

mostly plateau

hill-land or highland

mostly highland

mostly canyon

Reservoirs constructed in similar landforms even when they're in different parts of the country are enough alike to fit into six basic groups: canyon, plateau, highland, hill-land, flatland, and lowland (or wetland).

Reservoir Types

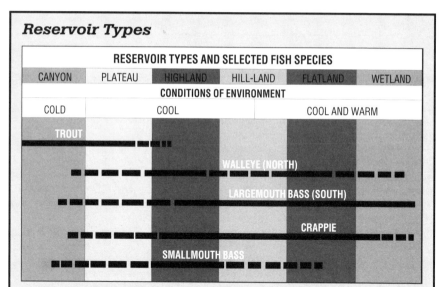

RESERVOIR TYPES AND SELECTED FISH SPECIES

CANYON	PLATEAU	HIGHLAND	HILL-LAND	FLATLAND	WETLAND

CONDITIONS OF ENVIRONMENT

COLD	COOL	COOL AND WARM

TROUT

WALLEYE (NORTH)

LARGEMOUTH BASS (SOUTH)

CRAPPIE

SMALLMOUTH BASS

Each reservoir category can sustain walleyes. Most sections of canyon reservoirs are, however, too deep to provide prime habitat. Likewise, some lowland reservoirs are too warm and fertile to support many walleyes. Walleyes generally thrive in plateau reservoirs, flatland reservoirs, and hill-land reservoirs, and often do well in highland reservoirs.

Canyon

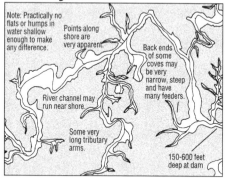

Note: Practically no flats or humps in water shallow enough to make any difference.

Points along shore are very apparent.

Back ends of some coves may be very narrow, steep and have many feeders.

River channel may run near shore.

Some very long tributary arms.

150-600 feet deep at dam

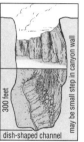

300 feet

dish-shaped channel

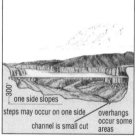

may be small step in canyon wall

300'

one side slopes

steps may occur on one side

overhangs occur some areas

channel is small cut

Plateau

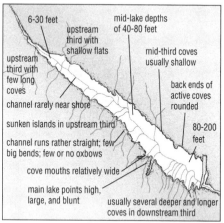

6-30 feet

upstream third with shallow flats

mid-lake depths of 40-80 feet

upstream third with few long coves

mid-third coves usually shallow

channel rarely near shore

back ends of active coves rounded

sunken islands in upstream third

80-200 feet

channel runs rather straight; few big bends; few or no oxbows

cove mouths relatively wide

main lake points high, large, and blunt

usually several deeper and longer coves in downstream third

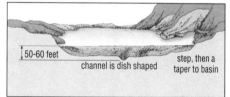

50-60 feet

channel is dish shaped

step, then a taper to basin

Highland

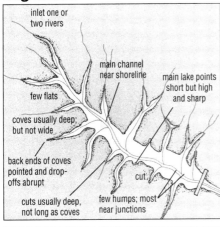

- inlet one or two rivers
- main channel near shoreline
- main lake points short but high and sharp
- few flats
- coves usually deep; but not wide
- back ends of coves pointed and drop-offs abrupt
- cut
- cuts usually deep, not long as coves
- few humps; most near junctions

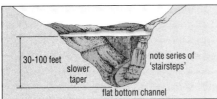

- 30-100 feet
- slower taper
- note series of 'stairsteps'
- flat bottom channel

Hill-Land

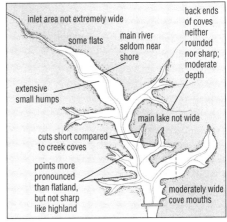

- inlet area not extremely wide
- some flats
- main river seldom near shore
- back ends of coves neither rounded nor sharp; moderate depth
- extensive small humps
- main lake not wide
- cuts short compared to creek coves
- points more pronounced than flatland, but not sharp like highland
- moderately wide cove mouths

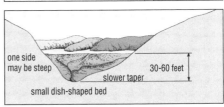

- one side may be steep
- 30-60 feet
- slower taper
- small dish-shaped bed

Flatland

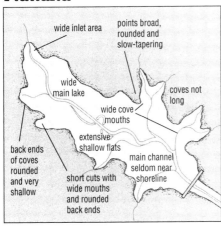

- wide inlet area
- points broad, rounded and slow-tapering
- wide main lake
- coves not long
- wide cove mouths
- extensive shallow flats
- back ends of coves rounded and very shallow
- short cuts with wide mouths and rounded back ends
- main channel seldom near shoreline

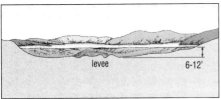

- levee
- 6-12'

Lowland–Wetland

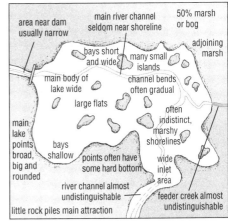

- area near dam usually narrow
- main river channel seldom near shoreline
- 50% marsh or bog
- adjoining marsh
- bays short and wide
- many small islands
- main body of lake wide
- channel bends often gradual
- large flats
- often indistinct, marshy shorelines
- main lake points broad, big and rounded
- bays shallow
- points often have some hard bottom
- wide inlet area
- river channel almost undistinguishable
- feeder creek almost undistinguishable
- little rock piles main attraction

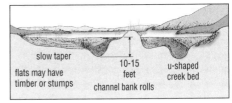

- slow taper
- flats may have timber or stumps
- 10-15 feet
- u-shaped creek bed
- channel bank rolls

Edge Effect and Structure

THE BIG PICTURE FOR WALLEYES

The previous chapters emphasize the importance that learning to classify waters and recognizing Calendar Periods play in determining fishing patterns for walleyes. Those ideas must be coupled with another set of factors before you can finally begin to find walleyes consistently. No angler can progress past the most basic stages of fishing without understanding the effect that edges and structure have on walleye location.

Long ago, scientific observers noted a pattern of animal behavior termed edge effect—the tendency of so many living things to respond to edges in their environment. An edge occurs where two different habitat areas meet—for example, where a meadow meets a forest. Many species of wildlife make use of such edges.

Not only are there edges, but there are also edges on edges. A meadow meeting a forest is an edge, and wildlife may use this entire edge. Certain species, though, confine their activities to only certain areas along this edge. The spot where a forest projects into a meadow, or perhaps the spot where a bunch of seedlings grow along an edge are examples of edges on edges. These areas often attract more wildlife than the rest of the edge.

Edge effect is important in fishing because fish, including walleyes, relate to edges. Sometimes the edge relationship is obvious, as when walleyes relate to the outside portion of a weededge. Sometimes it's subtle, as when walleyes relate to the edge of a baitfish school or the depth of light penetration. To be able to find walleyes consistently, you must learn to recognize edges—and edges on edges.

Structure and edges are closely related. *Structure* is a term coined by one of the most astute anglers of all time, Buck Perry, who said that structure was an area of bottom different from the surrounding area. Perry developed a fishing concept incorporating edge theory. His term for edge was *breakline*, and his term for an edge on an edge was *break*. So he called the outside edge of a weedline a breakline. And he called a pod of rocks along this outside weededge a break in a breakline, or a break on a break.

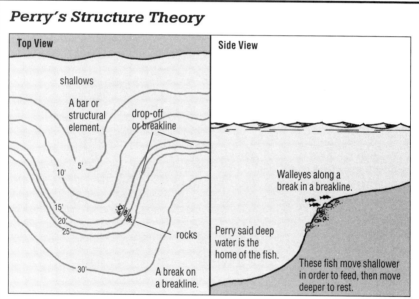

Perry's Structure Theory

Top View

shallows

A bar or structural element.

drop-off or breakline

5'

10'

15'

20'

25'

rocks

30'

A break on a breakline.

Side View

Walleyes along a break in a breakline.

Perry said deep water is the home of the fish.

These fish move shallower in order to feed, then move deeper to rest.

Buck Perry theorized that schools of gamefish lived in deep water and made periodic feeding movements into the shallows when active. They contacted physical changes in the bottom he termed structure. As they moved up, they held along rapid changes in depth called breaklines. Small areas of concentration along the breakline were called breaks, or breaks on the break. Fish that continued moving shallower might scatter across the shallows when they became more active.

We've since discovered many exceptions to Perry's structure theory, but it remains the cornerstone of modern fishing strategy.

But if every time you see an edge, or an edge on an edge, you assume that walleyes must be there, you're in trouble. Some edges are better than others. The next step is to learn to make judgments about the total environment you're fishing. Structure and edges on structure should be judged on the basis of how they combine with, are influenced by, and influence other environmental factors and the Calendar Period in which you're fishing.

For most anglers, the ability to make such evaluations successfully is a matter of experience. First, though, the angler needs to know how to play the game. That's what this book's first four chapters are about. In a lifetime, any angler can learn to catch walleyes on a favorite body of water, providing, of course, that the population of walleyes remains high. Most anglers today, though, make occasional forays to other bodies of water where walleyes are booming. The ability to fish successfully on a variety of waters depends on the processes we're discussing here.

But what are the principal factors that influence the productivity of certain structures and certain edges? Why are some structures and edges on structure better than others? And why are some structures productive during some Calendar Periods and not during others?

But if every time you see an edge, or an edge on an edge, you assume that walleyes must be there, you're in trouble.

In 1975, Al and Ron Lindner made the leap from fishing guides to tackle manufacturers to fishing information publishers, printing the first of a series of educational study reports entitled *The In-Fisherman*. The Lindners not only covered all the important basics, but they also dared to reach out and postulate new ideas, many of which went against popular concepts.

In the years since, *In-Fisherman* has forged ahead in exploring the intricacies of fish behavior in the underwater world. Much of what we have written since then confirms Buck Perry's original ideas. But we've discovered so many exceptions and contradictions along the way that we now consider them only guidelines.

Perry proposed structure fishing theory. We call our current understanding of the subject "modern structure theory." It incorporates more than just cover, the shape of the bottom, and changes in depth. Modern structure theory attempts to understand everything that occurs underwater—even how the tiniest plankton and baitfish affect gamefish movement and behavior in a particular environment at a particular time of year. Instead of considering only one item, modern structure theory focuses on the big picture.

MODERN STRUCTURE FISHING

In the early days, anglers were so bent on fishing drop-offs that all they looked for were changes in depth. But as we've suggested, a sharp drop-off by itself doesn't attract and hold fish. Fish must have a reason to be in that area. If it offers food, cover, and proper spawning conditions, chances are that fish will use it at least part of the time. When they do, they are likely to concentrate along a change in depth or some type of edge. Structure theory applies when the area attracts fish, but not when it's devoid of fish.

So don't just look for physical shapes—bars, humps, channels. Look for lake or river areas that fulfill a fish's seasonal needs. Then look for smaller areas—bars, humps, channels—that concentrate fish within larger areas.

Seasonal needs incorporate a variety of items. Some are universal and apply yearlong; others, like spawning conditions, are important only at certain times.

Walleyes in Shallow Lakes and Reservoirs

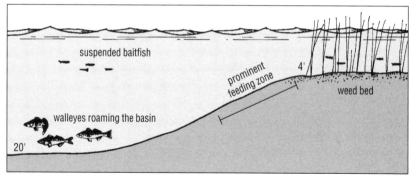

Shallow featureless basins and shallow shoreline cover with little or no deep water structure are hallmarks of fertile prairie waters and some shallow reservoirs. Walleyes often roam the basin area, making periodic feeding forays into extremely shallow shoreline cover or along shoreline drop-offs from 0 to 3 or 4 feet. In these dark water environments, this pattern is the norm. Pockets, points, and changes in shallow cover or shoreline tend to be better than straight sections.

Walleyes at Spawning Time

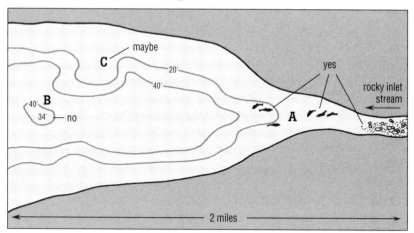

Structure isn't the only key to fishing success. Structural location and seasonal needs play a big role. At spawning time, walleyes are likely in or near rocky inlet stream *A*, especially at night. During the day, they might move to the first drop-off and lie along the edge, even if no distinct point or structural feature is present.

Deep sunken island *B* looks great but is poor at this time of year. Shoreline point *C* may produce, especially if rocks are strewn along the shore. After spawning, *C* will begin to attract fish. Eventually, some will move to *B*.

Food, though, is almost always key to attracting fish. If food isn't present, walleyes usually don't stay long. Beautiful-looking structure is often fishless.

Walleyes also need oxygen. Most gamefish can only tolerate oxygen levels below 5 parts per million for a short time. In most walleye lakes, oxygen is present in sufficient quantity throughout most areas except possibly below the thermocline in summer. Classic structure below the thermocline may be too deep for walleyes until after fall Turnover, when cooling water returns oxygen to the depths.

Temperature can be a limiting factor, too, but only in extreme cases. Walleyes can withstand temperatures near 100°F for short periods. The problem with temperature is more likely to affect baitfish directly. If water becomes too warm for baitfish to survive, walleyes will follow them to cooler areas.

In spring, water temperature is an indicator of the spawning cycle. Between 40°F and 50°F, walleyes are in the vicinity of spawning areas. They often arrive earlier and remain later if food is present. At this time of year, walleyes typically congregate around shallow rock or rubble shorelines, reefs, or inlet streams. Suitable spawning areas may adjoin deep water structure but may be miles away from classic points and humps.

Anglers who fish deep points or humps when walleyes are on gravel flats may be fishing structure, but their logic has backfired. Go where the fish are. Then find features that concentrate them within the area. Otherwise, it's like having a great seat on the 50-yard line before football season begins.

About cover—In most environments, cover increases the likelihood that an area will draw and hold baitfish and walleyes. It offers a billion hiding places for predator and prey. Cover can be weeds, wood, rocks, or manmade features, whatever's available. Where cover is present, expect fish to use edges or transitions between cover and open water or between different types or thicknesses of weeds.

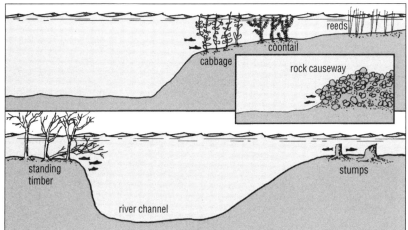

Cover

Cover usually enhances the ability of shallows to attract and hold baitfish and walleyes. In some waters, however, cover is lacking and fish use slick structures. In this case, bottom transitions or scattered rocks may concentrate walleyes.

This is structure theory on a microscale. Changes concentrate walleyes, providing that walleyes are in the area.

Deep water often contains little or no cover. Changes in bottom content may be key here, especially where changes in depth occur. For example, if the tip of an underwater point looks good, fish the primary drop-off all the way around the tip. Say you catch all your fish in one spot, a small rock slide. You can feel the difference with your sinker and see a visible change in signal strength on your depthfinder. Walleyes will have noticed and responded to the difference, too.

Prime elements of structure—Structure fishermen usually fish points, but they often ignore inside corners, the opposite of points. Inside turns can be good when suspended baitfish are present. Baitfish wandering in open water bump into the drop-off, then turn and follow it at the same depth. When they come to a corner, they stall, hovering in the area like confused tourists at an unexpected dead end. Walleyes and other gamefish use inside corners as productive feeding areas. The best inside turns occur along deep drop-offs, river channel bends, and shallow timber or weededges.

Even shallow shorelines or the outside edges of reeds can collect fish in such corners. Ask yourself: Do walleyes move shallowly in this type of environment? In lakes with clear water, they may do so only at night or during a strong wind. But in dark water, fish may move into 3 or 4 feet of water during the day.

Shallow walleyes—Shallow water walleyes are one of the hardest concepts for a hardcore structure fisherman to accept. But they're common in prairie lakes, many rivers, and impoundments with stained water. Cover edges in extremely shallow water can draw large groups of walleyes to feed on bullheads, shad, white

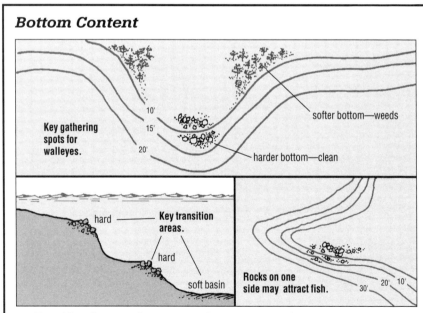

Bottom Content

Key gathering spots for walleyes.

10'
15'
20'

softer bottom—weeds

harder bottom—clean

hard

Key transition areas.

hard

soft basin

Rocks on one side may attract fish.

30' 20' 10'

Transitions between bottom type often concentrate fish, even without distinct change in depth. Bottom type can enhance or prevent weedgrowth, provide crevasses for bait to hide, or simply offer fish something different to relate to.

Corners

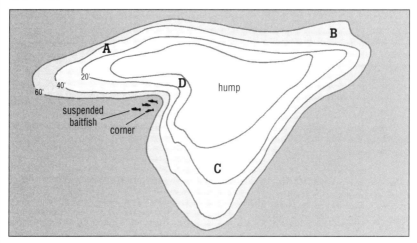

*Tips of points (**A, B, C**) are considered the best walleye spots, but sometimes suspended bait and walleyes concentrate at tight inside corners in the breakline (**D**). The corner can be on a deep hump or have shallow weeds, wood, or boulders on top.*

Suspension, Basins, and Flats
—Exceptions or Logical Options?

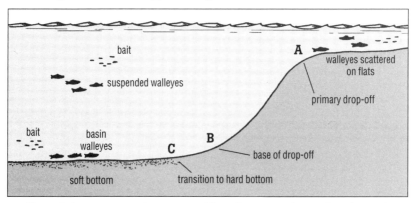

*Three obvious concentration spots on this underwater point are the primary drop-off (**A**), base of the drop-off (**B**), and the transition to soft bottom (**C**) where the hard bottom of the point meets the soft basin.*

*But in this case, the fish aren't there. Schools of baitfish sometimes rove flat, featureless areas—suspended, across the basin, and on shallow flats. Walleyes follow. These conditions occur on many waters at least seasonally. While **A, B,** and **C** usually are logical options, don't assume that fish can't or won't use flat areas.*

bass, or minnows, particularly during windy conditions.

So much has been written about walleyes using deep water structure that some walleye anglers have a hard time thinking shallow. But when water clarity is reduced, bait and gamefish readily move into shallow water.

Roaming walleyes—Some fishermen also find it difficult to believe that walleyes wander in open water, off bottom, responding to nothing except nonstructural factors like moving baitfish, sunlight penetration, possibly temperature variations, wind, seasonal migration, boat traffic, and a host of other factors. Anglers love catching fish on sharp drop-offs and classic structure because they're been told that's how it's done and how they have done it before. But if the fish are suspended, you may be wasting time fishing those classic spots. If you can't accept this, take a trip to Lake Erie, where millions of big walleyes roam open water. Seeing is believing.

Finally, walleyes also roam large, featureless flats. When you locate fish in such places, try to isolate a slight depth change, a transition in bottom composition, dips or rises, subtle weedcover, current, depth of light penetration—anything that indicates a structural reason for fish being there. Remember: it's always necessary to fish where the fish are. Drifting over huge, gradually sloping shallow flats on big lakes and reservoirs can be key, especially in wind.

The same goes for deep flats in the basin. In many lakes, 20- to 50-foot flat basins hold baitfish and walleyes. This is particularly true in early summer before strong thermoclines drop oxygen levels in the depths, forcing fish into shallower water.

More habitat factors—In a lake where walleyes are the major predators, you may find fish on classic structure, but if significant numbers of competing predators like

Complex Structures

Complex structures offer a variety of habitat options to attract walleyes all year. They offer more areas than small simple structures, but they usually hold many more fish—often multiple species.

pike, muskies, and bass are present, something has to give. If suitable habitat is limited, all species may use the same areas, but during different times of the day.

As a rule, simple structural elements hold the fewest fish, usually in a limited area. Large, complex structure contains a variety of fish-attracting areas, with bass on the flats, pike on the deep weedline, walleyes on twists and turns along the drop-off, muskies suspended off the side, as well as interaction among them.

Take the same structure, remove the competing predators, and walleyes may occur in all these spots, expanding to fill the available environmental niches. Expect the deepest fish to be active during the day, the shallowest to be most active during low-light conditions and in wind and at night.

Consider, though, that habitats change constantly throughout the year. Water temperature rises and falls. Light penetration varies as plankton blooms, then decreases. Weedgrowth flourishes, then dies. Baitfish hatch in incredible numbers, grow to edible size, then are preyed upon and diminish. Fish move from spring spawning areas to summer feeding spots to fall and winter holding areas before restaging for their next spawning run. Nothing remains the same for long. To survive, walleyes must constantly stage and adjust. If you don't follow them through their habitats and seasons, they'll leave you up the lake without a clue.

Perry's theory of active fish relating to edges and fish in general relating to physical shapes and changes in the bottom remains critical. But if you travel and fish different waters, you'll find that walleye behavior in a variety of freshwater habits ranges from classic to odd. In odd environments, odd behavior becomes the norm.

TEN QUICK TIPS FOR APPLYING STRUCTURE THEORY

It takes more than fishing magic baits or good-looking structure to catch fish. In-Fisherman's *Fish + Location + Presentation = Success* formula pieces together the environmental factors you must consider to locate fish so you can catch them.

Veteran walleye pro Mike McClelland offers the following gameplan for contacting fish on unfamiliar waters:

(1) Check bait shops and talk to anglers at boat ramps. Study lake maps. Assemble as much prefishing information as possible before you even get on the water.

(2) Observe what local boats are doing. Are they fishing deep, shallow, in between? Fishing aggressively with artificials or extracting neutral fish with livebait presentations? Fishing humps, points, shorelines, or other structures? Determine what's working, then use it as a starting point.

(3) Fish prominent structural features— big bars, humps, creek mouths, whatever—that attract fish at that time of year. They may not be the best spots, especially

Finding walleyes fast is a typical topic in In-Fisherman's annual Walleye Guide, which hits the newsstands once each year in the spring.

if fishing pressure is heavy, but they should provide clues to fish location and behavior. Study your lake map and begin fishing where fish should be. Then adapt.

(4) Use electronics. Scan 12- to 30-foot depths to find fish before you fish for them. Run drop-offs on prominent structure to see how fish are oriented.

(5) Determine a productive depth and pattern. Concentrate on the fish you've marked with a variety of techniques ranging from aggressive to slow and tempting. Don't waste more than a few minutes on fish that won't bite. Move on to other options.

(6) If you don't catch fish, move shallower rather than deeper. Walleyes deeper than 28 to 30 feet are usually tougher to catch than shallower fish, which tend to be more aggressive. Penetrate weedlines and move up onto the flat adjacent to the drop-off.

(7) Still no fish? Move extremely shallow—right up on the shoreline or along inside weededges. Concentrate on the windy side of the lake for aggressive fish. Look for rocks, piers, causeways—obvious fish-attracting structures. Consider cover and bottom content. Fish shorelines with distinctive lips rather than gradual tapers; these are the spots where walleyes can herd baitfish against the drop.

(8) Next check middepth flats with bottom bouncers, spinners, and crankbaits—presentations that cover lots of water quickly—searching for active fish.

(9) No fish? Could they be in open water? Will you have to troll? Look for suspended baitfish and gamefish near prominent structural elements. Put out trolling boards, crankbaits, and either weighted or leadcore line to take lures to the depth where fish are holding.

(10) Still nothing? Deep-lying fish are the last resort. Using slow livebait rigging techniques; fish the deep tips of structural elements where you see fish. If you see fish spread across the mud in a deep basin, drag bottom bouncers, spinners, and crawlers. Tough, slow fishing is often productive if faster, shallower, easier tactics don't produce.

Putting It All Together

Study hydrographic lake maps for clues to fish location and behavior. Some are accurate. Many only indicate good starting points. Consider the Calendar Period and the type of lake, river, or reservoir.

Fish structure—at the right time and place. Structure can be simple or complex, distinct or subtle, deep or shallow, covered or barren. Seasonal hot spots can be devoid of fish during the rest of the year.

Walleyes relate to their environment. So should you. The better you follow their movements, the better you can apply structure theory at the right times in the right places, even when little or no structure is available.

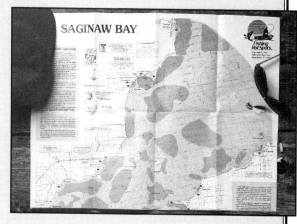

SAGINAW BAY

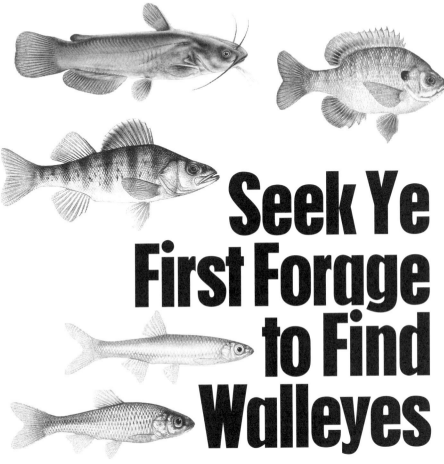

Seek Ye First Forage to Find Walleyes

**FOCUS ON
PREDATORY
RESPONSE**
_____

Walleyes usually eat what's abundant, readily available, and easy to catch. That varies. One shorecasting pattern that *In-Fisherman* Editor In Chief Doug Stange used to rely on was based on an influx of age-2 walleyes into a current area on a lake in Iowa. Each year about the second week of November, after a month of decent fishing for larger fish, small walleyes would move in. Fishing pressure steadily declined as anglers became frustrated with the nasty weather and small fish.

But if Doug kept fishing, if he stood there long enough and late enough into the midnight hours, and if he released enough small walleyes, eventually on a night or two, the small fish suddenly disappeared . . . and often on consecutive casts he'd poke 10-pounders with telltale lumps in their tummies. He cleaned a few of those big fish over the years. Din-din had always been 7- to 8-inch walleyes. Big Daddy walleyes didn't leave to seek traditional forage because the forage at hand was little brother Billy Bob.

In most bodies of water, however, walleyes do not typically forage on walleye young. Walleyes must eat, though, and except during the peak of the spawn, identifying forage plays a key role in walleye location. *Seek ye first forage to find walleyes* is a basic strategy for In-Fisherman staff members.

BULLHEADS, BLUEGILLS, AND CRAPPIES

That walleyes eat—indeed, rely on—bluegills, crappies, and especially bullheads during certain periods surprises some walleye anglers. I guess such prey sounds physically uncomfortable: How can something as wide and spiny fit down something (a gullet) so soft and narrow? Easily, apparently. Bullheads in particular are easy for walleyes to catch. So are yearling and age-2 and -3 panfish—bluegills and crappies.

Classic walleye lakes are moderately fertile. Crappies and bluegills do well in such lakes, and so do bullheads, up to a point. But all three species do even better in slightly more fertile bodies of water. So the best classic lakes in which walleyes key on these forage species have large, fertile bays—the equivalent of small, fertile lakes—adjoining them. Other good sites are necked-down areas leading from the main body of a classic walleye lake to an even more fertile lake, or, in the case of bullheads, necked areas leading to marshes.

As lakes pass the classic walleye stage and become more fertile, natural reproduction of walleyes drops, crappie and bluegill populations also drop, and bullheads boom. Many such bodies of water continue to be stocked with walleyes. Once introduced and equipped with aeration systems to prevent freeze-out, walleyes also boom, growing quickly and providing many more pounds of walleye per acre than many, if not most, classic walleye lakes. Bullheads are a primary forage in these lakes all year, even during winter, when walleyes root out dormant bullheads as they rest on the bottom.

That's hardly a primary pattern to help you contact walleyes eating bullheads. During spring, though, after walleye have spawned and are feeding aggressively, bullheads finish spawning in marshes and other fertile areas adjoining the main body of water. All sizes of bullheads continually move in and out of these areas. Necked-down current areas become prime spots because they focus fishing in a confined area. Bars near such areas also become high probability places to find walleyes.

Even tiny bullhead fry, travelling in small, dense pods, sometimes leave the shallows for the main lake. In classic lakes, bullheads group in weedbeds near fertile areas. In fertile lakes without many weeds, bullheads tend to roam, but they often group in greater numbers on the prevailing windward side of a lake.

Roughly the same pattern occurs in fall, when fertile areas adjoining the main

The Bullhead, Bluegill, Crappie Connection

A rea A—Bullheads move through this necked-down area during spring and fall. During fall in particular, bluegills and crappies may also move through this area. Current areas focus forage for walleyes and focus walleyes for fishermen.

Area B—This is a bullhead travel area during spring (spawning) and fall (feeding). This area remains good well into summer as pods of tiny bluegills continue to filter into the main lake. The lake side of the current area may also attract bluegills and crappies using the shallow bay just outside Area B.

Area C-1—Although the fishing is less focused, during many periods many more bullheads, bluegills, and crappies use weedgrowth on the deeper part of this bar. Troll a shallow-running minnow bait on a long line through this area after dark during spring and particularly during fall after the weedgrowth dies.

Area C-2—Bullheads, bluegills, and crappies spend much of the year in or moving in and out of the large fertile bay (Area E). This is the best area in the lake for long-line trolling (spring and fall) or working the weededge during summer. Be sure to work the bay side as well as the lake side of the edge.

Area C-3—Similar to *Area C-1*.

Area C-4—The least attractive area for bullheads, although weedgrowth may attract bluegills and crappies.

Area D—A prime area for wading anglers who fish during fall. Once the weedgrowth thins, bluegills, crappies, and some bullheads filter through the area, attracting walleyes after dark.

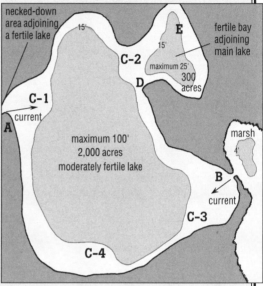

necked-down area adjoining a fertile lake

fertile bay adjoining main lake

15'

E

15'

C-2

maximum 25'

300 acres

D

C-1

current

A

maximum 100'
2,000 acres
moderately fertile lake

marsh
4'

B

current

C-3

C-4

Area E—If a fertile bay's large enough, as this one is, it harbors lots of bluegills and crappies. This is an important bullhead area, too. Troll around the rim of the bay during spring. During early summer, forage and walleyes suspend in the deeper water in the bay. Run baits through this open water.

During summer, forage moves back into the protective weedcover. Work the weededge during twilight periods. During fall, again troll around the rim of the bay. In most lakes, substantial numbers of walleyes reside in fertile bays most of the year.

lake warm quickly during nice weather (attracting bullheads) and cool quickly during bad weather (sending bullheads back to the main lake). Again, walleyes target bullheads at the mouths of necked-down areas or on bars adjoining fertile areas.

In classic lakes with large fertile bays adjoining the main lake, bullheads tend to move en masse into these areas. In many lakes, a large portion of the walleye population moves with them. Bars in these fertile bays become prime areas to troll at night. This pattern continues to be overlooked in many lakes. Instead, fishermen concentrate on classic rocky drop-offs in the main lake.

Young bluegills and crappies, often called "flats" because of their shape, first become readily accessible to walleyes during early summer when large schools of them suspend in open water immediately adjacent to the most fertile areas of the lake. Walleyes usually suspend, too, from late May into June in lakes and reservoirs from Iowa on the south into central Minnesota on the north.

Throughout summer, walleyes using weededges or holding on weed flats use panfish (and minnows and bullheads) as primary forage. Weeds protect the young forage until about September, when weedgrowth dies, exposing hordes of prey. Then walleyes go on a feeding binge, usually at twilight or after dark. These binges set the stage for some of the finest longline trolling of the year. Shorecasters can also take advantage of this pattern by wading and casting over weedy shallow bars. The key is to wait until the weedgrowth begins to die. First fish near-surface lures, then switch to baits that fish deeper, like leadhead jigs.

Tiny bluegills and crappies seined from barrow pits can be incredible bait if fished below a float in open water or through the ice. The tiniest flats are great perch bait. The best size for walleyes runs from approximately 1½ to 2 inches.

YELLOW PERCH

Angler surveys show that in several regions, yellow perch rank among the most popular sportfish because they're abundant and good to eat. Walleyes must have similar tastes, because where perch are common, young and adult walleyes select them as prey during most of the year.

Studies on Oneida Lake in New York indicate that perch are such an important prey that they can affect the strength of walleye year classes by buffering cannibalism. When young perch are abundant, walleyes selectively feed on them; when perch year classes are weak, walleyes feed on young walleyes, reducing walleye year classes.

In Mille Lacs Lake, Minnesota's premier walleye fishery, a huge hatch of perch can make fishing for walleye difficult, despite the abundance of walleyes. When natural prey are abundant, anglers' chubs, crawlers, and leeches lose their appeal.

In many lakes in the northern and central portions of the walleye range, yellow perch are the predominant prey once walleyes switch from invertebrates to a fish diet early in their first year. One key to successful walleye fishing in these regions is understanding this predator-prey relationship.

Juvenile and adult perch orient to structure, typically holding near bottom on points, humps, or deep flats connected to shore. The largest groups, often numbering several hundred fish, favor structural features like gravel shelves on sandy bars, slight depressions on humps, or small fingers on points. Many of these features have become classic "walleye spots" because groups of yellow perch holding there draw walleyes to them.

A Perch Pattern

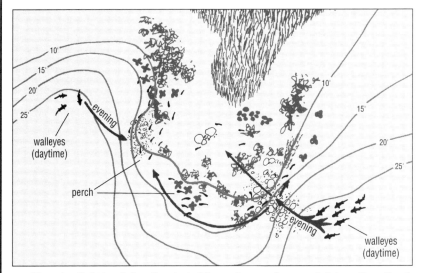

Changing light levels key the start of the walleye-yellow perch interaction. Perch that have been feeding over rock or gravel bars or along weededges rest as the sun sets. Walleyes that have been holding deeper and feeding little during the day approach these spots to prey on perch. The walleye's vision advantage lets it approach perch that are unaware of being stalked until it's too late.

In many mesotrophic and early eutrophic lakes, these spots may coincide with weedlines or clumps of sandgrass, eelgrass, or coontail where prey-size perch forage for invertebrates. In natural lakes, perch and walleyes tend to use the same areas each year because cover conditions and depth are constant. Where water level fluctuates, the angler's job becomes more complicated. A few additional feet of water often restrict plant growth, so perch shift to shallower areas. Falling water levels push perch and walleyes deeper.

Although walleyes eat perch during every season, peak feeding begins when perch gather in weedy bays, on weedy bars, or along brushy shorelines to spawn. This typically occurs from one to two weeks after walleye spawning ends, and when water temperatures have climbed into the upper 50°F range. Yellow perch don't begin spawning until they reach 5 or 6 inches at around age-3, but juveniles accompany adults into spawning areas, so walleyes of all sizes find suitable prey near spawning sites.

After spawning, perch move onto middepth flats or hold along breaks. They tend to group by size, with smaller fish holding shallower and larger fish deeper. During the day, walleyes often hold along deeper contours while perch feed in shallower water.

As dusk approaches, walleyes move up to feed. Perch are daytime feeders and rest on bottom during the night. Walleyes, in contrast, are less active during the day and feed instead at night. Their eyes are adapted to foraging well after dark because of the reflective surface on their retinas, the *tapetum lucidum*. This gives walleyes an advantage over fish that lack this adaptation, including perch.

Inactive perch nestled next to rocks or weed clumps become vulnerable to walleyes. The hot bite begins about half an hour before sundown and continues until full darkness. Bites may continue sporadically through the night, peaking a second time when the sky begins to lighten at dawn.

Feeding activity may occur on a 3-foot flat or on a 25-foot hump, depending on available structure and season. The general rule is that shallow action dominates during spring and fall, while deep spots are best in winter. During summer, feeding depths vary, with middepth spots (8 to 20 feet) most common.

Depth affects which presentations are most effective. In the shallows, drifting and casting crankbaits or trolling with an electric motor works best. In middepth spots (8 to 20 feet), try jigging, backtrolling livebait rigs, or setting baits under floats. Perch attract and activate walleyes, but walleyes also bite standard livebaits or lures. Perch-colored crankbaits often don't work better than black-backed or chartreuse models.

For deep duty during late fall or winter, jigging spoons or leadhead jigs tipped with minnows attract fish. Fish them precisely on slight bumps or turns on the structures where fish concentrate.

SHINERS

Throughout the walleye range, shiners are a top-selling livebait. Various members of the minnow family are prime prey because they form large schools; lack spines, speed, and other defenses; and inhabit almost every lake, river, and reservoir that contains walleyes.

The minnow family, Cyprinidae, is the largest in the world, containing over 1,500 species in about 275 genera. North America has about 280 species. While walleyes willingly consume most of these varieties, two species are of greatest importance in walleyes' diets and are therefore equally important to anglers.

The *spottail shiner*, a widespread species, ranges from the Georgia coast northwest into Saskatchewan. It grows to about 5 inches and travels in large schools, particularly at spawning time in late spring. Spawners gather on sand and gravel shoals at the mouths of small tributaries or along shorelines in the lower ends of creeks. Females broadcast their eggs over sand or algae.

Walleyes key on spawning groups because of their abundance and because other types of prey may not be as available at that time of year. Studies on Lake Erie show that spottail and emerald shiners constitute a large proportion of adult walleyes' diets during May and June. Later in summer, young-of-year yellow perch and gizzard shad become dominant prey as they reach edible size.

Spottails are popular baits in Iowa and Wisconsin, where dealers trap them along shorelines of lakes and backwaters of rivers. In other areas, redtail chubs, golden shiners, and fathead minnows are more available to bait collectors and so are sold in greater numbers. Walleyes sometimes prefer a certain type of minnow, for unknown reasons. But they usually eat what's most readily available.

The *emerald shiner* is important walleye prey in natural lakes, major rivers, and reservoirs. This species overlaps the range of the spottail but isn't present along the Atlantic coast. It extends west to British Columbia and in the central United States south to the Gulf of Mexico.

This popular bait is used live, salted, frozen, or preserved in chemicals. Walleyes in many areas focus on emerald shiners when they spawn in large groups of up to a million fish. Emerald shiners typically spawn a week or two after spottails and in similar but deeper habitat. This species spawns at night over a one- to two-week period, giving predators a greater opportunity to locate and exploit them at this vulnerable stage.

Emerald shiners live a maximum of three years, reaching a length of about 4 inches. Yet studies at Lake Erie showed that walleyes from 22 to 26 inches selected shiners as prey during spring and fall.

Though fathead minnows (or tuffies) are a popular bait, biological studies show they're not a common prey in natural situations. When they are an important forage, they're mostly preyed on by young-of-the-year walleyes.

Any minnow species may be a walleye favorite if the fish are abundant and walleyes can get to them. In the Columbia River, the fast growth of walleyes is attributed partially to their diet of peamouths and chiselmouths. These members of the minnow family, common in the Columbia and other West Coast rivers, reach 12 inches in length, providing a sizable meal for the Columbia's trophy-size walleyes. Like other minnow species, they spawn in spring on gravel or sand flats at dusk when water temperatures rise into the mid-50°F range. Walleyes follow chiselmouths and peamouths onto these shallow areas and feed until the minnows disperse.

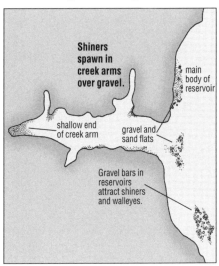

Shiner Spawning Sites

Shiners spawn in creek arms over gravel.

main body of reservoir

shallow end of creek arm

gravel and sand flats

Gravel bars in reservoirs attract shiners and walleyes.

Walleyes eat most of the 280 species of minnows found in North America. In spring, most species form huge schools to spawn, and predators seek them during this period. In lakes, minnows and walleyes concentrate near shallow gravel and sand flats. In rivers, spawning often occurs in riffles.

To capitalize on the walleye-minnow connection, locate likely spawning areas along gradually sloping banks, mouths of creeks, and other areas with shallow flats of sand and gravel. Spawning schools form within two weeks of ice-out in the North Country. Water temperatures in the mid-50°F to mid-60°F range prompt most minnow species to spawn. You'll see vast schools of minnows cruising spawning areas during daytime.

Walleyes attack the schools at dusk and after dark, so return then and cast across these areas with minnow baits or live minnows on light jigs. Trolling minnow baits or livebait rigs along breaks offshore of spawning sites can be effective, too, because fish hold there when they're not feeding.

CISCOES

The cisco, *Coregonus artedii*, ranges from the upper Mississippi River drainage and the Great Lakes basins north to Labrador and northwest to the Mackenzie River drainage, including lakes and rivers around Hudson Bay. Populations vary in growth rate, size at maturity, maximum size, and spawning time. This led early ichthyologists to

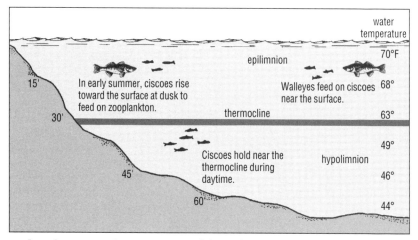

Summer Cisco Distribution

water temperature

epilimnion

70°F

15'

In early summer, ciscoes rise toward the surface at dusk to feed on zooplankton.

Walleyes feed on ciscoes near the surface.

68°

30'

thermocline

63°

49°

Ciscoes hold near the thermocline during daytime.

hypolimnion

45'

46°

60

44°

In early summer, ciscoes move toward the surface at dusk where they prey on zooplankton that rise at night. Walleyes prey on these ciscoes in open water. When surface temperatures rise into the mid-70°F range, ciscoes no longer follow zooplankton upward since water that warm is lethal to ciscoes. In some lakes, trolling near the thermocline takes walleyes that key on ciscoes in deeper, cooler water.

describe 22 subspecies. Most scientists now recognize a single species with many local variations.

Regardless of type, ciscoes—also known as lake herring or tullibee—are a favorite of walleyes wherever their habitats mesh. As coldwater fish that feed on plankton, ciscoes remain separated from walleyes for portions of the year and much of the day. To capitalize on the times when anglers can take advantage of walleyes' fondness for ciscoes, consider when ciscoes become the focus for walleyes.

In the oligotrophic to mid-mesotrophic lakes where ciscoes typically live, the fish remain in cool water during the day, often near or below the thermocline after surface waters warm in early summer. To feed on their preferred zooplankton, however, ciscoes must leave cool waters and rise toward the surface to follow plankton as they ascend at dusk. This brings ciscoes into the realm of walleyes, who rarely venture into water colder than low 60° F if warmer water is available. Cisco schools may hold within a few feet of the surface over water 100 feet deep, half a mile from the nearest shore.

In-Fisherman staff members often score best by trolling large minnow baits about 100 feet behind the boat. Speeds from 1 to 2 mph produce consistently, although faster speeds occasionally produce even better. Rapala minnows in size #13 and #18, Storm ThunderSticks, Magna Strike's 6-inch Grandma bait, and Cordell's Ripplin' Red Fin attract walleyes. As in other predator-prey interactions, find the walleyes and they can be caught on a variety of baits only slightly resembling what they're feeding on.

When surface waters warm into the upper 60°F and 70°F range, ciscoes no longer approach the surface, despite plentiful plankton. They remain near the thermocline, where walleyes apparently don't hunt them. After studying this midsummer phenomenon for years, *In-Fisherman* contributor Bruce Carlson surmises that "there seems to be a gap between the lower comfort zone of walleyes and the upper comfort zone of ciscoes. When ciscoes stop rising near the surface, walleyes switch to a diet of yellow perch."

In some mesotrophic lakes, walleyes refocus on ciscoes when declining oxygen in the hypolimnion forces ciscoes into the epilimnion, an event that may occur in August or early September. As ciscoes become stressed and die-offs occur, walleyes typically suspend from 25 to 35 feet down, preying on weakened ciscoes. Trolling crankbaits on downriggers or leadline is effective whenever concentrations of baitfish and walleyes appear on a graph. Run baits less than a foot above the walleyes for best results.

Ciscoes spawn from October through early December in water temperatures in the low 40°F range. They gather over humps that rise close to the surface, on points, or over shallow, hard bottom flats near shore, although some populations reportedly spawn much deeper. In the Great Lakes and some Canadian lakes, commercial netters take ciscoes for smoking; they are considered a delicacy. Frequent capture of large walleyes in cisco nets provides evidence that walleyes are keying on them.

Fishing at night just before ice-up is a challenge that few walleye anglers have accepted. The pattern has trophy potential, however. Al Lindner has taken some of his biggest walleyes by drifting light spoons baited with crappie minnows across spawning humps during fall.

Under the ice, walleyes and ciscoes are free to mingle, though walleyes rarely prey on ciscoes then. Perhaps the size of the ciscoes or their tendency to suspend under the ice keeps them safe from walleyes, which typically remain near the bottom during winter.

SMELT

Rainbow smelt, a coldwater member of the Osmeridae family, are often encountered by walleyes. Smelt are distributed throughout the northern hemisphere in marine, anadromous, and freshwater habitat.  They're common in cool waters rimming the east and west coasts of Canada but are not widely distributed in US inland waters outside the Great Lakes and deep, cold, well-oxygenated lakes in New England and Alaska. Smelt stocked into the Missouri River system have spread throughout the cooler upper impoundments, but water temperatures warmer than 60°F have prevented their expansion southward.

Smelt spawn in spring in water temperatures in the high 40°F or low 50°F range, usually on gravel bottoms. They run upriver from the Great Lakes in April, attracting fishermen armed with dip nets. Smelt are smoked, fried, or preserved as ice-fishing bait for pike and large walleyes.

Smelt feed voraciously on plankton, crustaceans, insect larvae, fish eggs, and fry. Many biologists believe that they eat walleye eggs and fry and that stocking them in nonnative waters was a poor decision. Smelt, however, provide a plentiful food source for walleyes in some large bodies of water.

In reservoirs, smelt often remain shallow in spring and early summer until water temperatures become too warm. Then they desert the back ends of shallow bays and suspend in the main deep body of the reservoir. Large schools of suspended smelt are stopped by the tips of the longest points where they

Reservoir Smelt Patterns

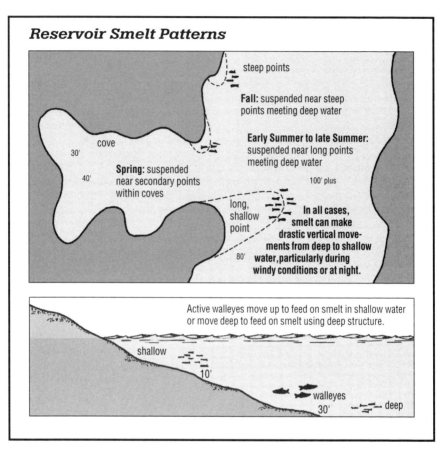

steep points

Fall: suspended near steep points meeting deep water

Early Summer to late Summer: suspended near long points meeting deep water

cove

30'

40'

Spring: suspended near secondary points within coves

100' plus

long, shallow point

In all cases, smelt can make drastic vertical movements from deep to shallow water, particularly during windy conditions or at night.

80'

Active walleyes move up to feed on smelt in shallow water or move deep to feed on smelt using deep structure.

shallow

10'

walleyes
30'

deep

meet deep water. In such spots, smelt occasionally move along or up onto the structure.

Walleyes frequent such areas, feeding shallow when smelt move shallow and suspending with or below the smelt when the baitfish drop deeper. In fall, smelt and walleyes move toward fast-dropping structures where they meet deep water. Both species are found deep or shallow, depending on conditions. Wind usually brings them up; calm conditions drive them deeper.

Great Lakes smelt provide consistent forage for lake trout and salmon, too. Once smelt leave bays and rivers in spring, they're frequently found in water over 100 feet deep during the day, moving shallower at night. Salmon and walleyes intercept the schools as they make daily vertical movements from extreme depths to shallower water.

Troll with downriggers, leadcore line, and trolling boards, or jig extremely deep. Smelt, typically 4 to 8 inches long with iridescent silvery sides, are easily imitated with minnow lures like a Rapala Minnow, Rebel Minnow, Bomber Long-A, Storm ThunderStick, or Bagley Bang-O-Lure.

Because melt may range far in the Great Lakes during summer, they become less important as an angling pattern until fall, when smelt and walleyes begin concentrating within major bays of natural lakes or at river mouths meeting big water.

SHAD

"In Lake Erie, shad is the major walleye prey," says Roger Knight, fisheries biologist for the Ohio Division of Wildlife. "Erie walleyes grow as fast as any walleyes in the world, and shad is the reason."

When walleyes have a choice of prey, they often choose shad. This demands a shallow- to mid-depth open water lifestyle. During winter in the north, when shad mortality is high, walleyes key on perch or other prey until midsummer, when young-of-the-year shad reach acceptable size. At that point, the switch is fast and wholesale.

Gizzard shad are a more important walleye food source than threadfin or American shad, which seldom coexist with walleyes. Notable exceptions are Columbia River walleyes, which feed heavily on American shad in summer and early fall, and walleyes in Elephant Butte Reservoir in New Mexico, which prey heavily on threadfin shad.

Gizzard shad range as far north as the St. Lawrence River and the Great Lakes, west to the Dakotas, and south to Mexico and Florida. In walleye country, shad spawn in 1 to 10 feet of water in May, June, and July in water temperatures of 63°F to 73°F. Immediately after spawning, they return to deeper water.

Adult gizzard shad are vegetarians, grazing on drifting fields of algae—unique for North American fish of their size. They can reach weights of over 5 pounds. In some environments, especially rivers, shad feed on bottom. But in most lakes, they suspend over large transitions between shallow and deep water or over large flats 20 to 40 feet deep. Where algae covers the surface in dense blooms, however, they may move as shallow as 4 feet. Deep basin areas rarely hold shad, with the exception of reservoirs where 50- to 80-foot depths occur close to shore. Even then, shad use only the top 30 feet of the water column, where their source of food is most abundant.

Because shad depend on free-floating plankton, they tend to collect in downwind areas after several days of wind from the same direction. Walleyes follow the shad.

This means suspended fish. Approaching walleyes who have keyed on shad involves a step-by-step approach. Obtain information about where to start from other fishermen, tackle retailers, or biologists. Use sonar to track clouds of baitfish. Shad are nomads that seldom relate to structural elements. The best fishing could be over table-top mud fields or near classic structure. Wherever it's centered, it often changes overnight, because shad roam.

Step two is to troll. Once you locate shad, productive presentations include longline trolling, downrigging, and leadcore line. Diver-planers and snap-on weight systems are effective, too.

Two zones produce the most fish. One is just beneath or in the lower portion of the school, within 5 feet of bottom. Before and after feeding sprees, walleyes rest on bottom. (Walleye pros on Lake Erie report catching fish near bottom with mud still clinging to their scales). One theory is that these bottom-resting fish adjust to the pressure change by rising slowly, pausing along the way to reorient themselves. If sonar shows hooks suspended just above bottom, target these fish. They're usually preparing to feed.

Walleyes that key on shad often are loosely grouped over an area the size of a football field or larger. Trolling is the most efficient way to catch these fish. When shad are working shallow algae fields, cast jigs with plastic shad bodies, or try shad cranks or rattlebaits.

Crankbaits that imitate shad are effective, but minnow-shaped lures, rattle-baits, jigging spoons, spinner rigs, and other techniques work as well or better for suspended walleyes. The key is to locate the target zone, then move something through that depth at the right speed.

Bodies of water with impressive populations of huge walleyes and shad include Saginaw Bay, Lake Erie, Bay of Quinte, and impoundments of the Mississippi River. Where shad and walleye coexist, walleyes usually grow fast and stay fat. And shad don't compete with young walleye fry for food, so perhaps no other forage base is so perfectly suited to maintaining trophy walleye fisheries.

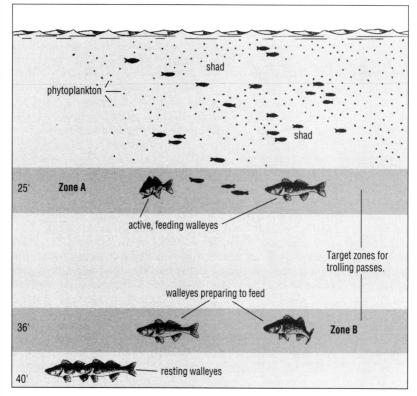

The Shad-Walleye Connection

phytoplankton

shad

shad

25' **Zone A**

active, feeding walleyes

Target zones for trolling passes.

walleyes preparing to feed

36' **Zone B**

40' resting walleyes

*This scene is typical of Lake Erie. In Saginaw Bay or Bay of Quinte, walleyes and shad feed 5 to 10 feet down over depths of 12 to 25 feet. Trolling passes on Erie are made with downriggers, leadcore, or planing divers, so depth of presentation can be determined exactly. In Saginaw Bay and Quinte, crankbaits are often run behind planer boards, with no depth-gaining device—maybe one Rubbercor sinker. Sometimes walleyes actively feeding (**Zone A**) are harder to entice than fish preparing to feed (**Zone B**).*

ALEWIVES

Alewives can become so prolific that in habitats where they thrive, walleyes feed so quickly and efficiently that anglers have little chance to compete. On the other hand, hordes of hungry alewives can also wipe out a year class of walleyes in certain environments.

Fishery managers still occasionally use the alewife to create a consistent forage base for walleyes, especially in reservoirs. The most recent introductions have been in Nebraska, where alewives perplexed anglers and biologists by creating a fat-and-happy megaload of walleyes that local anglers couldn't catch.

Originally, alewives invaded the Great Lakes through the St. Lawrence Seaway. They were first identified in Lake Ontario in 1873, and now occur in all the Great Lakes and lakes connected to them by channels or short streams. Fishery managers and "bucket biologists" have further increased the range of the alewife. Shad first appeared in New York's Lake Otisco in 1961, then quickly disappeared. Alewives appeared in 1966 and have continued to thrive.

In open water, alewives feed primarily on zooplankton, but they invade the shallows to spawn in late spring when water temperatures reach about 58°F (peak spawning occurs at about 64°F), just as juvenile "pin eye" walleyes are absorbing the last of their egg sacks and are becoming easy marks for hungry, tightly massed hordes of alewives. Alewives are adaptive pelagic fish that can spawn over any kind of substrate. As walleyes grow, they quickly turn the tables. As forage, alewives produce some of the fastest growth rates in all of walleyedom. As you see, the relationship between walleyes and alewives is a sort of double-edged sword.

Fisheries biologists determined in 1960 that alewives would be good prey for walleyes in Nebraska's newly formed Merritt Reservoir. "Merritt has consistently produced trophy walleyes ever since," says Monte Madsen, fishery supervisor for the Nebraska Game and Parks Commission. Elwood Reservoir and McConaughy, newer reservoirs filled in the late 1980s, were also stocked with alewives when shad proved too fickle. Results have been mixed, according to Madsen.

"Alewives selectively devour larger zooplankton needed by other juvenile fish in the system," Madsen says. "And they feed on fish larvae, meaning they affect other populations as a predator. But there are positives, too. Shad don't do well in these reservoirs because of the cold, deep water. Alewives do well. And, unlike shad, the biggest alewives are forage even for average-size walleyes. They never outgrow predation."

Fishing guides around the country agree that when alewives move in, anglers have two options: change tactics or change lakes. Walleyes feeding on alewives get fat, but not lazy. Their feeding strategy involves barreling pell-mell into the tightest available pod of alewives, mouths open. It's easy pickings in terms of calories gained versus calories expended, but it does involve exertion, as suggested by the aggressive way walleyes feeding on alewives slam into lures.

"When shad gave way to alewives in Elwood (Elwood Reservoir, Nebraska), all my old honey holes went dry," says Dan Ferguson. "It became impossible to find fish on structure. The walleyes were gone, even though the lake was brimming with fish. Big fish. Obviously, we were doing something wrong."

Ferguson stumbled on a pattern while bass fishing. "We kept catching walleyes by slow-rolling spinnerbaits in shallow water during late spring and early summer," he says. "I thought it was a fluke, but it kept happening. Then I noticed it was the alewives that were drawn to gold blades. They followed the lure, surrounding it in a big swirling mass. Then I saw a walleye charge, the alewives scattered, and there was that big juicy spinnerbait.

"Walleyes chasing alewives hit like a freight train," Ferguson adds. "It's not some picky tic-tic kind of bite. In fact, they hit so hard they sometimes snap 8-pound test. I had to give my clients baitcasting equipment with 14-pound test line."

The following year the spinnerbait bite tapered off. "The water was stained, so we experimented with rattling baits like Mann's Loudmouth crankbaits and Rattlin' Rogues. The key is to get away from classic main lake structure and start prowling the backs of bays, in reeds and grass where bass should be. It works right through July until alewives move out of the shallows."

Meanwhile, Keith Hendrickson, a guide for 14 years on Lake Michigan's Big and Little Bays de Noc, says, "The fishing goes through big changes when the alewives roll in." Alewives suspend most of the year, but they move shallow to spawn sometime between mid-May and mid-June throughout the Great Lakes, staying shallow through July most years.

"Alewives first appear in the shallows closest to deep water," Hendrickson explains. "Walleyes feed on them off shoreline-connected points. Shortly thereafter, alewives are everywhere and everything eats them—pike, smallmouths, walleyes, perch.

"Alewives force you to change tactics. Anglers who fish structure start complaining by the first weeks of June, when the alewives typically arrive. Bay de Noc becomes a suspended fishery. Trolling crankbaits behind boards works. Using sonar, find schools of alewives off steep-sloping shoreline banks. Alewives usually are 12 to 25 feet down over 22- to 45-foot depths."

Sometimes the walleyes are right on top in Bay de Noc, Hendrickson notes. "You won't see them on sonar because they spook away from the boat. Wherever you see alewives on sonar, especially on flat, calm, sunny days, put at least one unweighted Rapala behind an outside board. Try Shad Raps, Hot'N Tots, or Deep ThunderSticks on the other lines.

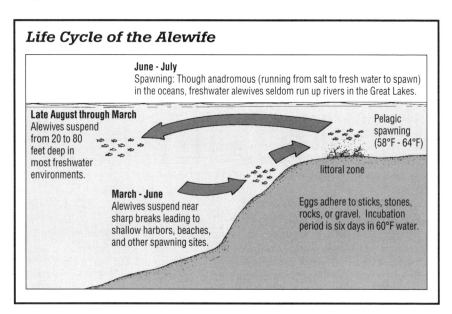

Life Cycle of the Alewife

June - July
Spawning: Though anadromous (running from salt to fresh water to spawn) in the oceans, freshwater alewives seldom run up rivers in the Great Lakes.

Late August through March
Alewives suspend from 20 to 80 feet deep in most freshwater environments.

Pelagic spawning (58°F - 64°F)

littoral zone

March - June
Alewives suspend near sharp breaks leading to shallow harbors, beaches, and other spawning sites.

Eggs adhere to sticks, stones, rocks, or gravel. Incubation period is six days in 60°F water.

"At times you can throw crankbaits all day and catch fish," Henderson says. "Other days you need an almost motionless presentation. When walleyes chow heavily on alewives all night, they become torpid. When that happens, the only way to catch any during the day is to locate them on sonar (usually suspended 20 to 25 feet down) and to drop tiny jigs under slipfloats. A 1/32- or even 1/64-ounce jig with a tiny piece of crawler dropped right on their nose is the only thing that works. The water has to be calm for the pattern to work."

But if Hendrickson had his druthers, he'd choose jigging the weeds during the daytime. At midday, Hendrickson says, alewives move out of the shallows, but walleyes stay behind, tucked into pockets and edges of huge main lake weedbeds. "Cast jigs and minnows or drift slipbobbers and jigs with crawlers along the edge to pluck a few walleyes.

"Night fishing is best, but most of my clients don't want to go out at night," Hendrickson adds. "Even if they do, I seldom take them. Bay de Noc walleyes are easy at night. I'm concerned about the numbers of big fish taken. Casting or slow trolling a Rapala along weededges is just too deadly at night."

Ferguson, meanwhile, also depends on jigging spoons. "When alewives move out later in the morning, they suspend over 50 or 60 feet of water (in Elwood Reservoir), and the walleyes often are beneath them. I work the nearest point at the depth I graphed the fish, bouncing a Hopkins Spoon or Manns Man-O-Lure off the bottom."

In Elwood, alewives are the primary forage for walleyes. In Muskegon Lake in Michigan, walleyes switch from perch and shad to alewives and back again after the alewives disperse back into Lake Michigan. Bay de Noc walleyes start feeding on alewives sometime in June and stay on them right through fall. So the walleye-alewife connection varies from area to area. In some waters, such as Oneida Lake in New York, alewives may not be the primary walleye forage, while in other waters, walleyes feed on little else.

During summer in waters where alewives or shad are a primary walleye forage, silver- or grey-pattern "fat" crankbaits are favorite baits for triggering walleyes holding in open water.

In many instances, though, it isn't necessary to match the hatch so much as to be in the key area where walleyes are interacting with prey. Then it's a matter of presenting a bait that's as attractive or more attractive than the prey. Spinner rigging, for example, often triggers walleyes when more realistic fare doesn't produce so well.

CRAWFISH

Largemouth and smallmouth bass, as well as the other black bass species, are notorious crayfish eaters. Rock bass, catfish, and a few other species often eat craws, too. But what about walleye?

Jig fishermen and riggers will testify that walleyes and saugers feed on or close to bottom most of the time. And the shallow feeding grounds of walleye, like weededges and rockpiles, are usually home to several species of crayfish. In our experience, however, craws rarely turn up in the walleye gutpile.

A review of scientific studies of walleye diets reinforces this observation but also documents waters where walleye eat substantial numbers of craws. Diet studies in several major walleye fisheries have found no walleye predation on crayfish in Lake Erie, Lake Oahe, Lake Sakakawea, Lake Vermillion, Mille Lacs, and the Columbia River. Many studies in other waters have revealed no craws in walleye bellies.

Dr. John Kelso found that walleyes in Blue Lake, Manitoba, began eating crayfish in July and continued through August, but not into fall. Kelso considered craws a minor component of the walleye diet, along with leeches and caddisfly larvae.

Fritz Johnson and John Hale of the Minnesota Department of Natural Resources studied populations of smallmouth bass and walleye in several Canadian Shield lakes to check competition between the two species. In Pike Lake, 47 percent of the walleye examined contained crayfish, which comprised 18 percent of food volume. Smallmouths relied more on crayfish—half of the stomach volume of 60 percent of smallmouths contained them.

In a study of walleye, smallmouth bass, and pike in Ontario's Kaministiquia River, S. A. Stephenson and Walter Momot found that adult walleye diet consisted of 97 percent fish, with crayfish, worms, and insects making up the rest. Northern pike diet was similar, but smallmouth bass fed primarily on crayfish (87 percent of total volume).

According to fish nutritionists, the walleye's preference for fish and other invertebrates is wise. Crayfish contain about the fewest calories per gram of any animal food except jellyfish, sponges, and echinoderms (starfishes, sea urchins). Some nutritious fish like shad and shiners have nearly double the calories per gram of craws. Ecologists wonder what makes the antagonistic and not-very-nutritious crayfish so popular with bass, rock bass, and a few other fish.

Crawfish-color crankbaits often score well on walleye, and bass anglers often catch big 'eyes on jig-and-pig or jig-and-craw combos that imitate the crustacean. The lures may appeal to the opportunistic nature of most predators, including walleyes, but they mimic natural prey in only a few waters.

Advanced Walleye Prognostication

PREDICTING HOT BITES

You've assembled a massive tackle box. The boat is rigged and ready, the batteries are charged, and the electronics are humming. An impressive arsenal of rods is battened down in the lockers, and reels are spooled with premium line. You're ready. Now you face the question that overrides all others: "Where to fish?"

What now? Mirror, mirror on the wall, where's the biggest walleye of them all? Well, you already have favorite destinations—places that produced in the past. And you've been wanting to expand your range and follow more hot tips. And you try to make it to the nearest world-class fishery once a year, even though it's an 8-hour drive.

Predicting the bite is one integral factor in consistent fishing that is often over-looked. Knowing where to fish shouldn't always be a matter of reading out-door news reports or waiting to hear how your buddies fared. Biologists prognosticate all the time. It's part of their job. Tapping into their data gives you an advantage.

On any body of water, some years are better than others. The controlling fac-tor is year-class strength. When natural reproduction rates are high and condi-tions are ideal for lots of young walleyes to hatch and thrive, walleye fishing may improve dramatically 2 to 5 years down the line—the time required for walleyes to reach harvestable size. Technically, that's where "recruitment" comes into play: as far as fishery managers are concerned, fish recruited into the ranks of har-vestable size count most. For another 5 to 7 years, a healthy year class of walleyes may provide excellent fishing, if pressure, pollution, and other factors don't remove them from the picture.

That's the key concept. Finding and following an exceptional year class of walleyes through the years will improve your fishing. Finding two or three prime year classes only a few years apart in the same reservoir, lake, or river can provide

What's A Good Year Class?

For a good year class to exist, a number of conditions must be optimum at the time of the spawn.

Where natural reproduction occurs, suitable spawning habitat must be present. For walleyes, this means gravel or gravel mixed with rock in relatively shallow water (2 to 8 feet). When water tempera-tures reach about 48°F, spawning usually peaks. Sudden and severe cold fronts at this critical time can push fish off spawning areas. Con-tinued bad weather may influence how many fish spawn and how successfully.

But ample habitat under prime conditions doesn't guarantee a good spawn. In rivers and reser-voirs, rain or heavy snowmelt can transport extraordinary loads of silt into the system, burying the unhatched eggs, which need oxy-gen to survive, thereby killing sub-stantial numbers. In some areas, a supersuccessful spawn can only occur when winter or spring pre-cipitation is lower than normal.

Aside from being buried, wall-eye eggs can survive most things other than being eaten. In years when prolonged cold spells delay hatching (normally a 10- to 18-day process), eggs are vulnerable for a prolonged period of time to preda-tion by baitfish, suckers, crayfish, bullheads, and other nest robbers.

Once hatched, the young alevins can suffer high mortality rates if water temperatures dip back into winter temperature ranges. Floods can sweep them out of sheltering areas. Young fry are susceptible to predation by such unlikely enemies as smelt and insects, along with the usual host of bass, perch, and birds. Finally, young walleyes can starve for lack of adequate prey in rearing areas, as determined by weather, water, and other conditions. An early spawn and subsequent cold fronts can be brutal on such fragile little fish.

If the serendipitous occurs—if conditions conspire to bring the most walleyes to spawning areas at

a decade or more of great fishing. It requires a little research, something to do when ice-fishing's slow or the season's closed.

HOMEWORK

Two facts more than any others determine what kind of walleye bite a lake is likely to have: (1) an abundance of walleyes—several strong year classes, and (2) normal-to-low numbers of forage fish. Walleye and forage populations are principal factors in determining where a good bite might occur, but other factors like fishing pressure and weather may also play major roles. To make predictions, you need background information on these and other variables.

Biologists use three primary methods to obtain information about year-class strength: electroshocking, netting, and creel surveys. In high-profile fisheries, biologists obtain information through all three methods. In other waters, they may use only one or possibly none of these methods because of a lack of time or money. Even so, a surprising number of lakes, reservoirs, and rivers are tested for population strength every year.

With information from these three forms of research, biologists can compare

the right time under prime conditions, if the hatch is successfully carried off, if predator counts are low, shelter is good, and forage is high—lots of young walleyes hatch. But another critical hurdle must be jumped. Young-of-the-year walleyes that don't find adequate prey in summer may be too small and weak to escape predators and survive the winter.

If significant numbers survive their first winter, odds are they'll become a super year class in several years, barring other potential disasters—environmental problems like freeze-out and pollution, or biological disasters like disease and lack of forage. Then, when the year class edges into the catchable size range, great year classes begin showing up in creel surveys and test nets.

Only then can you be certain that a great year class exists, the kind of year class that increases odds for fishermen. But knowing and catching are flip sides of the same coin. Fishing should be good

for another 6 years or more, unless a major bloom of perch, shad, smelt, or ciscoes keeps walleyes so fat and happy they're impossible to catch, or anglers crop the year class too quickly, or weather conspires against you every time you visit the fishery, or . . .

data with previous surveys and with information from other bodies of water. This indicates how the population compares to past years and to other fisheries. They can determine which year classes are the strongest by the numbers of fish appearing in each size category.

"Fisheries like Oahe, Saginaw Bay, and Erie are unique, in that nearly every year class is strong," says Dave Fielder, fishery biologist for the South Dakota Game, Fish, and Parks Department. Perhaps more than anything else, that's what defines a world-class fishery: good hatches, good survival rates, and adequate if not abundant forage on a consistent basis. "Most lakes are fortunate to have one good year class going at a time," Fielder concludes.

A good year class is determined by a number of factors. According to Denny Schupp, senior research biologist for the Minnesota Department of Natural Resources, it starts with good habitat, lots of natural reproduction, a late spring, and fast-warming trends in northern waters. "With a late spawn and a fairly rapid warmup, the odds are good," Schupp explains. "An early spring subjects young fry to unstable weather. Born early, they often suffer through severe cold fronts that retard production of forage (plankton). Floods and cold snaps can wipe out the majority of a year class through stress and starvation. So, for most bodies of water, exquisite timing is necessary to pull off a good year class."

Perhaps more than anything else, that's what defines a world-class fishery—good hatches, good survival rates, and adequate if not abundant forage on a consistent basis.

In New York's Oneida Lake, however, spring weather has very little to do with year-class productivity, according to Professor Emeritus Dr. John Forney, who is still working at the Cornell Biological Station he once headed. "Whether a year class is good or bad on Oneida is largely controlled by cannibalism," Forney says. "The only really abundant predator is the walleye. How intense the cannibalism becomes depends on the abundance of shad." In other words, if shad numbers are low, Mama's a dangerous beast.

Oneida differs from Mille Lacs and lakes like Glen Elder in Kansas in another way. Almost two thirds of the recruitment during most years arises from stocking, whereas Mille Lacs and Glen Elder experience phenomenal natural reproduction. "Spring weather patterns have no effect on egg or hatchling survival, which is high in a hatchery," Forney says.

Lakes differ. In some lakes, walleyes are the major predator. In others, they're just another face in the crowd. Burbot, pike, largemouths, muskie, smallmouths, and crappie may help to diminish a massive bloom of perch in 6 weeks to 2 months in one lake, while the same kind of bloom in a similar lake where predation is provided primarily by walleyes may slow fishing for a year or more.

Blooms of forage fish like perch and shad affect walleyes positively, but they often hurt fishing. And, according to Schupp, conditions that elicit a supersuccessful walleye hatch are nearly identical to those that bring on a massive bloom of perch, the primary forage fish of most walleyes in the Midwest. Above-average-to-phenomenal numbers of young walleyes need those little perch to survive, but massive hatches also keep adult walleyes fat, happy, and healthy. Often this means the years that promise good fishing in the future can be poor fishing years.

"That's exactly what happens sometimes at Glen Elder," according to Kyle Austin, district fishery biologist for the Kansas Department of Wildlife and Parks. "Sometimes we just have too many shad for fishermen to compete with."

Glen Elder Reservoir on the Solomon River system normally covers 12,586 acres. During periods of heavy rain, the pool may swell to 33,000 acres. Austin remembers the floods of 1993: "When the lake grew, shad kept spawning to fill the void," he says. "So when the lake drew back to 12,586 acres, we had 33,000 acres worth of shad. As a fishery manager, I have mixed emotions. The walleyes are plentiful, fat, and happy, but nobody can catch any."

The good news is, once the walleyes knock down that bumper crop of shad, they're going to be plentiful, fat, and hungry. The bad news is, there can be no guarantee that shad won't bloom again. The only way to know is to call biologists working there in late fall and ask them what their tests revealed about the shad population. That will give you a good idea about the ice bite. And at winter's end, biologists scan shorelines for dead shad to determine the severity of the winterkill. "I like to see a good winterkill of shad," Austin admits. "A good winterkill means a good bite in spring."

In Oneida, strong winds right after the perch spawn can be deadly. "Perch eggs take 10 days to 3 weeks to hatch, depending on water temperatures," according to Les Wedge, regional fisheries manager for the New York Department of Environmental Conservation. "After the eggs are laid, a strong wind can wash them onto the beach. Temperature has a limiting effect, too. A late spring means slow growth, and walleyes don't prey heavily on perch until the perch reach at least an inch in length."

A boom in local forage populations doesn't mean the same is happening elsewhere. Perch may spawn too deep in some lakes for wind to be a factor. And lakes that are not connected to flooding river systems with booming shad populations could experience normal shad production while those fed by the river systems are booming.

"But similar things happen in similar lakes over a broad region," Schupp says. "The years 1966 and 1979, for example, had strong year classes all over the region. Conversely, 1965 was a bust all over. The synchrony of year classes can be striking even in lakes separated by several hundred miles."

The reverse is also possible: two lakes in the same area with strong year classes in different years. For example, a large, deep lake that warms slowly is likely to have a significantly later spawning window than a smaller, shallower lake just down the road. Several weeks can make quite a difference. Walleye fry in the larger lake may avoid severe weather and starvation by hatching slightly later in spring.

A massive hatch that survives the summer doesn't, however, secure the future of that particular year class. If growth is poor during that first critical summer, over-winter survival is typically poor as well.

A massive hatch that survives the summer can't, however, secure the future of that particular year class. If growth is poor during that first critical summer, over-winter survival is typically poor as well. In Minnesota's Lake Mille Lacs, the DNR runs test netting operations in late August to monitor the growth of walleyes during their first year. "I count on good survival if they reach 6 inches," Schupp says. "Six inches is good. Five inches or less means a shortage of prey at midsummer, so they won't be as healthy. Winter could take a heavy toll."

The crux of all this information is that biologists keep track of year-class strengths in lots of waters. In some cases, it's done to maintain population strength through regulation. For example, based on annual population estimates for walleyes and forage species, biologists tweak size limits on Oneida: "If walleyes are too abundant for the forage base, we drop the minimum length to 12 inches," Wedge says.

"And if the walleye population drops below a certain density, we raise the minimum length to 18 inches."

Biologists often sample for preyfish in late summer or early fall to monitor numbers and sizes. "If it weren't for shad, we wouldn't have any forage, so we like to keep track of them," Austin says. "We net them in August to check their size. If they're 70 millimeters or smaller, they're the right size for predation. If they're bigger, they're outgrowing the walleyes."

For biologists, factors like size and numbers of young walleyes in late summer figure into predictions about year-class strength but not about next year's bite. Statistics on prey size and numbers, however, can help predict what anglers can expect through winter and spring. Good records show annual notations on both predator and prey abundance and size. An ongoing chart can point you to high-percentage waters for next year and years beyond.

CRYSTAL BALLS

To begin making predictions, you need information about two variables: (1) the relative abundance of walleyes, and (2) the relative abundance of their primary forage. The first part is easy. The strength of the walleye population is a known factor on many lakes across the country. Part two isn't so easy. Many lakes are not tested regularly for baitfish populations. But intermittent data are better than no data at all.

The optimum condition to look for when predicting a bite is a high population of walleyes— several good year classes— and a relatively low population of primary forage fish.

The optimum condition to look for when predicting a bite is a high population of walleyes—several good year classes—and a relatively low population of primary forage fish. This may not be the optimum condition for maintaining healthy fish, and it may mean a significant reduction in young-of-the-year walleyes— the newest year class—through cannibalism, but it's a marvelous situation for bending rods.

"I developed an index for comparing year-class strength several years ago, and it's now used in the field by many of our biologists," Schupp says. "Basically it's a simple comparison. What is the catch of young-of-the-year walleyes and how does that catch compare in both size and numbers to previous years? If walleyes are abundant and growing fast, we have high numbers. If they're growing slowly, we have low numbers. That's basically it."

With 35 years of experience on Oneida, Dr. Forney knows a little about predicting walleye bites. "I can make predictions about walleye bites, but I wouldn't want to publish them," he laughs. "Predicting bites on Oneida depends on forage abundance. In spring, when forage numbers are low, walleyes are highly vulnerable to anglers. That vulnerability decreases in summer, when prey is more abundant. Past bites have been controlled by the population densities of yellow perch. Before gizzard shad disrupted the equation, the ups and downs of perch populations offered the most reliable method of predicting the bite.

"Shad almost disappeared from Oneida for 20 years," Forney reports, "but they're making a strong comeback. For the past 10 years, every good year class of walleyes corresponded to an abundance of shad. The Catch 22 on Oneida is that low numbers of shad mean good fishing but poor year-class survival because more young walleyes are cannibalized by adult walleyes."

According to Wedge, "Shad now buffer the perch, protecting them from heavy predation by walleyes. And shad protect walleyes from angling because they're not as hungry."

In lakes with strong perch populations, walleye bites often slow between late June and mid-July, when young-of-the-year perch have grown past 1 inch. When shad are most numerous, fishing is poor in July and August and sometimes right through winter. Shad are prolific, hatching in huge numbers in May or June, depending on latitude. In winter they stress easily in cold water, becoming easy pickings for predators. "Sometimes walleyes in Oneida store so much fat from feeding on shad in summer and fall that they rarely feed in winter," Wedge says.

Relative Abundance of Walleye Year Classes in Oneida Lake

Year Class	Catch/Haul (age 1)	Predicted Contribution of Year Class to Fishery (age 4)
1979	0.09	32,000
1980	1.44	296,000
1981	0.60	183,000
1982	0.63	150,000
1883	0.24	45,000
1984	0.28	73,000
1985	0.53	128,000
1986	0.05	21,000
1987	3.32	521,000
1988	0.06	25,000
1989	0.31	82,000
1990	0.49	119,000
1991	2.19	413,000

PRACTICAL APPLICATION

Knowing the dynamics of this predator-prey relationship might have helped you predict the bite on Oneida in 1993. A call to biologists in the fall of 1992 would have revealed that two good year classes were moving through the system—the 1987 class at 20 inches and the 1991 class at 15 inches. And forage numbers were down.

The ice bite that following winter was tremendous, according to Forney. The winterkill of shad was high, and June 1993 was among the coolest on record. "All we know about factors limiting shad numbers is that a warm June brings high hatching success," Wedge adds.

This had an effect on walleye morphology. "Our 6-year-old walleyes were smaller in 1993 than they were at age 5," Wedge reports. "They experienced a 10 to 15 percent weight loss over the winter and didn't gain it back during summer." With shad numbers way down and a cold early summer keeping perch smaller than those walleyes normally eat, walleyes should have been biting.

And they were. "The biomass of walleyes was high, the biomass of prey down," Forney says. "Test netting in fall for both predators and prey seems to predict the success of the winter and spring fishery. Fishing was excellent during the winter of 1993. Anglers had a good summer, too, though not so outstanding as we might have predicted."

Variables can all be predicted. Maybe the weather was so bad last summer that walleyes didn't feel well enough to bite all the time. But Forney indicated that walleyes did bite better in July and August than during previous years.

Back in Minnesota, Schupp found similar variables indicating similar bites. "In 1985, the last time we had a really bad year for walleyes on Mille Lacs, was one year after a huge bloom of perch," Schupp says. "During the fall of 1984, trawl catch rates for perch were exceptionally high compared to previous years. Consequently, the spring and summer of 1985 were terrible for walleye anglers on Mille Lacs. And it's happened again: a massive hatch of perch in 1992 shut down fishing in 1993."

Year-Class Chart—Glen Elder Reservoir, Kansas

Researching a lake can be as easy as calling a biologist and asking, "How much do they have to eat and how likely are they to bite?" But a more thorough record will help you for years to come.

When researching a lake, call the state natural resources department and ask for the fishery biologist most familiar with that body of water. Ask the biologist about the maxi-

Choosing the right place to fish often is more important than having all the right lures and other tools.

mum age walleyes reach in that environment. If it's 12 years, ask for a quick rundown on all the year classes, good, bad, and mediocre, over the past 12 years. Ask also about the average length of each of the year classes.

Also remember to ask: (1) Are any of those 12 year olds still present in the system, and if not, what are the oldest fish in the system? (2) How fast do walleyes grow in that system? How big is a 12 year old now? (3) Ask for an estimate of fishing pressure, season-by-season. And (4) What is the main forage base and are forage populations expected to be high or low this year? Why?

Now you can start a chart. From that point, add data concerning the size and number of fish you catch in the lake you've researched to see if your catch ratios compare with the data from the biologists. For example, if the strongest year class is supposedly 5 years old and averages 18 inches, keep records to see what percentage of your catch is from that year class. Your results should indicate something about the relative strengths and weaknesses of each year class moving through the system.

Several years ago, Schupp predicted that 1995 would be a banner year on Mille Lacs. "I might have to hedge on that a little," he laughs. "The last time we had so many perch, fishing was poor for over a year, then things gradually improved until 1988, a banner year for fishermen. But something big is going to happen soon. An abundance of walleyes from super year classes in 1988 and 1991 are getting fatter and healthier because fishermen aren't having much luck getting them to bite."

Forage densities also affect other aspects of walleye behavior. Schupp found that well-fed walleyes don't move much. "We plotted the movements of tagged walleyes in Leech Lake against angler success—fish caught per hour—and plotted that statistic against the abundance of perch on a seasonal basis," Schupp says. "As the abundance of perch peaks, walleye movement slows. As the abundance declines, walleye movements increase." Yin and yang. Walleyes may not bite

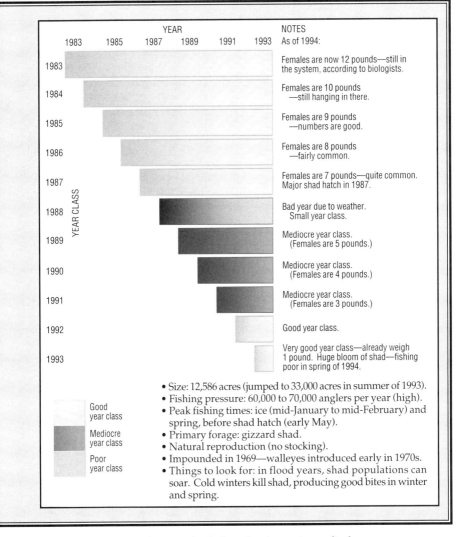

	YEAR						NOTES
	1983	1985	1987	1989	1991	1993	As of 1994:
1983							Females are now 12 pounds—still in the system, according to biologists.
1984							Females are 10 pounds —still hanging in there.
1985							Females are 9 pounds —numbers are good.
1986							Females are 8 pounds —fairly common.
1987							Females are 7 pounds—quite common. Major shad hatch in 1987.
1988							Bad year due to weather. Small year class.
1989							Mediocre year class. (Females are 5 pounds.)
1990							Mediocre year class. (Females are 4 pounds.)
1991							Mediocre year class. (Females are 3 pounds.)
1992							Good year class.
1993							Very good year class—already weigh 1 pound. Huge bloom of shad—fishing poor in spring of 1994.

YEAR CLASS

Good year class
Mediocre year class
Poor year class

- Size: 12,586 acres (jumped to 33,000 acres in summer of 1993).
- Fishing pressure: 60,000 to 70,000 anglers per year (high).
- Peak fishing times: ice (mid-January to mid-February) and spring, before shad hatch (early May).
- Primary forage: gizzard shad.
- Natural reproduction (no stocking).
- Impounded in 1969—walleyes introduced early in 1970s.
- Things to look for: in flood years, shad populations can soar. Cold winters kill shad, producing good bites in winter and spring.

well when forage numbers are high, but they're easier to find.

On most lakes, one year class often stands out every 5 or 6 years, but a super year class is rarer. "About every 10 years, we see a super year class on a good walleye lake," Schupp says. A super year class requires a fortuitous combination of events that are difficult to predict.

The only way for biologists to know for certain that a good year class exists is to follow it from the year it's born until it reaches harvestable size. The only way to do that is to continue netting every year—sometimes several times a year. "A lot of effort is needed to collect this kind of information," Schupp says. "And it's expensive."

The information also is needed by biologists performing studies that ultimately affect how fisheries are managed and protected. "A study on Lake Erie correlated strong year classes of walleyes with a late spring and fast-warming waters," Schupp says. "Long-running records are needed to perform analyses like that. Wisconsin has a similar situation on Lake Escanaba, including the longest-running record in the freshwater world on angler harvest, population size, year-class strength, growth rate, and other walleye data, an absolute treasure to biologists all over the world.

"But is it realistic for an angler to try and find the best circumstances for fishing by using the same data?" Schupp asks rhetorically. "It could be, depending on how the angler goes about it." And so long as the angler is willing to accept the occasional failure, who's better adapted to accepting failure than a fisherman?

Finding people like Schupp, Forney, and Austin who are willing to prognosticate may be the hardest part of the equation. That's one reason why making your own predictions may become invaluable in future seasons.

Another reason is that simply choosing the right place to fish often is more important than having all the right lures, rods, reels, and other tools. Letting that process evolve into something approaching logic, as opposed to depending on blind luck and hearsay, can represent a giant step forward in your fishing success.

Is there a rationale for predictions? "We have to do it," Austin says. "Fishermen want to know. After 2 or 3 years, you get caught up in the rhythms of fluctuating populations, and sometimes you're actually right about these things."

Many bodies of water depend on supplemental stocking to ensure year-class strength. Even on stocked waters, however, year-class strength varies.

Those Wandering Walleyes

LAKES, RIVERS, AND RESERVOIRS— TRACKING STUDIES VERIFY HOW WALLEYES REACT

In-Fisherman has long believed that blending science with everyday fishing theory and observation is one of the best ways to arrive at solutions to fishing problems. *In-Fisherman* magazine was the first to include reviews of scientific research within the magazine, the first to employ a certified fishery scientist as a staff editor, and the first to write reviews of ultrasonic fish tracking studies.

Since the mid-1950s, when transmitters were first used to follow fish, more than 20 projects have examined walleye movement patterns. The first telemetry study of the walleye was conducted by Dr.Charles Holt on Lake Bemidji, Minnesota, in

1973. Over the intervening years, trackers have studied walleyes in lakes, rivers, and reservoirs, verifying how they tend to react within specific environments. We offer here selected reviews of tracking studies that best illustrate how walleyes act in environments often visited by anglers.

RIVER MOVEMENTS

Telemetry studies have found that walleyes move extensively in the Mississippi River. Where lock and dam structures fragment the river, walleyes swim upstream and downstream through the structures before and after spawning and at other times when flow is high. Throughout the year, walleyes use habitat in the main channel, channel border areas, shoreline features like wing dams, sloughs with running water, and backwater lakes.

As part of his master's thesis at St. Mary's College, James Fossum used ultrasonic transmitters to follow walleyes in Pools 3 and 4 of the Mississippi River, in the first riverine telemetry study of walleyes. Though early tags lasted only 15 days, Fossum found that individual fish varied greatly in the extent and timing of their movements.

In ensuing years, biologists noted walleyes' variable behavior within single bodies of water. It seems that walleyes aren't programmed to behave in a single way, but instead learn the dangers of their environment and its feeding opportunities as they grow. This poses challenges to anglers, who must go beyond thinking like a fish to thinking like one of several groups of fish.

Mississippi River, Pool 13—John Pitlo, a fishery biologist with the Iowa Department of Natural Resources, conducted a series of telemetry studies in Pool 13 of the Mississippi River, a 34-mile-long pool between Iowa and Illinois. Pitlo, who has spent much of the past 18 years following radio- or sonic-tagged fish, is an expert in this type of research.

During summer, he found, most walleyes spend most of their time near wing dams and closing dams. Wing dams extend toward the main river channel, while closing dams run roughly parallel to backwater areas. River engineers built both types of structure to divert flow to the center of the river in order to maintain a channel for barges.

In Pool 13, most such dams are attractive to walleyes and other fish. In other pools, particularly downstream, where dams have silted in and lost their biological and navigational function, the Corps of Engineers routinely dredges the channel.

River walleyes move farther, faster than walleyes in most lakes and reservoirs, making river fish more difficult to find during some yearly periods.

Walleyes begin using wing dams after spawning, when river levels decline. When water levels remain high, walleyes enter sloughs with running water and side channels that offer timber and other cover that block current. Although walleyes are suited to life in current, they often seek refuge in protected areas off the main river.

Walleyes, Pitlo discovered, typically stay near wing dams during low flows of summer but also remain on these structures into midfall if heavy rains don't raise the water level. When high flows occur during summer, walleyes move to side channels, where they hold downstream of standing or fallen timber.

Even during the highest flows, however, walleyes don't enter river "lakes" or backwaters lacking current until late fall or winter. Although excessive current causes problems for walleyes, it also allows more efficient foraging by carrying potential prey and directing the movements of baitfish.

In late winter, Pitlo found, several walleyes move into the tailrace of Lock and Dam 12, where they remain until the spawning period. After spawning, however, walleyes rarely stay in the tailrace.

Wing Dams on Outside Versus Inside Bends

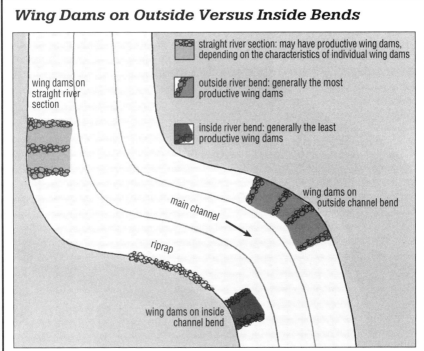

Studies on the Mississippi River show that walleyes feed and rest near wing dams during summer and fall. When river levels rise, however, they typically leave wing dams and enter side channels where timber provides current breaks. John Pitlo's telemetry studies showed that walleyes prefer wing dams located on straight runs or on outside bends of the river.

In those locations, current sweeps the dams and eddies, creating deep holes on the downstream side. Pitlo also found that dams with about 5 feet of water flowing over the top at normal pool levels attract more fish.

In addition to placing transmitters in 48 walleyes, Pitlo placed transmitters in 42 sauger. Sauger differ in habitat preference during most seasons. They favor the tailwater in fall, winter, and early spring, occasionally moving into backwater lakes after spawning. Except for these occasional movements into slack water, sauger tend to choose areas with faster current than walleyes do.

During summer and fall, many sauger stay along the border of the main river channel, while walleyes rarely stay in this habitat except where wing dams extend toward the river channel. Walleyes remain in border areas during winter if river level and flows are low. When flows increase, sauger move to wing dams, while walleyes tend to evacuate wing dams for side channels or backwaters.

Due to the obvious importance of wing dams as walleye habitat, Pitlo studied these structures more closely and found, as you might expect, that walleyes prefer certain types of dams. About 5 feet of water flow over the top of the best dams during normal pool levels. These are located at outside bends or along straight river sections. Here, current is stronger and scours deep holes on the downstream side of the dam. Although active walleyes tend to hold on the upstream face of the dam, they also rest in the eddy behind the dam.

Wing dams are very attractive to fish. Biologist Rod Pierce, now with the Minnesota Department of Natural Resources, studied wing dams during his years at the University of Wisconsin–Stevens Point. Pierce collected 52 species of fish from 6 wing dams in Pool 13, including all popular gamefish and many smaller species.

Mississippi River, Pool 8—During the same period as Pitlo's study, Jim Holzer and Kenneth Von Ruden of the Wisconsin Department of Natural Resources followed 19 radio-tagged walleyes in Pool 8. Their fish were more mobile than Pitlo's, with one wandering up to Pool 5 to spawn and another moving into the Chippewa River to spawn.

Walleyes in this pool, they found, spawn at several sites offering reduced current and reed canary grass. Spawning in weeds, first noted among walleyes in the Lake Winnebago system, also occurs in the Upper Mississippi. Pool 8 is connected to gravel pits, and several walleyes enter the pits after spawning and remain there for the summer.

On portions of the upper Mississippi River, walleyes spawn on reed canary grass instead of "traditional" rock-rubble banks. We would never have known without tracking.

In October, walleyes move to large sloughs with reduced current or into gravel pits. No fish remain in the main channel when water temperature falls into the 50°F range. The fall shift coincides with heavy fall rains that increase flow. Walleyes typically remain in their chosen fall location throughout winter, though a few fish still move between protected holding areas, even in midwinter.

Cedar River, Iowa—Vaughn Paragamian of the Iowa Department of Natural Resources followed 31 radio-tagged walleyes in the Cedar River and its tributaries in eastern Iowa. The Waverly Dam blocks upstream migration on the Cedar; 92 percent of all telemetry locations were within 6 miles of the dam. Several fish, Paragamian found, move up tributary streams to spawn but soon return to the Cedar.

During summer, walleyes stay near current breaks in areas with gravel and cobble substrate. During the heat of summer, walleyes in the Cedar sometimes move into the deepest pools (up to 10 feet deep). This behavior hasn't been described in the Mississippi River, probably because river depths there are much greater. In the Cedar, however, water temperature doesn't vary from surface to bottom. Perhaps walleyes shift deeper during the day, not to find cooler temperatures but reduced current or shade.

> *During summer, walleyes stay near current breaks in areas with gravel and cobble substrate.*

As river flows decline in late summer, walleyes move upstream where a series of pools with gravel, cobble, and boulders offer cover and feeding opportunities. During fall, active fish also hold downstream of brush and submerged logs located in current, moving into pools to rest. In October 1986, when a fall flood raised water levels, walleyes moved downstream to refuge in backwaters and flooded timber. They hold along riprap only in fall, and it is not a preferred form of cover in the Cedar.

When water temperatures drop into the the mid-40°F range in late fall, walleyes move into deep pools to overwinter. Pools range from 4 to 9 feet deep and provided protection from current. This seasonal scenario probably represents a common pattern in small midwestern warmwater rivers.

Luxapalila Creek, Mississippi—The Tombigbee River supports a native population of walleye, the most southern of the walleye range. Construction of the Tennessee-Tombigbee Waterway extensively channelized the river and threatened walleye habitat. Additional threats to the river include channelizing, dredging gravel riffles, and removing brush and snags. In 1986 and 1987, Roger Kingery, at the Mississippi Cooperative Fish and Wildlife Research Unit, radio-tagged walleyes to document spawning areas and habitat preferences throughout the year.

In Luxapalila Creek, walleyes favor wood cover on the creek bottom for shade and current breaks and because baitfish inhabit snags and brush. Walleyes held near wood in 73 percent of Kingery's telemetry locations, entering backwaters only during floods.

During summer, walleyes remain in limited areas and seem to feed primarily at night. Kingery feels that walleye movements are restricted because forage fish concentrate in small areas and because water temperatures near the upper limit of walleye tolerance force fish to conserve energy as much as possible. During summer, walleyes inhabit the coolest available water. They become active as twilight fades or as the moon sets in the evening and remain active until sunrise.

Kingery notes that plans for damming, dredging, and removing snags would reduce walleye cover and spawning habitat in the Tombigbee Waterway.

LAKE MOVEMENTS

Lake Bemidji, Minnesota—Lake Bemidji, a 6,400-acre eutrophic lake in northern Minnesota, supports a strong walleye population. In 1973, Dr. Charles Holt, now retired from the faculty of Bemidji State College, assembled a research team including college and high school students to conduct what apparently was the first telemetry study of walleyes. They wired radio tags to the back muscles of 18 walleyes and followed them for periods of up to one month during spring, summer, and fall.

Walleyes, the team found, stay above the 15-foot contour and tend to hold at a constant depth as they swim. When they encounter the many bars that extend perpendicular to Lake Bemidji's shore, they either turn and backtrack or follow the structure without crossing its shallower contours. Walleyes usually move in the direction of the wind instead of moving into it, as is sometimes assumed.

Changes in water clarity do not affect the depth walleyes occupy. Holt noted that during 1973, tagged fish occupied progressively shallower water from spring to summer to fall. In 1974, however, depth remained similar during the three seasons. Lake Bemidji becomes progressively more turbid as the seasons progress, perhaps countering the common pattern of walleyes moving deeper in summer and fall.

Walleyes move least during summer (no tracking was done during winter). Holt theorizes that high abundance of young perch provides abundant forage for walleyes, so they have little need to roam in summer. Total distance moved ranges from 0.5 mile to 11 miles, reiterating the marked range of behavior among individual members of this species.

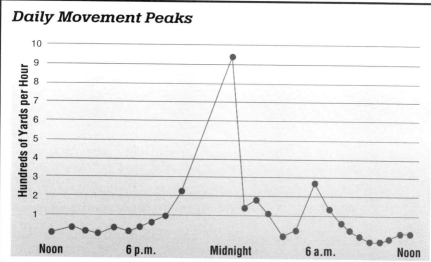

Daily Movement Peaks

Tracking studies prove what anglers have observed for ages—walleyes are most active at night, with peaks at dusk and dawn. This graph is based on John Pitlo's study on West Lake Okoboji, but Les Ager's results were almost identical, based on the behavior of walleyes in Center Hill Reservoir, Tennessee. An exception to this rule may be during the Prespawn Period, when walleyes move toward spawning sites throughout the day.

West Blue Lake, Ontario—Dr. John Kelso first used temperature-sensitive ultrasonic transmitters to observe walleyes after locating them in West Blue Lake, Ontario. This narrow, steep-sided lake thermally stratifies in late May, with a thermocline from 20 to 33 feet, depending on season. It's typically ice covered for six months.

During this late-summer and fall study, Kelso found, water from the surface to the top of the thermocline ranges from 51°F to 59°F, while water below the thermocline is 39°F to 45°F. Walleyes are found exclusively in water from 51°F to 52°F, suggesting that they shun colder and warmer water at this time. Obviously they always stay above the thermocline.

Walleyes typically move along breaks parallel to shore. During daytime, they remain suspended offshore but usually within 100 yards of it. As daylight wanes, they move toward shore, swimming at a constant depth. As sunrise nears, they return offshore.

Total movements range from 1 to 5 miles per day in this large lake. Daily average speed is just a quarter of a body length per second because movement is slight for much of the day. During peak activity, they move as fast as 3.7 body lengths per second.

Walleye activity peaks just after dusk as fish make short, fast bursts, perhaps catching perch, their primary prey in West Blue Lake. Walleyes are also active just before dawn. This bimodal peak of activity, termed crepuscular, has been reported in several behavioral studies of walleyes and is supported by anglers. Walleyes see well in low light and can more easily capture preyfish that elude them in daylight.

West Okoboji Lake, Iowa—John Pitlo began his telemetry career in graduate school at Iowa State University when he implanted temperature-sensitive ultrasonic transmitters into 9 walleyes collected in West Lake Okoboji, in northwest Iowa. This 3,800-acre mesotrophic lake stratifies in summer, and the hypolimnion is low in oxygen during late summer. This clear water lake features points, bays, large bars with sand and gravel, and thick beds of cabbage, coontail, and sandgrass growing as deep as 25 feet.

Five of the 6 walleyes Pitlo tracked extensively stayed in shallow eutrophic bays with dense weedbeds, spending most of their time in water from 10 to 16 feet deep. Weed walleyes establish activity centers that they then occupy for most of the summer. These activity centers range from 17 to 190 acres, again illustrating the individuality of fish in a population.

Walleyes with activity centers along faster-breaking contours move less, probably because weedbeds are narrower. Fish living on more gently sloping

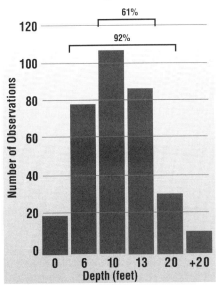

Weed Walleyes

In West Lake Okoboji, five of the six walleyes that John Pitlo tracked through the summer remained in thick weedbeds. They were found in 10 to 16 feet of water about 61 percent of the time. West Okoboji is clear, and weeds grow deeper than 25 feet in summer. In murkier lakes, weed walleyes hold shallower.

structures move more throughout the vast weedbeds that grow there.

West Okoboji offers plenty of "classic" walleye structure, including sand, gravel, and rock bars with little vegetation. A substantial portion of the lake's walleyes favor weedier and shallower water than most anglers typically fish. Fishing experiences and other telemetry studies suggest that this is a common pattern in mesotrophic and eutrophic walleye waters.

During summer, walleyes in West Okoboji follow daily patterns, holding in weedbeds or near the outside weededge during the day, moving somewhat shallower at night, presumably to feed. They stay shallower during cloudy or windy days. Activity peaks from around 8 p.m. till midnight, with a minor peak from 5 to 8 a.m.

Walleyes occasionally undertake what Pitlo terms "exploratory excursions" to other parts of the lake, after which they return to their activity center. Remarkably, fish swim directly across open water to reach spots and return the same way, suggesting that they possess a well-developed directional sense and knowledge of large parts of the lake.

In Pitlo's study, a lone deep walleye remained all summer within an activity center less than a quarter mile in area. During the day, it held off a rocky bar about 30 feet down. It moved up the bar to feed at about 18 feet but never approached the weedbeds that held many other walleyes. As Kelso found in West Blue Lake, walleyes follow contour lines when travelling, except when venturing shallower to feed.

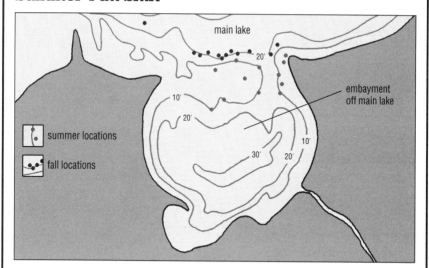

Summer-Fall Shift

West Lake Okoboji typifies a productive, mesotrophic walleye lake. During summer, many walleyes hold in weedbeds located on a large bar that extends off a shoreline point. In fall, weeds die and thermal and chemical stratification break up. Walleyes shift deeper but stay within a few hundred yards of their summer home ranges.

Fall home ranges are smaller and located more precisely on structure breaks. Fish are more catchable then to an experienced structure fisherman than when they're scattered in shallow water.

These Iowa walleyes occupy much warmer water than walleyes in Ontario, though considerably cooler water than walleyes in Luxapalila Creek in Mississippi. During summer, their average body temperature is 72°F, with a range from 70°F to 77°F.

In October, deep and shallow walleyes move deeper as water cools and aquatic plants die. In Pitlo's study, 3 walleyes in a huge weedbed on a broad bar moved to the 20-foot contour off the east side less than 200 yards from their typical summer positions.

Advances in understanding the ways of walleyes has lead to increased angler success and satisfaction.

Pitlo tested for correlations between walleye movements and various environmental factors, including barometric pressure, wind, cloud cover, and water color. Although none of the relationships is statistically significant, he notes that walleyes stay deeper and move less when barometric pressure is high.

Chautauqua Lake, New York—Radiotelemetry studies by Don Einhouse and his advisor, Dr. Jim Winter of the State University of New York at Fredonia, document walleyes using weeds and describe another pattern in Chautauqua Lake walleyes. Seneca Indians named the lake, which means bag tied in the middle, for its two basins and constricted middle. The southern basin is weedy and eutrophic, with a mean depth around 11 feet, while the northern basin is mesotrophic, with a mean depth of 26 feet.

Winter and his colleagues implanted 128 transmitters, although as in all studies, transmitter failure, fishing, and natural mortality reduced the number of fish providing usable data. Most fish, they found, occupy weedy habitat in 6 to 13 feet of water, similar to the range Pitlo found that Okoboji walleyes prefer. These weed walleyes, weighing less than 4 pounds, remain in a portion of a bay all summer.

Larger walleyes (5 to 9 pounds) behave in two ways: one group stays near weeds but switches areas frequently. Another group nomadically roams offshore areas, usually suspending at mid-depths. Some of these fish travel throughout the entire lake during the summer. Anglers trying new trolling techniques on mesotrophic lakes in summer have been amazed by catching more and bigger walleyes than most folks believe inhabit the lake. Offshore waters throughout the country haven't been effectively fished yet, so what are we waiting for?

Walleyes in Chautauqua show peaks in activity related to light intensity, but they don't move shallower after dark, as fish in other waters sometimes do. They also show a distinct preference for outside weededges, unlike walleyes in West Okoboji. Walleyes form feeding groups when schools of prey, primarily perch, concentrate in spots. At other times, however, individuals are solitary. After spawning, walleyes return to feeding areas they occupied the preceding summer.

Like walleyes in Lake Okoboji, Chautauqua walleyes move deeper in fall. Some fish from the shallow southern basin move to the northern basin before ice-up.

Lake Wissota, Wisconsin—Joe Kurz and other biologists with the Wisconsin Department of Natural Resources radio-tagged walleyes in Lake Wissota, a flowage on the Chippewa River. With the Wissota Power Dam scheduled for relicensing by the Federal Energy Regulatory Commission (FERC), the Wisconsin DNR wished to check on spawning habitat, wintering locations, and movement patterns to evaluate how the dam affects the fishery.

The flowage is weedy, turbid, and does not stratify. During summer, radio-tagged walleyes hold in weedbeds in about 3 feet of water. They move little during the day but roam shallow areas at night, presumably hunting. In fall, walleyes remain in the same areas, though they occupy woody habitat more as weeds die.

During the annual winter drawdown, walleyes move into the old river channel, holding as deep as 25 feet. Their movements are minimal during winter, when they group in deep holes with bass, pike, and panfish.

Biologists are concerned that winter drawdowns in this shallow, fertile impoundment may hurt fish populations by restricting natural movements, reducing oxygen levels under the ice, and damaging habitat and cover exposed to ice They suspect that other flowages may be similarly affected. Final recommendations to FERC have not been made.

RESERVOIR MOVEMENTS

Center Hill Reservoir, Tennessee—While in graduate school at Tennessee Technological University, Les Ager performed the first telemetry study on reservoir walleyes, surgically implanting ultrasonic transmitters in 29 fish from Center Hill Reservoir. The U. S. Army Corps of Engineers operates this highland reservoir for flood control.

Center Hill walleyes display many movements characteristic of lake fish, with some variations. Daily movements by individual fish range from 48 yards to over 0.5 mile, with most activity from November through February. From April through September, walleyes are most active at night, with activity peaking around midnight. From October through November, activity peaks at dawn and dusk. From January through March, activity doesn't vary significantly at any time of day or night.

Walleye home ranges, which Ager defines as the area that fish repeatedly traverse, are not so large as in large lakes or river systems. Half the regularly

Reservoir walleyes act much like their counterparts in lakes and rivers. Habitat differences, though, also mean subtle behavioral differences.

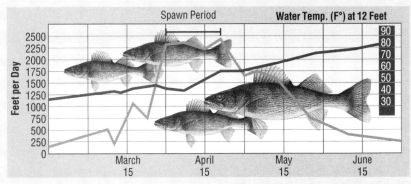

Average Daily Movement/Water Temperature

Spawn Period · Water Temp. (F°) at 12 Feet

Average daily movement rate of walleyes based on weekly observations and water temperature in Lake Shelbyville, Illinois. Rising water temperature in conjunction with the yearly period moves walleyes through Prespawn into Spawn and finally into summer patterns. Walleyes move only a little in cold water, begin to move a lot during Prespawn and Spawn, then settle into more static summer patterns.

monitored fish establish home ranges. These ranges are smallest in summer (29 to 83 acres) and largest in winter (73 to 187 acres). Walleyes wander most in fall, and during spring they migrate to spawning areas.

Ager notes that walleye anglers tend to fish the shoreline as they do for bass, but tagged walleyes favor offshore areas instead, with 60 percent of all locations more than 30 yards from the bank. Walleyes typically suspend from early summer through fall, when thermal stratification reduces oxygen levels below the thermocline. In warm months, they seek the coolest oxygenated water.

During summer, walleyes stay in the headwaters of tributary streams, where the substrate is rocky and the baitfish abundant. Current or cooler inflows also may attract walleyes. Fish in these areas remain closer to shore than they do in the reservoir.

After thermal stratification occurs in fall, walleyes move out to the main channel of the reservoir. In late fall and winter, they hold in deep channels of tributaries. Ager observes that walleyes do not react to a boat moving overhead, even in less than 10 feet of water, a finding that coincides with Pitlo's in West Lake Okoboji.

Lake Mackenzie, Texas—During his graduate studies at Texas A & M University, Tim Schlagenhaft implanted ultrasonic transmitters in 9 walleyes and 13 largemouth bass in Lake Mackenzie, a 500-acre reservoir in the Texas Panhandle, to check for potential competition between the two species. This reservoir is deep, clear, and has a steep shoreline.

In summer, he found, 76 percent of all walleye locations are along rocky shorelines. Fish are always shallower than 21 feet, probably because dissolved oxygen is low below that depth.

After turnover, walleyes move offshore and deeper. As the reservoir continues to cool, walleyes move even deeper, down to 49 feet in winter.

Schlagenhaft found that largemouth bass favor brushy coves in spring, fall, and winter, with some using rocky shorelines in summer. Habitat overlap with walleyes is slight.

Seasonal Shifts in a Reservoir

Walleyes stocked in reservoirs where they don't naturally occur often spawn on riprap. In Canton Reservoir, Oklahoma, and other impoundments, walleyes established home ranges in the lower end of reservoirs, holding along creek channels or submerged islands. In Canton Reservoir, fish concentrate close to humps in fall, with only a few fish using the channel. In Center Hill Reservoir, Tennessee, however, walleyes move from the upper ends of tributary creeks to deeper channels in fall.

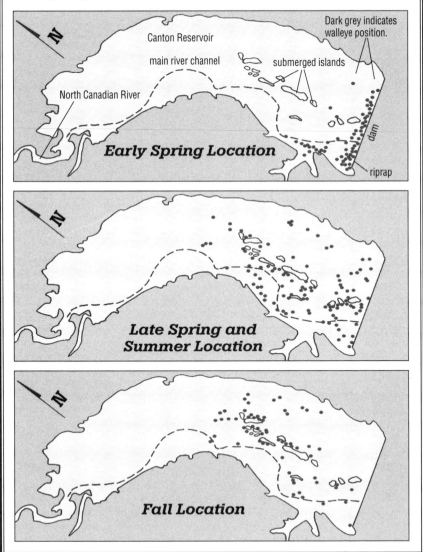

N

Canton Reservoir

main river channel

submerged islands

Dark grey indicates walleye position.

North Canadian River

dam

Early Spring Location

riprap

N

Late Spring and Summer Location

N

Fall Location

Canton Reservoir, Oklahoma—Greg Summers of the Oklahoma Fishery Research Lab implanted ultrasonic transmitters in 50 adult walleyes in Canton Reservoir, a 7,900-acre impoundment on the North Canadian River in northwestern Oklahoma. After spawning on riprap near the dam, walleyes concentrate around submerged islands in the lower half of the reservoir and near the main river channel. From May through November, over 80 percent of walleye locations are within 200 yards of submerged islands.

From April through October, walleyes move progressively upstream but never more than 1,200 yards upstream of the dam. In November, they shift closer to the dam.

Meredith Reservoir, Texas—Biologists James Parks and Joe Kraai of the Texas Parks and Wildlife Department placed ultrasonic transmitters in 19 walleyes to study their behavior in Meredith Reservoir, the premier walleye fishery in Texas. Large areas of Meredith have steep banks with rock and boulders. Aquatic weeds and brush are scarce.

Like the walleyes in Canton Reservoir, fish spawn on riprap near the dam, moving upstream to establish home ranges in the lower half of the reservoir. During summer, walleyes remain less than 25 feet deep, typically within 150 feet of shore. Walleyes favor shorelines with brushy cover but also use rocky banks.

The researchers found fish in open water about 21 percent of the time and near offshore submerged islands about 13 percent of the time. Home ranges are generally large, ranging from 348 to 6,220 acres. During the study, Meredith's surface area varied from 8,600 to 10,000 acres due to water level fluctuations.

Illinois Reservoirs: Lake Shelbyville, Fox Chain o' Lakes, Clinton Lake—In Illinois, the Department of Conservation stocks millions of walleyes to supplement populations in 49 impoundments across the state. Biologists try to collect adult brood fish on their spawning grounds, concentrating their efforts on three large reservoirs—Clinton, Shelbyville, and the Fox Chain o' Lakes. Collecting spawners is difficult, however, because the timing of the run varies, and information on the most common spawning sites has been lacking. In some years, the spawn is completed in two weeks or less.

As a result, the supply of ripe females has not met the demand for production of young fish for stocking. To better define spawning areas and the timing of the run, biologists R. C. Heidinger and B. L. Tetzlaff surgically implanted ultrasonic transmitters in 74 walleyes from 1½ to 9½ pounds and tracked them over three years. They followed the fish primarily from late November through June, since movements surrounding the spawn were of most interest.

Lake Shelbyville—Lake Shelbyville is an 11,000-acre flood-control reservoir on the Kaskaskia and West Okaw rivers in east-central Illinois. The Y-shaped impoundment stretches 20 miles from the dam to the upper end, with a maximum

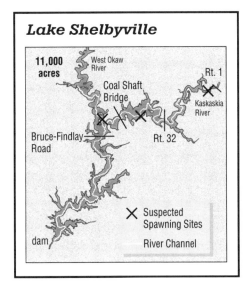

Lake Shelbyville

11,000 acres

West Okaw River

Coal Shaft Bridge

Rt. 1

Kaskaskia River

Bruce-Findlay Road

Rt. 32

dam

✕ Suspected Spawning Sites

River Channel

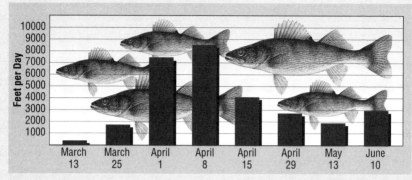

Average Daily Movement

Average daily movement of walleyes during 24-hour tracking periods at Lake Shelbyville, Illinois. Movement is most pronounced during the Prespawn, Spawn, and Postspawn Periods.

width of approximately one mile and an average depth of 19 feet.

In fall, biologists placed transmitters in 19 walleyes and monitored them as they wintered in standing timber off main lake points or near channel bends in the upper third of the reservoir near the meeting of the two main channels. A brief staging period was observed in late February. By mid-March, some walleyes began moving upstream, following the Kaskaskia River channel, while others remained downstream. This shift began as ice cover began to decay, which made tracking difficult.

Prespawn Movements: A week after breakup, as water temperatures climb through the upper 40°F range, 60 percent of the tagged walleyes are moving upstream, while the rest make no directional moves. Walleyes move most during this period, averaging about 1½ miles per day, and fish move along the submerged river channel. One particularly eager fish has been tracked moving almost 3/4 mile per hour and swimming over 6 miles.

Spawning: By mid-April, water temperatures edge into the low 50°F range, and spawners apparently find their preferred sites. Movements decrease. Walleyes carrying the ultrasonic tags use three main spawning areas. One is a large flat about 3 feet deep, located near an island at the lower end of the West Okaw River channel.

A second site, a submerged ridge, is 4 feet deep on top, with a substrate of gravel, sand, and mud, and located in the Kaskaskia arm. A third site is in a riffle far upstream in the Kaskaskia River. Fish that spawn in the upper river spawn earliest. Postspawn fish move downstream while other walleyes are still spawning in the upper reservoir. In May, most walleyes move downstream to the main body of the reservoir.

During the Postspawn Period, walleyes apparently forage in shallow areas (less than 10 feet deep) near shore, off points, or along flats. Shelbyville's turbid water color apparently keeps them shallow during the day in all weather conditions.

When biologists tracked a second set of walleyes two years later, they found that some fish spawn in the lower end of the reservoir as well as upstream. This finding suggests that two or more subpopulations may exist in Shelbyville, as has been documented in large natural lakes.

Fox Chain o' Lakes—During fall and early spring, biologists placed transmitters in 14 adult walleyes caught in two of the lakes in the Fox Chain o' Lakes—Channel Lake and Lake Marie. This chain, a series of glacial moraine lakes in northeastern Illinois, was joined early in the twentieth century by constructing a lowhead dam on the Fox River and dredging channels between lake basins. The nine lakes in the Fox chain cover about 6,500 acres.

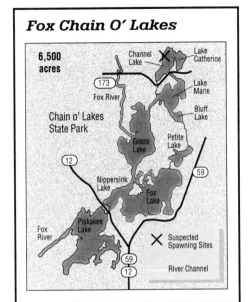

Fox Chain O' Lakes

During winter, walleyes were captured in deep holes in two of the lakes. Ice cover was 15 to 20 inches and fish held about 25 to 28 feet deep. Three of the tagged fish were next to each other. Daily movements increased toward the end of February.

Prespawn Movements: During the first week of April, walleyes concentrate in Lake Marie, where they winter. Fish appear to stage on two large, main lake points where depth is 10 to 20 feet.

Spawn: Walleyes remain on those points for the next two weeks, suggesting that they spawn there. None of the tagged walleyes moves into the Fox River to spawn, suggesting that one group of walleyes lives entirely in the lakes. Sampling in the Fox River during spring fails to capture adult walleyes, so perhaps few if any walleyes spawn there.

The Fox chain is stocked with walleye fry raised from broodstock caught from the lake, which may perpetuate this trend. After spawning, walleyes disperse into a variety of habitats, but generally remain in the more northern lakes. In general, walleye movements vary more among individuals there than they do at Shelbyville.

Clinton Lake—Biologists implanted transmitters in 20 walleyes from Clinton Lake, a central Illinois 5,000-acre nuclear power cooling reservoir that was filled in 1978. The reservoir is V-shaped; its two arms follow the two branches of Salt Creek. Average depth is 15 feet. A large warmwater discharge from the power plant flows from a canal at temperatures as high as 111°F, creating a large heat sink.

Two of the tagged walleyes were collected from the warmwater discharge. One returned quickly to it after being released in another cove. Another tagged fish joined it, as well as presumably many untagged walleyes. During this period in December, the discharge was about 46°F, 10° warmer than the rest of the lake. As in Lake Shelbyville, walleyes favor timbered coves during winter.

At ice-out in mid-March, most walleyes hold in creek channels in open parts of the reservoir. None are present in the warmwater discharge.

Prespawn Movements: During the last week of March, several fish holding in diverse spots move up the North Fork of Salt Creek, holding in the creek channel. One male walleye has apparently sensed the spawning urge strongly, for he moves 2 miles in one hour. During the first week of April, walleyes move out of

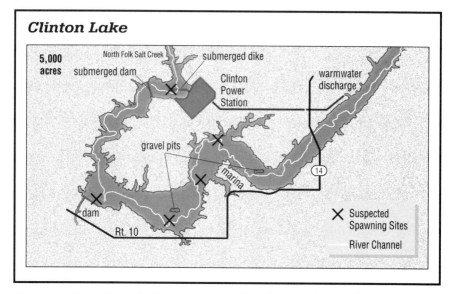

Clinton Lake

5,000 acres

North Folk Salt Creek
submerged dam
submerged dike
Clinton Power Station
warmwater discharge
gravel pits
marina
14
dam
Rt. 10

X Suspected Spawning Sites
River Channel

the channels and into shallower water, primarily on points or flats. Ten of the walleyes move to within 0.5 mile of the dam.

Spawn: Biologists feel that most walleyes spawn during a week in mid-April when water temperatures climb from 47°F into the low 50°F range. One walleye spawns on the face of the dam, while several others apparently spawn on submerged dams and dikes and along riprap banks near the power plant. Other groups of fish spawn on flats near the creek channel or near submerged gravel pits. During spawning time, some walleyes occupy adjacent creek channels, suggesting that some fish move into deeper water during the day between nocturnal spawns. The spawning sites are exposed to prevailing winds.

Another group of walleyes apparently spawn in the lower reaches of the North Fork branch of the reservoir, while another group moves up the river channel. Some fish may move farther upstream into the river itself. After the spawn, several walleyes move directly to the warmwater discharge, where they remain for several weeks, presumably feeding on baitfish concentrated there.

Principles of Wind and Walleyes

THE WIND. AN EVER-PRESENT FACTOR AFFECTING WHEN, WHERE, AND HOW WE FISH FOR WALLEYES.

The vastness of the Dakota prairies is immediately impressive. So is the size of the reservoirs where those old walleyes reside. But besides the fine fishing, it's the wind that leaves a lasting impression on fishermen who visit.

The Dakotas aren't the only place where the wind whistles a tough tune. Lake Powell (Utah-Arizona) is an amazing and miserable place when a 30-mph blow sends massive waves careening from canyon wall to canyon wall, left-right, right-left, and even back into the wind. Find cover or die.

Covering Your Presentation Trail

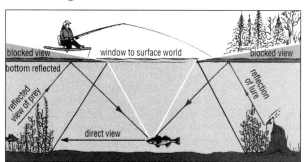

In addition to a direct line of sight underwater, fish can see surface objects and activity through a circular area above them. The view is distorted by the refraction of light. Objects like anglers are likely to appear very small. Around this "window to the surface world" is an area where light from the bottom reflects off the surface of the water and then back down to the fish. Ripples and waves break up these images. Fish may detect obvious motion in these areas, but may not be able to tell exactly what's there.

But then 6-footers are 6-footers wherever they swell, from Lake Erie to Lake of the Woods. And those who "ralph" robustly in 3-footers on a famous walleye lake like Mille Lacs are unlikely to fare much better in similar swells on other famous fisheries such as Winnebago or Oneida or Saginaw Bay.

Walleye fishermen love and hate the wind. It's wonderful to be there on a June morning, 75°F, sun peeking over the horizon, a soft and steady south breeze wrinkling the surface. You're a picture of confidence as you use your electric trolling motor to move precisely and quietly along a breakline. If you want to jig, you can jig. If you want to use a livebait rig, you can feel exactly what's happening as it tickles bottom. Add a few walleyes to this fine stew, and you're at one with the world, in control of your life, and quite possibly convinced you're one of the world's great walleye fishermen.

But 24 hours later, temperature 47°F, gale-force wind driving rain from the northeast, you frantically attempt a "controlled" drift. But where are you? Peeking over the top of your fogged over glasses, you realize your bait is riding 20 feet down over 117 feet of water.

Numb fingers slip from the handle of the kicker motor. As you turn and reach, a wave busts over the back of the boat into your face, driving a trickle of razor-edged ice water past the protection of your rain suit, around your neck, down the small of your back, past the belt above your behind, and finally down that perfect passageway where rubber meets the road. *Aiieeyah!* If only your fingers would function, you'd gladly write a suicide note on a dollar bill.

On the one hand, wind can concentrate walleyes, turn them on, and cover your presentation trail, making it more difficult for fish to detect you when you wade or troll. On the other hand, it can complicate boat control, disperse fish, turn them off, and make fishing dangerous. So wind is friend and foe, fearsome force for good fishing and bad—an ever-present factor in where, when, and how we fish for walleyes. Wind also is a factor not completely understood.

But most anglers do know things about wind and walleyes. And most of what's known is probably correct. For example, *Concentrate on structural elements on the windward side of the lake* is a solid rule. But that steadfast axiom leaves questions unanswered. Any structural element? Shallow-lying structural elements? The windward side of shallow structural elements? How deep is shallow?

And those are just a few simple questions. Some topics lie beyond what the average advanced walleye fisherman considers important. Potentially more important questions aren't asked because few fishermen know enough about how wind affects the movement of water to pose sophisticated questions and possibly to arrive at answers that mean more consistent fishing.

That's the quest here—first, for questions that in time lead to answers that aren't widely known to help you become a more sophisticated and successful walleye fisherman. So here we focus on basic concepts—principles—of how wind affects the water in which walleyes live. Examine what you already know from a new perspective. Lay a foundation to draw from in predicting how wind affects walleyes.

BACKGROUND

The sun ultimately is responsible for currents in bodies of water. Temperature variation in different levels of the atmosphere causes winds. The interactions of the earth's rotation on its axis, its revolution around the sun, and the movement of our solar system produce global wind patterns.

On either side of the equator, winds typically blow from east to west—the trade winds that powered mercantile fleets of yesteryear. North of the Fortieth Parallel, which runs roughly through Philadelphia, Indianapolis, Denver, and Redding, California, winds blow predominately from west to east—the westerlies. These are the potent blows that whip the western plains and gather momentum as they cross middle America, sweeping past the Great Lakes toward the East.

Add to this mix the *Coriolis force*, which is generated by the rotation of the earth and causes air and water to deflect to the right in the northern hemisphere (left in the southern hemisphere). The intensity of the Coriolis force increases from nil at the equator toward the poles.

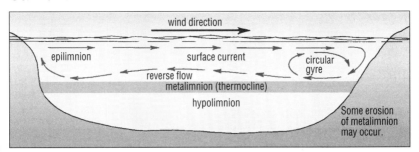

Current Direction

Steady wind from one direction establishes a directional surface current moving toward shore. The shore diverts the flow downward and back across the lake in the opposite direction.

If the surface current is strong, it may continue to circulate near shore in a circular gyre. Plankton may collect in this current. Schools of baitfish often congregate here, and walleyes follow.

Warm circulating water erodes the upper portion of the metalimnion. During summer, calm warm days restore this layer. In fall, circulating water hastens Turnover.

CORIOLIS FORCE

If wind affects walleyes, then Coriolis force affects your fishing. Say you assume, as many good fishermen do, that a half day or more of wind from a consistent direction creates a current moving toward structural elements on the windward side of the lake. You're correct. But Coriolis force bends water currents to the right of the wind direction. In large lakes like Ontario and Superior, the current bends as much as 45 degrees.

As lake size and depth decrease, the angle of deflection is reduced. Limnologists studying 9,600-acre, 80-foot-deep Lake Mendota (Wisconsin) found currents deflected about 20 degrees to the right of the wind. Assume, then, that in most lakes the deflection is slightly to the right.

Coriolis Force

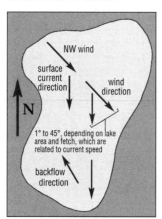

The surface of the earth spins at about 66,600 miles per hour. (Gravity keeps us from flying off the face of the earth.) This velocity affects the direction in movement for all objects. Drain a bathtub in the northern hemisphere, and the water swishes down in a clockwise direction (reversed on the other side of the equator). Winds and water currents tend to circle in the same direction.

In the northern hemisphere, wind-caused currents move to the right of wind direction. The amount of deflection is related to the size of the lake. Maximum deflection of 45° occurs only in the ocean or the world's largest lakes.

Degree of deflection increases with current speed, which is affected by wind speed only up to a critical point of 14 to 18 mph. Stronger winds don't speed currents or increase the angle of Coriolis deflection.

Currents rebound after contacting shorelines and are again deflected in a clockwise direction in the northern hemisphere. In a huge lake, the result often is one or more vast circular currents flowing clockwise.

Rebound Current

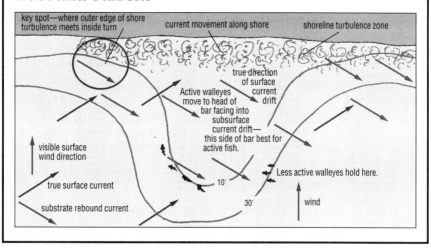

Not only does surface current move in a different direction from the wind, but a substantial *subsurface reverse current* also moves in the direction opposite the wind—10 to 20 to perhaps 30 degrees farther to the right. First figure the to-the-right deflection of the surface current; then note that below this surface current a reverse current rebounds, like a pool ball bouncing off a cushion, at another angle to the right of the surface current.

This often overlooked current affects walleye position near middepth structural elements. Fish in shallow water usually face into shallow surface current. But fish holding deeper than about 5 feet often face the opposite direction, into a reverse current.

Say the wind is blowing onto a bar that drops abruptly into 4 feet of water just offshore, then slopes to 10 feet, then plummets to 30. The tip of the 10-foot dropoff is a key area. Most fishermen consider the wind and the wind-generated current washing this bar. And because walleyes usually face into current, they picture walleyes facing the wind.

The direction walleyes face affects presentation. Presentations should move toward or quarter in front of walleyes, instead of sneaking up on them from the rear. In this case, most walleyes probably face the rebound current moving in the opposite direction of the wind. Retrieving baits offshore will therefore be more productive.

Currents that hit shorelines also are deflected clockwise, which affects fish position and location. Say you're fishing a plateau reservoir, though it could be any body of water where walleyes gather along wind-blown shorelines. Wind blowing into shore produces a right-moving current. Follow the shoreline drop-off to the right until you meet a bar. The inside turn on the side of the bar that meets the current is likely to hold active fish. The tip of the point on the current side of the bar is also likely to hold active walleyes.

Predator Position

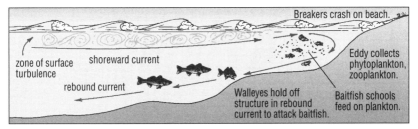

zone of surface turbulence

shoreward current

rebound current

Breakers crash on beach.

Eddy collects phytoplankton, zooplankton.

Walleyes hold off structure in rebound current to attack baitfish.

Baitfish schools feed on plankton.

Many factors affect the direction and strength of wind-caused current, so anglers must understand the physical principles, then assess conditions as they occur in a lake. Areas where current turns abruptly form eddies where water follows a circular course. Islands, humps, and shorelines are obvious current breaks that often cause upwind eddies.

Strong directional currents collect debris and organisms incapable of strong swimming. Baitfish, including shad, yellow perch, bluegills, and shiners, may quickly congregate to feed on abundant plankton. Larger predators also appear and may hold offshore, facing into the rebound current, or may invade the turbulent shallows to chase prey.

In this example, crankbaits or jigs would be good presentations near shore. Slipfloat rigs worked on the outside of the eddy might take walleyes holding off the first break.

But in early spring or late fall, when the water's cold and the fish aren't active, the back side of the tip of the point (a bit removed from the current) is more likely to hold fish. Perhaps the side of the inside turn away from the wind-generated current also holds inactive fish.

When picking presentation options, consider current direction and speed. Preyfish, and the walleyes that eat them, orient to current.

When picking presentation options, consider current direction and speed. Preyfish, and the walleyes that eat them, orient to current. Baits moving with current mean more fish because such presentations seem more natural and remain longer in the walleye's strike zone.

Don't troll crankbaits into surface current deflected along the shoreline. Troll with the subsurface current, in this case coming into the inside turn or coming into or along the tip of the point.

Consider this scenario from a different angle. The surface current is moving slightly clockwise of the wind. To work the deeper lying rebound current that is moving even more to the right, move with the wind, but slow your approach with drift socks or your outboard motor. Use your outboard or electric trolling motor to adjust your direction of drift.

If these scenarios confuse you at first, sketch a lake. Draw the wind direction. Add arrows slightly to the right to depict the general direction that surface water flows.

Where this current contacts a shallow bar or bank, draw surface current channeled to the right along the shore or bar. Now add arrows to depict a rebound current deflected almost in the opposite direction—again, this current is deflected clockwise and runs deeper. Now draw walleyes facing this deeper lying current. Also draw fish facing the surface current, particularly where it contacts sharp breaking structural elements.

Suppose you anchor to cast jigs at fish positioned near the tip of the 10-foot drop-off. Consider their position—probably facing into a rebounding current caused by the wind. Cast past the fish and bring the bait toward or quartering in front of them. A good option is to anchor off the point in deep water and cast into the shallows, bringing the jig from the flat toward deeper water.

Surface wind will push a slipfloat rig in to the point, but this isn't the most effective way to move a bait past walleyes that probably are facing the other way. Correctly set slipfloats move slowly past walleyes; they're still an option to catch fish. Slipfloat presentations are more deadly, however, where walleyes face into wind-caused surface currents at the edge of or over shallow flats.

For most fishermen, factoring in the potential effects of Coriolis force and rebound currents provides a new view of the real world of walleyes. But there's more.

WAVES AND SURFACE TURBULENCE

What you're about to be told has never been a secret, has a major effect on fishing, yet remains a mystery to most fishermen. Although wind causes the surface of the water to roll into travelling surface waves, very little water actually moves laterally. Instead, the wind raises water, which then curls in a circular pattern as gravity pulls the molecules downward—not unlike a wave travelling along a jump rope.

After wind has blown steadily for several hours, the tug-of-war between wind and gravity creates near-surface currents that move slowly, even in a strong wind. Watch, for example, the movement of neutrally buoyant debris—a piece of vegetation, perhaps—suspended just below the surface. The very slow drift of an

Waves

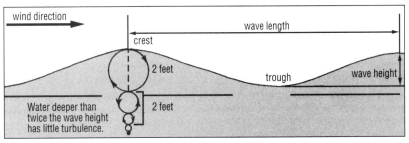

wind direction

wave length

crest

2 feet

trough

wave height

2 feet

Water deeper than
twice the wave height
has little turbulence.

A series of circular currents of decreasing size occurs below a wave, each with a diameter equal to half the one above. Water deeper than twice the wave height has little turbulence. When the ratio of wave height to wave length decreases, whitecaps form as gravity pulls over the crest of the wave and wind blows off water as spray.

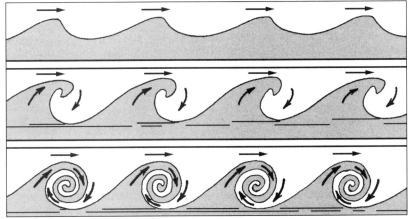

Waves appear to roll across the surface, but the water within them moves up and around without shifting position horizontally.

object just below the surface contrasts with that of a floating object pushed by wind, which may move faster than 10 mph in a stiff breeze.

This surface movement, contrasting with the "stationary" water below, is why drift socks slow boats that are being blown across the surface of the water. A sock is a parachute anchored in the relatively stationary water below. Drift speed can be cut by 10 to 90 percent, depending on the size of the drift sock (or socks) and the size of the opening in it.

The rolling action of waves creates surface turbulence, but *only to a depth about twice the height of the waves.* If waves crest at 3 feet, then water at 6 feet is only slightly affected, although slow-riding currents may move through those depths.

The wave-caused zone of turbulence offers an important edge that focuses the activity of prey and predators. First, both prey and predators moving through open water may travel just below this edge. Second, prey like shad or bluegills, which hold near the surface in calm conditions, are forced deeper along this edge when waves increase.

Wind's Effects On Walleyes

The wind's effects on walleye location, position, and disposition depend on several physical and biological characteristics of the lake. The slope of bottom and its depth affect how waves break and how current curls away from shore. The composition of the bottom sediment determines whether a mudline forms and also affects its size and duration. Amount and type of aquatic weeds as well as baitfish species and behavior affect walleyes' foraging patterns, too.

In *Scene 1*, waves roll across a shallow flat and break on a gradually sloping shoreline. If waves exceed 18 inches in water less than 3 feet deep, turbulence extends from the surface to bottom. Eddies form across the flat as circulating water turns to flow offshore. Phytoplankton and zooplankton accumulate in the eddy and slosh along the banks, stimulating baitfish to feed.

Walleyes may enter the shallow turbulent zone for short feeding forays, particularly at dawn, dusk, and after dark if waves persist. Mudlines provide shade that may also give walleyes a sense of security in shallow water and a feeding advantage over preyfish. Lighter sediments are held near the surface by current, so water may be clearer near bottom.

Rebounding currents push mudlines farther from the bank, so after days of directional wind, the outer edge of the mudline may be 100 yards offshore. These spots lack significant current, baitfish concentrations, and structural features, so walleyes rarely feed along these edges.

Walleyes also concentrate where rebound currents pass over a lip or breakline. Predators have access to deeper holding areas and shallow feeding opportunities. By casting toward shore and retrieving crankbaits or jigs, you can pull baits toward waiting walleyes. Light jigs wash naturally in bottom-hugging current, but you may miss bites in the turbulence. Heavier leadheads trigger active fish and are easier to fish effectively.

In *Scene 2*, winds buffet a steep, rocky bank and create a larger but more concentrated eddy near shore. If turbulence is strong, baitfish and

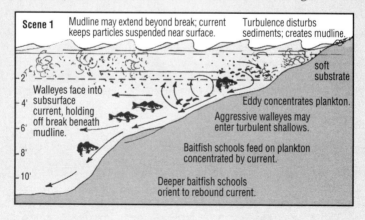

Scene 1
Mudline may extend beyond break; current keeps particles suspended near surface.
Turbulence disturbs sediments; creates mudline.
soft substrate
Walleyes face into subsurface current, holding off break beneath mudline.
Eddy concentrates plankton.
Aggressive walleyes may enter turbulent shallows.
Baitfish schools feed on plankton concentrated by current.
Deeper baitfish schools orient to rebound current.

predators may hold outside the eddy, each taking advantage of feeding opportunities.

Turbulence doesn't cause much turbidity because substrates are coarse. In clear lakes, walleyes typically hold deeper during the day, facing into the rebound current. Find these fish with sonar, then test their catchability by trolling or casting crankbaits. If bottom doesn't drop precipitously, backtrolling livebait rigs with floaters or inflated crawlers can score fish.

In darker-colored lakes, expect walleyes in turbulent shallow water along shorelines or offshore reefs. Slipfloat rigs and minnowbaits work both day and night.

When waves hit weedy shorelines, such as in *Scene 3*, weeds bend shoreward under the force of onshore surface current. Because the brunt of the force is buffered by weed stalks, minnows and small panfish hold in the lower portions of the stalks for shelter. Wind provides walleyes easier entry into dense weedbeds, and they feed among stalks or along the inside weededge. Shallow-diving minnowbaits and in-line spinners run across bent weed stalks are two productive lure options.

A weed face also deflects current down the break where less active walleyes hold, facing shoreward. Drop a baited jig down the face of the weedbed and bump it off the break.

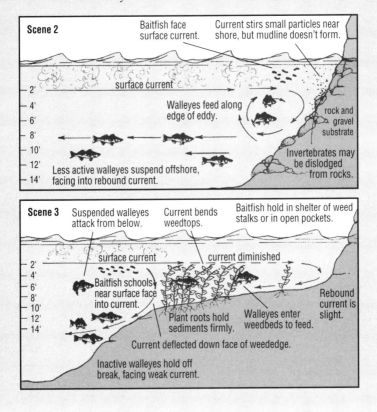

Scene 2

Baitfish face surface current.

Current stirs small particles near shore, but mudline doesn't form.

surface current

Walleyes feed along edge of eddy.

rock and gravel substrate

Invertebrates may be dislodged from rocks.

Less active walleyes suspend offshore, facing into rebound current.

Scene 3

Suspended walleyes attack from below.

Current bends weedtops.

Baitfish hold in shelter of weed stalks or in open pockets.

surface current

current diminished

Baitfish schools near surface face into current.

Rebound current is slight.

Plant roots hold sediments firmly.

Walleyes enter weedbeds to feed.

Current deflected down face of weededge.

Inactive walleyes hold off break, facing weak current.

Predators attack from below, forcing prey upward against the edge of turbulence. When prey are forced into the turbulence, they lose equilibrium. Schools break into disarray, and baitfish that drop back into the stable water below become slightly disoriented and vulnerable to attack.

Wavelength, which plays a role in the amount of turbulence, is the distance between successive wave crests. The typical ratio of wave height to wave length ranges from 1:100 to 1:10. A low ratio (1:100) causes swells, typical of calm days on the ocean. When wave height increases toward a ratio of 1:10 (choppy waves), whitecaps form as each wave collapses and its crest blows off as foam.

In small lakes, wave height at a given wind speed isn't related to lake depth. But in large lakes, wave height and wave length increase with depth. The maximum wave height is a factor of the distance the wind blows without interruption (fetch).

Waves may reach 8 or even 10 feet on Oahe Reservoir (South Dakota) or on Winnebago (Wisconsin). Lake Superior's vast area and depths to 1,300 feet produce the largest inland waves on the continent, up to 35 feet—woe be the *Edmund Fitzgerald*, which capsized and sank in a November gale that produced waves of that magnitude.

As waves approach shallow water, their velocity and wave length decrease because of the resistance of land. The circular motion of waves changes to an oval movement and then to a back-and-forth slosh when waves crash as breakers. Across shallow flats or rock bars, wind-induced turbulence may extend to bottom, forcing crayfish, larval insects, and bottom-dwelling baitfish from shelter.

This shoreline turbulence creates important fishing patterns. Mudlines that form in reservoirs with clay or shale banks attract walleyes during the day. The best areas are on or near major structural elements—bars or creek channels—that hold walleyes at that time of year. The fish there hold in deeper water when the wind isn't blowing.

Once wind begins blowing into a shoreline, a rebound current sets up and sweeps into deeper water. Soon walleyes follow the current onto the edge of the flat. Eventually, the fish may move across the flat and feed near the turbulence along the shoreline if the flat is deep enough to allow them to move in without being buffeted by wave-caused turbulence.

Walleyes tend to use shorelines with a lip—an immediate drop-off of a foot or two. Once you have found a shoreline with a lip, look for secondary structural elements such as rock piles or points along the shoreline.

Beyond this general pattern, search for more specific patterns caused by current moving to the right along windward shorelines. Active walleyes tend to hold on the current side of points and inside turns.

Another overlooked pattern for walleyes during summer occurs when wind sweeps weed-choked bars where baitfish usually lie hidden from walleyes. In lakes, most of these bars run 8 to 15 feet deep at the outside edge, where a weedwall rises almost to the surface to meet open water.

Once surface current bends the tops of the weedwall, it flattens weeds on shallower parts of the bar. If the directional wind continues into the evening, walleyes roam these bars at night. Often the fish hold just below the zone of wave-caused turbulence. In 2-foot waves, walleyes hold 4 to 6 feet down. In 1-foot waves, walleyes hold 2 to 4 feet down.

One option is trolling high-riding, minnow-imitating plugs like the Cordell Red Fin far behind the boat. Or try a tandem-hook spinner rig (#3 Colorado blades) with a crawler, which will catch fewer weeds. Better still, once you find a bar that holds fish, cast minnowbaits as you position your boat with a trolling motor.

THE TEMPERATURE EQUATION

The surface flows and rebound currents that we've described occur during all seasons, in warm and cool water. Combine these movements with the different densities of water at different temperatures, and the effects of wind become even more significant.

Water is densest at 39°F, so at ice-out (surface temperature 34°F to 36°F) water readily mixes in moderate winds. As surface water becomes heated by the sun, it becomes less dense and floats on cooler water. This density gradient reduces circulation between layers of different temperature.

Summer stratification into three layers is the large-scale result of warming and density differences. Even strong summer winds fail to mix these layers. But smaller-scale temperature variances do occur.

On a sunny summer day, the top 3 inches of water may be several degrees warmer than water a foot down. And while swimming in a lake, you encounter cold pockets that send you shivering to the surface. These same cold pockets may eventually be moved by wind-caused currents to areas that attract or repel walleyes.

A strong directional wind, for example, can pile a layer of warm surface water against a bank. During summer, this upper-70°F water may be too warm for coolwater species like walleyes or pike, causing them to shift deeper or to move offshore, even though schools of warmwater prey like minnows and shad are concentrated in warmer water.

Due to gravity, this bulk of warm water squeezes out a mass of cooler, denser water lying just above the thermocline. The colder water sets in motion a rebound current that may concentrate coolwater preyfish like alewives or smelt.

Wind and the Thermocline

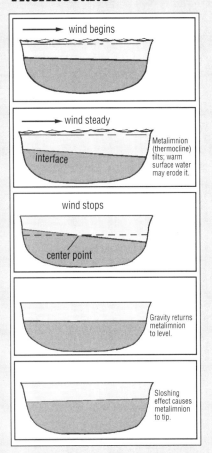

wind begins

wind steady

interface

Metalimnion (thermocline) tilts; warm surface water may erode it.

wind stops

center point

Gravity returns metalimnion to level.

Sloshing effect causes metalimnion to tip.

For most of the summer, the metalimnion acts as a barrier to walleyes. They prefer the warmer oxygenated water of the epilimnion. Currents in the epilimnion drift along the top of the metalimnion. Strong surface wind creates distinct subsurface current that forms waves in the denser metalimnion. The metalimnion may also tilt. In each case, walleyes move to avoid the colder water of the hypolimnion.

Picture pockets of warmer or colder water as drops of oil in water. Colder, denser pockets tend to sink through warmer water. Warmer, less dense pockets tend to float on colder water. But both pockets can be moved by surface or subsurface current.

In the Great Lakes, fish follow temperature plumes or ***thermal bars*** that confine coolwater or warmwater prey. Savvy anglers use thermal bars to find trout and salmon miles offshore. Electronic temperature meters capable of checking temperature in the depths and infrared images drawn by satellites are valuable tools.

For Great Lakes walleyes suspended offshore, currents and water masses of different temperature are important because of their effects on preyfish and

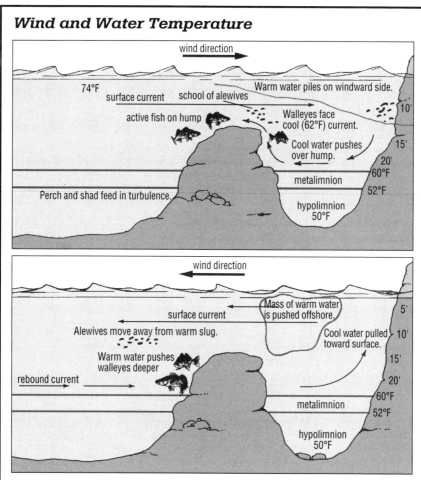

Wind and Water Temperature

Wind and water temperature often interact to alter fishing conditions. If surface temperatures are cool, a wind-driven slug of warm water can trigger walleye feeding in shallow areas. But this coolwater species may abandon attractive structures when winds pile hot surface water onto them.

Warm water tends to float on the surface. But when winds displace warm water, cooler water from the depths is drawn upward. Ambient temperature and the temperature preferences of prey species and walleyes determine the changing nature of fishing patterns.

Consistent fishing depends on anticipating wind-caused shifts in water temperature and monitoring changes on the surface and at depths with electronic thermometers.

walleyes. But they're also important on smaller waters.

A cold rebound current eventually may be forced toward the surface by an offshore bar, forming a cold pocket of surface water surrounded by warmth. With or without an influx of prey, this new water may stimulate activity in walleyes. Due to its greater density, this cool pocket will drift downward. But it may be renewed over hours or days by continuing cool currents.

At wind speeds between about 5 and 15 mph, a phenomenon called *Langmuir circulation* may also occur. Currents near the surface form columns of convection as surface water is pushed over slightly cooler water below. The surface water turns downward, forcing cooler water up. Langmuir currents are visible as streaks on the surface that align slightly to the right of the wind direction (again, due to the Coriolis force).

Langmuir Streaks

streaks of organic material including invertebrates, algae, pollen

wind direction 5 to 15 mph surface current

5' deep

"Tubes" of surface water, drawn to illustrate effects of Langmuir circulation.

Currents near surface move in helical pattern.

Small upwellings of cooler water occur between Langmuir streaks.

Adapted from R. Wetzel, *Limnology* (1983).

These streaks contain floating debris, including algae, pollen, and invertebrates. Between the streaks are zones of upwelling where cooler water from the depths has been forced to the surface. In oceans and the Great Lakes, upwelling areas are among the most productive fisheries. On smaller lakes and reservoirs, these areas also are productive. Concentrations of microorganisms in the streaks draw baitfish that in turn draw predators like walleyes.

Wind-induced currents are subtle, but temperature variances are invisible. The first step is recognizing that these thermal bars and upwellings occur in lakes and that they can dramatically affect the location of preyfish and walleyes. Systematically charting and anticipating these shifts is an advanced step that few walleye anglers have taken.

The last few years have seen increasing focus on open water walleye fisheries and the fabulous catches there. The next breakthroughs in using temperature profiles to find walleye will by necessity occur in Lake Erie, Saginaw Bay, Bay of Quinte, and other big waters. Fine-tuning these techniques to small lakes will provide a challenge into the twenty-first century.

These few examples of wind-induced fishing opportunities begin to suggest how much could be written on the topic if we had pages available to illustrate patterns. Indeed, a book of patterns could be produced, given the variety of lake basins and structural shapes, plus 360 degrees of wind direction and variables like water color and baitfish species.

All-Time Walleye Greats

TWENTY YEARS OF IN-FISHERMAN MASTER ANGLER DATA IN REVIEW

During the past 20 years, nearly 2,000 walleyes have come to scale and tape, entries in In-Fisherman's highly exclusive Master Angler Contest. Collectively, these large fish offer hints of wisdom about the walleye's world. Which waters, for example, have been the best producers of big fish? And what about monster walleyes, those fish surpassing 14 and 15 pounds? The best times to pursue huge walleyes? What baits have been best? And much more, here in capsule form.

THE MEGA WATERS
ALL-TIME GREATEST TROPHY WALLEYE FISHERIES

Here are In-Fisherman's listings of bodies of water, number of trophy walleyes recorded, and staff comments on each.

1. Western Basin of Lake Erie, OH (78 entries)—This water offers a superb opportunity for anglers in small (under 20 feet) inland fishing boats to catch big walleyes during spring and fall, or to fish from 6-man charter boats that provide necessary tackle during spring, summer, and fall. Great ice fishing opportunities exist when portions of the basin freeze during January and February. Arguably, this is the king of walleye fisheries. While fish size generally peaks at around 10 pounds, top size is increasing, with several 15-pounders caught in recent years.

2. Columbia River, OR-WA (64)—Multiple fish over 10 pounds are possible nearly anytime on this gigantic river system. Angler attention is focused below massive power dams, typically in or within a few miles of tailraces. During the day, fish vertically with heavy jigs or slow troll three-way rigs with either floater-crawler snells or minnow-imitator crankbaits. At night, when many of the largest walleyes are taken, try trolling large diving crankbaits that dive to the 20- or 25-foot level. Peak trophy fishing occurs in the low flow periods of fall and winter, with a good though more scattered summer bite. From late March through early June, a high flow allows salmon smolts to migrate downstream, resulting in massive current that curtails walleye fishing.

Walleyes That Make 10s Look Like Peanuts

AL NELSON
22 lbs. 11 oz.
Greers Ferry, AR, 1982

ARNOLD BERG
19 lbs. 15¼ oz.
Columbia River, OR-WA, 1990

3. Little Bay de Noc, MI (49)—This large shallow bay off the north end of Lake Michigan hosts small- to medium-size walleyes all year, plus a late fall and winter trophy fishery once walleyes migrate into the bay from the big lake, beginning in October. Many tactics produce fish: open water planer board trolling with crankbaits; structure fishing with livebait rigs, jigs, and jigging spoons along shoreline drop-offs, weedlines, and the edges of humps; longline trolling the shallows at night with minnow-imitator crankbaits. Also, excellent ice fishing for hawg walleyes exists from about Christmas throughout winter.

4. Upper Mississippi River, WI-MN-IA (39)—Classic big river fishing conditions exist below dams during spring and fall, from Minneapolis-St. Paul down to the Quad Cities of Illinois and Iowa. Even below this traditional stretch, winter fishing for walleyes and sauger extends all the way down to St. Louis. Focus on eddies, wing dams, and any current breaks within a mile or so of dams where fish congregate during low water. Vertical jigging with jig-and-minnow combos, three-way rigs baited with minnows, and bladebaits or jigging spoons excel in cold water. In the upper Mississippi, big walleyes are present in sections downriver from dams all summer, though they also spread into numerous current-deflecting areas like wing dams and flooded timber.

5. Lake Sakakawea, ND (32)—This windswept Missouri River reservoir is developing a stronger walleye population along the east end of the lake; the western extremity has long been known for producing the best numbers and size. Most big walleyes are caught in the Van Hook Arm area during windy conditions in October and early November, when big 'eyes move shallow into mudlines. Cast

MERLE FARLEY, JR.
17 lbs. 13 oz.
Greers Ferry, AR, 1986

MAX JACOBS
17 lbs. 8 oz.
Greers Ferry, AR, 1981

BRUCE BOWERS
17 lbs. 7 oz.
Kinzua Dam, PA, 1992

STAN SEIVEWRIGHT
17 lbs. 7 oz.
Boysen Reservoir, WY, 1991

BILLY RAY
17 lbs. 3 oz.
Gauley River, WV, 1990

STEVE DAULTON
16 lbs. 10 oz.
Columbia River, OR-WA, 1991

DARRYL LANDYGO
16 lbs. 10 oz.
Red River, MB, 1994

TRACY MCCONNELL
16 lbs. 9 oz.
Horsetooth Reservoir, CO, 1992

jigs and minnows toward shore, or troll bottom-bouncer rigs and crankbaits through mudlines. Large sauger also are taken with vertical jigging tactics, often as deep as 30 to 35 feet.

6. Red River, MB (30)—One of the better bets for 8- to 12-pound fall-run 'eyes moving upriver out of Lake Winnipeg. The Lockport Dam area north of Winnipeg traditionally concentrates both fish and fishermen. Vertical jigging with jigs and minnows takes big fish until freeze-up. Some anglers also fish the system through the ice. Spring fishing produces big 'eyes, though the system is better known for big channel catfish beginning in June and lasting through early summer.

7. Mille Lacs, MN (29)—Summer and winter walleye opportunities abound, from deep midlake structure to shallow rock reefs on Minnesota's most popular walleye lake, a scant hour's drive from the Minneapolis metro area. Spring fishing keys along shoreline rock points and sandflats, particularly at night. Longline troll floater-diver plugs, or anchor and fish lighted slipbobbers and leeches at dusk. In summer, deep mudflats in the central basin are key areas. Use slipsinker livebait rigs tipped with leeches or three-way rigs with spinners and crawlers. Also, when the wind blows, walleyes move up onto shallow rock reefs where bobber presentations and crankbaits excel. In fall, longline troll minnow imitators along shoreline rock points when big walleyes follow spawning ciscoes into shallow waters at night. During winter, deep fishing with jigging spoons on midlake mudflats produces 'eyes of all sizes.

8. Greers Ferry Reservoir, AR (26)—Home of the world record walleye, Greers Ferry still contains a few giant walleyes, though the population over 18 pounds appears to have dwindled. Traditionally, most fish are caught at night in February or March, when big 'eyes run up the three forks of the Little Red River to spawn. At night, troll deep-diving crankbaits like Rebel Deep Runners across the tops of shallow spawning shoals and through adjacent deeper pools. During the day, drift through pools and vertically fish with jigs and minnows. Best fishing generally occurs a few days after spring rains muddy the water and raise the water level, attracting fish upstream. Never a numbers game, the reservoir nevertheless provides an opportunity for fish of historical proportions.

The Top Twenty Largest Kept Walleyes

Water	Date	Weight	Moon Phase
*1. Greers Ferry, AR	03/14/82	22 lbs. 11 oz.	
2. Greers Ferry, AR	02/10/89	20 lbs. 10 oz.	
3. Columbia River, OR-WA	02/20/90	19 lbs. 15 oz.	
4. Greers Ferry, AR	02/28/81	19 lbs. 2 oz.	
5. Columbia River, OR-WA	04/09/90	18 lbs. 12 oz.	Full-1
6. Greers Ferry, AR	01/11/82	18 lbs. 4 oz.	
7. Greers Ferry, AR	03/13/86	17 lbs. 13 oz.	Dark
8. Greers Ferry, AR	03/02/81	17 lbs. 8 oz.	
9. Greers Ferry, AR	01/11/82	17 lbs. 7 oz.	Full+3
10. Greers Ferry, AR	03/01/83	17 lbs. 7 oz.	1/2Dark
11. Allegheny River, PA	01/22/92	17 lbs. 7 oz.	Full+3
12. Boysen Reservoir, WY	12/28/91	17 lbs. 7 oz.	
13. Green Lake, WI	10/02/85	17 lbs. 5 oz.	
14. Greers Ferry, AR	03/24/87	17 lbs. 4 oz.	
15. Gauley River, WV	02/05/90	17 lbs. 3 oz.	Dark
16. Greers Ferry, AR	02/18/81	17 lbs.	
17. Allegheny River, PA	11/25/89	16 lbs. 15 oz.	Dark-3
18. Greers Ferry, AR	03/08/83	16 lbs. 14 oz.	
19. Columbia River, OR-WA	03/08/91	16 lbs. 10 oz.	Full-2
20. Red River, MB	12/10/94	16 lbs. 10 oz.	Full+2

*Present world record as recognized by the Fresh Water Fishing Hall of Fame.

Many of the largest walleyes ever caught have been entries in the Master Angler contest, including the newly proclaimed world record walleye weighing 22 pound 11 ounces, caught in 1982. Members of the In-Fisherman staff were on hand to see this fish; Bill Lindner photographed the monster the day after it was caught from a feeder river running into Greers Ferry.

Windows of opportunity for huge fish open and close (and, of course, may reopen) on certain bodies of water. The window seems to have closed on Greers Ferry, where no huge fish have been entered since 1989. Surely, though, a few monsters probably still exist. Meanwhile, the window probably remains slightly ajar on portions of the Columbia River, although no Top Twenty fish have been entered since 1990, and no 20-pound fish have ever been entered from the Columbia.

As we have often discussed in articles in *In-Fisherman* and our sister magazine, *Walleye In-Sider*, chances for producing monster walleyes are dramatically reduced at each juncture in the weight progression beyond about 15 pounds. A walleye approaching 20 pounds could still be produced in many waters, including Greers Ferry and the Columbia, plus southern waters such as Bull Shoals, and perhaps western waters such as Boysen. But no one water seems a predictable choice right now, as Greers Ferry was a decade ago.

Most anglers, of course, would be happy with a fish approaching 14 or 15 pounds. Although not indicated by our Top Twenty chart, Tobin Lake, Saskatchewan, has emerged as the top water to produce fish of this size. Seems likely the Tobin window will remain open for several more seasons, although as you might expect, fishing pressure has already increased dramatically, especially during September and October, top times at Tobin.

Haunts of the Mutants
(Prolific Monster Producers)

Top Fisheries and Their Production of Walleyes over 32 inches (releases) or 13 pounds (kept fish)

Water	Monsters
1. Columbia River, WA-OR	35
2. Greers Ferry, AR	22
3. Georgian Bay, ON	12
4. Lake Erie, OH-PA-NY	9
5. Red River, MB	8
6. Tobin Lake, SK	7
7. Bay of Quinte, ON	6
8. Allegheny River, PA	5
9. Banks Lake, WA	5
10. Cloud Lake, ON	4

The chart doesn't tell the entire story. Master Angler has been around for 20 years, but the majority of fish have been entered during the last decade. The chart therefore tends to underestimate the present maximum trophy potential of some waters while overestimating others. All of the Tobin entries, for example, have been caught since 1991, while most Greers Ferry entries occurred before 1989. Meanwhile, Columbia River entries have been evenly spread over the past 15 years.

Other waters don't shine so brightly because most of the large fish caught there haven't been entered in Master Angler. Bay of Quinte and Georgian Bay are two waters not entered that produce many monster walleyes each season.

Lake Erie is another story. Again, most of the huge walleyes caught probably aren't entered in Master Angler. But this, too, is a water where for many years large fish topped out at about 10 pounds. Things appear to be changing. As suggested earlier, more trophy walleyes are present in Lake Erie than in most bodies of water on the list, combined. If the tendency of fish surpassing the 10-pound mark continues, Erie could rewrite the Master Angler record list during the next decade.

9. Georgian Bay, ON (24)—Huge and mysterious, the bay and islands area has yet to be fully explored, though many large river-run 'eyes are caught in fall. The French and Moon rivers produce fish as large as 15 pounds in October and November. During the rest of the year, big walleyes apparently disperse into the maze of islands and deeper water lying offshore—a great place to explore for trophy walleyes, pike, smallmouths, and world-class muskies.

10. Lake Saganaga, MN (23)—Focus on early-season river runners and crankin' reefs at night in summer for fish over 10 pounds. Not considered a numbers walleye fishery, this deep, clear lake trout lake nonetheless is home to some huge fish. Minnesota's 17-pound state record was caught in the Saganaga River in May. After spawning, walleyes disperse downstream into the big lake. Some are caught on traditional livebait rigging tactics during the day, but during summer, most walleyes are caught at night on top of shallow, midlake rock reefs. Trophy hunters, this one's for you.

11. Saginaw River, MI (23)—The Saginaw River in eastern Michigan flows into Saginaw Bay of Lake Huron. Loads of big fish opportunities exist in late winter and early spring when walleyes make an upriver spawning run into the Saginaw and the connecting Tittabawassee River. Vertically fish current breaks with a jig and minnow. Ice fishing is possible on the Saginaw at times, while the Tittabawassee generally remains ice-free. Most big walleyes leave the system and move into the bay in summer.

12. Bay of Quinte, ON (23)—A superb fall, winter, and spring trophy fishery— some of the best trophy walleye fishing in Canada. Untold numbers of big walleyes move into the bay area from Lake Ontario in fall, wintering somewhere within the generally flat, shallow expanse of protected water. Ice fishing is big business, with numerous services supplying rental shacks and guides. In spring and fall, open water angling produces both numbers and size on traditional jigging, rigging, and crankbait tactics. During summer, most of the large walleyes return to deeper, cooler Lake Ontario, though the bay remains a nursery area for small to midsize fish.

13. Lake Manistee, MI (16)—Large Lake Michigan walleyes inhabiting the river mouth area at Manistee produce hawgs for those willing to sacrifice shut-eye. Anglers cast crankbaits or jig and twistertail combos at night across shallow slab piles within the lake. Spring and fall are best, though some fish are caught throughout summer. Longline trolling minnow-imitator crankbaits along the breakwater and at the river mouth at night produces big walleyes all through the open water season. Jigging spoons occasionally produce, too.

The Top Ten Largest Released Walleyes

Releasing large walleyes didn't become common until about 1986. Today, just over 70 percent are released, many after also being weighed—digital scales make it quick and easy to get an accurate weight without harming fish.

The weight-to-length ratio of large walleyes may vary widely, given the body of water, subsequent life span, and forage sources. Lake Erie fish, for example, generally grow faster and live a shorter time than fish from top waters on the Canadian Shield. Few Erie walleyes presently surpass 32 inches, at which point they may weigh almost 14 pounds. A 32-inch shield fish is likely to weigh several pounds less. But the same shield fish may also live 10 years longer and at 35 inches weigh 15 pounds.

Ultimately, though, even an exceptional fish can hold only so much weight at a given length. To approach world record class, walleyes must be at least in the 38-inch range, and more likely near 40 inches.

The longest of most recent releases (1995) was until recently the Saskatchewan release record, a 34-inch fish from Tobin Lake. The fish weighed 15 pounds 12 ounces. The angler is Tim Geni.

Water	Date	Length	Moon Phase
1. Lake O'Sullivan, PQ	05/15/89	36 in.	
2. Columbia River, OR-WA	03/18/92	35.75 in.	
3. Cabonga Reservoir, PQ	07/03/88	35 in.	
4. Oneida Lake, NY	07/24/87	34.5 in.	Dark-1
5. Columbia River, OR-WA	03/29/92	34.5 in.	
6. Oneida Lake, NY	01/23/89	34.375 in.	Full+2
7. Tobin Lake, SK	10/08/95	34.25 in.	Full
8. Black Lake, ON	05/18/95	34 in.	
9. Lake Erie, ON	08/01/88	34 in.	Dark-1
10. Lake McConaughy, NE	04/25/95	34 in.	

14. Lake of the Woods, MN-MB-ON (20)—This spectacular walleye fishery for both numbers and size, at the junction of Minnesota, Manitoba, and Ontario, is loaded with mazes of islands, reefs, bays, and inlets. Many walleyes run upriver to spawn in spring, then drop back down to the deeper main lake as the water warms. Focus on reefs adjacent to the big open portion of the lake 'til June, then move out to midlake reefs in summer. Use classic livebait rigging or spinner rigging tactics along the tops or bases of rock reefs meeting water over 20 feet deep. In late summer, downrigger trolling on vast, open Traverse Bay has evolved into a top tactic for suspended 'eyes topping 10 pounds.

Moon Phase Monsters

(Master Angler Walleyes Caught During Days of Lunar Influence)

1.	Full Moon	61
2.	Full + 3 Days	53
3.	Full + 1 Day	50
4.	Full - 1 Day	47
5.	Dark Moon	47
6.	Full + 2 Days	46
7.	Full - 3 Days	44
8.	Dark - 1 Day	43
9.	Dark + 2 Days	43
10.	Full - 2 Days	41
11.	Dark - 2 Days	40
12.	1/2 Full Moon	37
13.	Dark + 1 Day	37
14.	Dark - 3 Days	32
15.	1/2 Dark Moon	31
16.	Dark + 3 Days	30

689 total moon fish out of
1,254 possible fish = 55 percent

Based on empirical observation, the In-Fisherman staff has long held that moon phases can influence the angling outcome for lunker walleyes during certain periods. Such empirical observation is difficult to document. So in 1986, we began asking anglers to identify the moon phase in which their catches were made.

Since then, 1,254 walleyes have been recorded, with 689 caught during intervals of influence—the day of the half moon, plus the 3 days before and after both full and dark moons. During a 10-year period, 55 percent of those 1,254 ten-pound or larger walleyes were caught under lunar influence.

The period of the full moon seemed particularly important to the production of big fish. Catches during September 1988 are somewhat representative: of the 21 award walleyes caught that month, 12 were taken during one of the days of full-moon influence.

The question remains, however, if the full moon isn't simply more influential on the fishing habits of anglers—more anglers fish then—thus explaining the increase in catches during certain periods, particularly during fall. Remember, too, that the moon periods identified in our "Best Fishing Times" monthly charts cover 16 out of 30 possible days in the typical month—or about 53 percent. Fifty-five percent isn't statistically more significant than 53 percent.

Our empirical observations stand, however: during certain periods, we believe moon phase has a bearing on the activity of trophy walleyes. And as in the past, we'll continue to tell you that in specific articles, when our observations suggest that moon phase is noteworthy.

The Baits

The right bait at the right time, presented in the right way—the right presentation depends on where walleyes are holding, what they're feeding on, the season, and other factors. We've spent over 20 years discussing these factors relative to catching big walleyes.

Well-known patterns have emerged: longlining shallow-running floater-diver plugs over shallow shoals in spring and fall; shorecasting the same baits at the mouth of feeder creeks and feeder rivers or in dam tailwater areas in spring and fall; spinner-rigging the edges of main reservoir flats in early summer or the open water in large lakes during summer; and many other patterns specific to certain bodies of water or types of water.

Just a few observations. Livebait rigging remains the traditional means to catch walleyes. But it's a comparatively slow presentation tending to be inefficient for searching out the limited numbers of big fish usual in most environments. Only when the whereabouts of big fish are known and those fish are in a negative or neutral feeding mood does livebait rigging usually produce better than one or more popular approaches with lures, sometimes in conjunction with livebait.

Plugs generally offer the right combination of attracting and triggering characteristics—shape and other visual attractors, as well as a wobble that stimulates a big fish's lateral line, usually the first indication for these fish that something worth checking is swimming nearby. Meanwhile,

the jig & minnow combo, used extensively during spring and fall in rivers and throughout the season on big fish waters in Canada, is a significant step beyond

ALL-TIME BEST PRESENTATIONS (GENERAL CATEGORIES)

Presentation	Trophy Walleyes
1. Diving Plugs	518
2. Jig & Livebait Combos	324
3. Jig & Plastic Combos	96
4. Livebait Rigs (with bait)	94
5. Spinner Rigs (with bait)	78
6. Spoons	58
7. Hair Jigs (without bait)	28
8. Weight-Forward Spinners (with bait)	22
9. In-Line Spinners (with or without bait)	12
10. Bladebaits	10

livebait rigging because it maintains the ability to present livebait precisely while allowing the angler to cover more water.

So on the one hand stands the most natural presentation of all, livebait rigging, and on the other, a more efficient means of presenting unnatural items that when presented well catch fish more efficiently and do a good job of presenting the illusion of something natural. In between lie a host of other options, many of them combinations.

The Liveliest Bait

1.	Baitfish	304
	Minnows	*213*
	Shiners	*35*
	Chubs	*25*
	Suckers	*15*
	Fatheads	*10*
	Sunfish	*6*
2.	Nightcrawlers	140
3.	Leeches	110
4.	Livebait (bait unknown)	48
5.	Waterdogs	11
6.	Leopard Frogs	9
7.	Crayfish	4
8.	Waxworms	3
9.	Roe (Egg Sacks)	2
10.	Clam Meat	1

Bait, especially bait used in combinations such as the jig & minnow, remains a vital part of walleye fishing. This is a quick look at the bait used when respondents were willing to share the information. Just one question: who was using clam meat?

15. Tobin Lake, SK (19)—Over the past 3 or 4 years, Tobin has become the most intense trophy bite in Canada each October. Literally hundreds of 10-pound walleyes are caught each fall, with mid-teen fish possible. The 17-pound provincial record has been broken several times. Try livebait rigging with leeches (no live minnows allowed), jig fishing with nightcrawlers, or trolling large diving crankbaits along the channel edge in about 20 feet of water. In recent years, however, a good early bite tapered off later in the season, perhaps due to increasing fishing pressure or low water, low flow conditions that failed to concentrate fish as in recent seasons.

16. Allegheny River, PA (18)—Unheralded in walleye circles, the Allegheny is probably the most productive trophy walleye fishery in the Northeast, other than the lower Great Lakes. This large river, with its numerous dams, concentrates walleyes and sauger in fall, winter, and spring. With a milder climate than that of the Upper Midwest, the Allegheny offers boat fishing most of the winter season. Use jigs and minnows, focusing on current breaks formed by manmade structural elements like concrete walls, bridges, and faces of dams.

17. Lake Oahe, SD (18)—High fish populations have resulted in a strong crop of 8-pounders, with an occasional larger walleye, along with lots of 2- to 4-pounders. Fishing pressure has increased, but the reduction to a 4-fish limit has helped to reduce harvest. Classic bottom-bouncer-spinner-crawler tactics excel, though vertical jigging and casting jigs or crankbaits to windswept shorelines produce under favorable conditions.

Undoubtedly, the biggest breakthrough is recent success with planer board-crankbait trolling tactics at In-Fisherman Professional Walleye Trail tournaments. Troll shoreline contours near drop-offs, then move offshore where you see baitfish or big fish suspended over open water.

18. Fox River, WI (17)—Spring and fall runs from Green Bay produce walleyes up to 10 pounds, along with good numbers of smaller fish. The dam at DePere is the focal point of fish activity, though bridges and other manmade, current-deflecting structure also are good. Jigging is popular, though in recent years, casting Rapalas into exceedingly shallow water at night has become a popular presentation.

19. Lake Geneva, WI (17)—An occasional large fish is caught, a holdover from past glory years. This deep, clear lake supports a two-story stocked trout fishery, along with pike and bass. In early spring, try shorecasting at night along rock points at the entrance to Williams Bay. In summer, either drift nightcrawler rigs at about the 30- to 35-foot level along extensive deep flats in the eastern end of the lake, or longline troll minnow imitators or spinner-crawler harnesses over cabbage weeds. Fish at night to avoid excessive boat traffic.

Trophy Peaks

(Most Frequently Occurring Months)

1.	July	184
2.	October	183
3.	June	180
4.	May	153
5.	September	148
6.	August	143
7.	April	140
8.	November	124
9.	March	121
10.	February	86
11.	January	59
12.	December	58

Data such as these are difficult to figure concisely. July, while generally not considered prime time for trophies in most waters, can be a peak period in many Canadian waters and on portions of the Great Lakes. After June, July is the month in which the greatest number of anglers fish most often.

October is peak time for trophies in most environments. November, too, but angler participation is down by then. Likewise participation during ice season. The best time to go remains whenever you can. Vital, though, is noting the identified peak periods for the waters you fish. It would be a shame, for example, for you to live near Lake Erie and not note the influx of huge fish into shoreline areas during fall.

20. Missouri River, SD-ND-MT (16)—Most large fish occur in lakes Oahe and Sakakawea, in the Missouri River section between them, and in Fort Peck Reservoir, Montana. Traditional reservoir tactics apply in the impounded sections. Within the shallower, fast flowing river portions, jig eddies. Also troll current breaks along shorelines at the 8- to 15-foot levels with Shad Raps or similar crankbaits. Note that shallow sandbars often form in midriver, yet there may be a deep slot of flowing water between the sandbar and the shore that attracts fish.

TWENTY MORE GREAT TROPHY WALLEYE WATERS

1. Lac Seul, ON (16)—Gigantic Lac Seul boasts a heavy population of small walleyes and fewer large ones. A slot limit prevents overharvest and allows some fish to reach trophy size. During summer, offshore reefs focus most of the walleye activity, with fish caught in the 18- to 25-foot range. Jigging, livebait rigging with leeches or crawlers, and bottom-bouncers to minimize snags all produce lots of small fish, with an occasional whopper.

2. Banks Lake, WA (15)—Off the beaten path of most lower Columbia River anglers, Banks is a good bet for big fish. Use techniques similar to those popular on the Columbia—jigs, three-ways with either livebait or a minnow-imitator crankbait, and trolling large crankbaits. The powerful current found in the Columbia is absent here, making Banks a good alternative during April, May, and June.

3. North Saskatchewan River, SK (15)—The river section running into Tobin Lake is best known for giant 'eyes. Although it receives less fishing pressure than Tobin, it offers a similar potential for monstrous fish. Explore upstream in late summer and early fall with jigs, livebait rigs with leeches or crawlers, and trolled crankbaits.

4. Cloud Lake, ON (14)—Despite popular opinion, we haven't been everywhere, folks. This one's off the beaten path for our staff, though we know it's one of many lakes in this region with the capacity to produce walleyes over 10 pounds. Typically, focus your efforts at or near river mouths in spring. Then follow the fish in transition as they move to adjacent main lake structures in summer. Fish the bases of humps where the hard bottom of the drop-off meets the soft basin. Jigs and bottom-bouncers are tough to beat.

5. Lake Ontario, ON-NY (13)—The eastern end of the big lake hosts a good open water trolling fishery, more for size than numbers, from early summer through fall. Try planer board trolling tactics with crankbaits. In spring and fall, big walleyes run into the St. Lawrence and toward rivers in the Black Bay region. During cooler months, try fishing the general mouth area of Black Bay-Henderson Harbor or up into the St. Lawrence.

6. Winnipeg River, MB (12)—Like the Red River, this fishery is good in fall for big fish running upriver from Lake Winnipeg, with a pretty decent spring fishery as well. Most attention focuses in the dam area near McArthur Falls, though jigging, jigging spoons, bladebaits, three-ways, and crankbait trolling are successful in the river portion all the way out to the main lake.

7. Saginaw Bay, ON (12)—Open water trolling produces lots of 8- to 12-pounders during summer and fall, once postspawn fish drop out of the Saginaw River. Suspended walleyes relate to shad or alewife forage within the shallow inner bay and ciscoes or smelt in the deeper water northeast of the Charity Islands. Trolling with Hot 'N Tots and planer boards is the number-one tactic, though recent In-Fisherman Professional Walleye Trail events have been won with snap weights, silver spinners, and crawler harnesses. Also, reefs and weedbeds within the bay are at times loaded with midsize fish that fall to jigs and jigging spoons. The bay develops a decent winter ice bite once shoreline ice becomes safe around Christmas.

8. Rainy River, MN-ON (11)—Exceptional numbers of walleyes run upriver from Lake of the Woods in fall, throughout winter, and into spring, with loads of 4- to 8-pounders and occasionally fish over 10 pounds. Most years, open water conditions from April 1 until the season closes April 15 draws thousands of anglers for one of the best bites anywhere. The fall bite isn't as intense, though the average fish size is bigger. The stretch from Baudette up to Birchdale Rapids is prime for vertical jigging and three-way rigging with minnow imitators.

9. Kaskaskia River, IL (11)—Most large walleyes probably are caught below the Lake Shelbyville dam in March by anglers night-fishing from the bank. Cast

---

Moon Phase Effects on Catches from Certain Waters

Bay of Quinte, ON	58% during full moon
Crow Duck Lake, MB	78% during moon phases
Eagle Lake, ON	78% during moon phases
Lac Seul, ON	80% during moon phases
Lake Oahe, SD-ND	67% during moon phases
Minnesota River, MN	56% during moon phases
Missouri River, SD-ND-MT	52% during moon phases
North Saskatchewan River, SK	61% during moon phases
Starvation Reservoir, UT	81% during full moon cycles of September & October

The effect of moon phase on catches from specific fisheries? A few top waters show no indication of a strong lunar-influenced bite. Others show strong preferences for the draw of the moon.

jigs or crankbaits from shore, focusing on eddies. The rest of the year, fish disperse downstream toward Lake Carlyle. Some walleyes are caught within Shelbyville Reservoir, but bass become the primary target.

10. Seminoe Reservoir, WY (10)—One of the top western walleye fisheries for both numbers and size, Seminoe is a great spring and early summer fishery. Irrigation demands and dropping water levels can dry up boat launches and make access difficult by late summer or early fall. Many walleyes are caught on main lake points during the day to bottom-bouncer trolling tactics. Most large walleyes probably are caught on crankbaits trolled along shorelines at night during summer.

11. Wisconsin River, WI (10)—A strong numbers fishery with the potential for size, the Wisconsin's best walleye catches and most of its large fish traditionally are caught during March below dams at Lake Wisconsin, the Wisconsin Dells, Castle Rock Flowage and Petenwell Flowage by anglers vertically jigging eddies and current breaks. The rest of the year, fish disperse to shallow downstream areas filled with sandbars, where they receive little attention.

12. Starvation Reservoir, UT (9)—The big fish population may have ebbed in recent years, but Starvation still is the best trophy walleye option in Utah. Same western walleye story—bottom-bouncer tactics, trolled crankbaits, livebait rigs. Try night fishing for lunkers.

13. St. Lawrence River, NY-ON (9)—This big river environment features a fall run of fish from Lake Ontario, in addition to a resident population of small to midsize walleyes, pike, bass, and monster muskies. Strong current focuses walleye activity along deep humps and islands that break current flow. Heavy jigs, crankbait trolling, and other deep water tactics are good for big fish anytime, with October and November being prime for hawgs.

14. Cherry Creek Reservoir, CO (9)—This 860-acre recreation reservoir in the south-central Denver metro area has a maximum depth around 30 feet. Despite its small size, walleyes topping 10 pounds are caught there each year, with many fish between 19 and 23 inches. Trophies primarily are caught in spring and through the ice. In summer, boat traffic makes fishing difficult.

15. Des Moines River, IA (9)—Small by most walleye river standards, most of the Des Moines's large fish are caught in spring below dams that block upriver walleye movement. The stretch below the Lake Saylorville dam perhaps offers the best opportunity for consistent spring walleye activity. Much of the fishing is from shore or in small boats. Jigs and crankbaits are best suited to fishing shallow eddies from a boat. Shore anglers perhaps rely more on jigs and three-way rigs baited with minnows.

16. Merritt Reservoir, NE (8)—This probably is the best trophy walleye opportunity on the central plains south of the Dakotas. Fishing along the face of the dam in April produces nice 'eyes for shorecasters fishing with crankbaits and jigs. Boat anglers may elect to troll minnow imitators along the face of the dam. During summer and fall, try bottom-bouncer tactics or livebait rigs on main lake points.

17. Lake McConaughy, NE (7)—On the rebound from low walleye, high forage years, McConaughy is producing big walleyes again. Deep leadcore trolling with crankbaits for walleyes probably originated on this impoundment and is still good for summer and fall activity. In spring, focus along the face of the dam, primarily at night.

18. Allegheny Reservoir, PA (7)—A few big walleyes are caught each year, primarily by the few anglers who rig livebait with crawlers in summer and minnows in fall. Fish main lake points or timber edges at about the 20- to 30-foot level. This is a good candidate for eastern anglers looking for a decent shot at big walleyes.

19. Crow Duck Lake, MB (6)—Expect a strong population of fish up to 8 or 9 pounds, with an occasional larger fish. Livebait rigging on main lake points with leeches or nightcrawlers produces numbers and size. Cast crankbaits across shallow reefs at night.

20. Boulder Reservoir, CO (6)—This 540-acre reservoir on the north side of Boulder has a maximum depth of 40 feet. It is heavily stocked with walleyes, with many fish around 5 pounds and some exceeding 10. In-Fisherman Professional Walleye Trail pro Tom Johnson says most big walleyes are likely to be caught near the face of the dam by shore anglers; others are caught by boat anglers using traditional western tactics. Boat access is by permit only, with most anglers fishing this bowl shaped impoundment from small boats or belly boats for a mixed bag of walleyes, trout, and other species.

Peak Trophy Bites

PEAK TROPHY TIMES AND PLACES AS REVEALED BY MASTER ANGLER DATA

Top Ten	Peak Trophy Bites	Happening Baits
Lake Erie, OH	April & Dec.	Jigs-Bait, Plugs, Erie Dearies
Columbia River, OR-WA	March & Sept.-Oct.	Jigs & Shad Raps-Shadlings
Little Bay de Noc, MI	Resoundingly November	Rebel Fastrac, ThunderSticks
Upper Mississippi R., MN-WI-IA	March-April	Jig-Minnow Combos
Lake Sakakawea, ND	August & Frozen Water	Jig-Minnow Combos
Red River, MB	Sept.-Oct.	Jig-Minnow or Shad Raps
Mille Lacs, MN	Sept.-Oct.	Rapalas & Rig-Leeches
Greers Ferry, AR	Resoundingly early March	Live Bream or Rebel Plugs
Georgian Bay, ON	June	Rapala Minnows
Lake Saganaga, MN	May-June	Gotta be a Leech (90%)
Other Hot Bites & Sleepers		
Saginaw River, MI	Jan.-Feb.	Jig-Minnow or Rapalas
Bay of Quinte, ON	Frozen Water (Dec.-Feb.)	Jigs or Spoons
Lake Manistee, MI	Late Aug. & Sept.	Fat Raps & Rapala Minnows
Lake of the Woods, ON-MB-MN	July	Rig-Crawler or Rebel Plugs
Tobin Lake, SK	Sept.-Oct.	Jigs, Livebait (leeches)
Allegheny River, PA	Coldwater (Oct.-Dec.)	Jigs & Livebait
Missouri River, SD-ND-MT	April & Nov.	Rapala Minnows
Lac Seul, ON	June-July	Jig-Livebait Combos
N. Saskatchewan River, SK	Resoundingly October	Rig-Minnow Combos
Seminoe Reservoir, WY	July	Spinner Rig-Crawler Combos
Winnipeg River, MB	Resoundingly October	Jig-Minnow Combos

Chapter 10

Perspectives in Passing

Select Topics On Walleyes

PERSPECTIVES ON SOME OF THE MOST ASKED QUESTIONS IN WALLEYE FISHING

Spawning walleyes: harvest, protect, or harvest selectively?

Harvest a 10-pound walleye from a Canadian Shield Lake, and it could take up to 20 years to replace it. Pull a 10-pounder from Saginaw Bay, and it could be replaced in 6 years or less.

Walleye fisheries differ, and few things highlight that point so well as the sometimes controversial harvest of walleyes during the spawning season. Most data indicate that harvesting walleyes while they spawn has no effect on a population, implying that only a few successful spawners are necessary to negate overall mortality in most years. Other

Does it hurt all species at all times to allow harvest during the spawn? No.
—

data indicate the opposite, especially during years when floods, predation, or extended and extremely low winter temperatures hurt recruitment.

Many lakes and rivers in the U.S. have no closed season for walleyes. Some, like Lake Ouachita, Lake Cumberland, and other southern impoundments, get so little pressure on walleyes that closed seasons are unnecessary. Others, like Lake Erie and Lake Winnebago, maintain such extensive natural recruitment that normal angling pressure has little apparent effect on the population.

Perhaps allowing extensive harvest of big walleyes concentrated in shallow water never does a fishery any good. In the case of Lake Erie, however, it seems to do little harm, though some anglers and charter captains dispute that. Contrast Erie with the Canadian Shield, where overharvest of big spawners can set a system back a quarter century or more. So, should fishing be allowed during the spawn?

Michigan shortened its walleye season in the St. Mary's River and the entire Upper Peninsula, moving the closing date back from March 15 to the former date of February 28. Recommendations based on information gathered by fisheries biologists over the years indicated that walleye populations suffered from increased harvest during the spawning season, according to Bill McClay, lake management specialist for the Michigan Department of Natural Resources.

"Lots of those fish start spawning during the first couple weeks of March," he says. "We watch populations closely and have 20 years of data on Bay de Noc walleyes. The population returned through stocking and by giving spawners a chance to contribute. In the judgment of biologists serving that area, walleyes should be protected for those additional 2 weeks. But we continue to evaluate such regulations," McClay continues. "Some species can be regulated statewide, while others can't. Does it hurt all species at all times to allow harvest during the spawn? No. We allow steelhead fishing during the spawn. Seasons are set to allow enough individual spawners to maintain the population.

"Some fishing for spawning walleyes is likely to occur somewhere in the state

Shallow spawning walleyes are vulnerable to various forms of illegal harvest, such as spearing and netting.

every year. But based on our data, that won't hurt population levels." The season in the Lower Peninsula remains open from the last Saturday in April to March 15.

Not far away, Wisconsin anglers enjoy a year-round fishery in Lake Winnebago. Ron Bruch, Oshkosh area fisheries supervisor for the Wisconsin Department of Natural Resources (WDNR), describes it as "the largest natural walleye hatching system in the world. It covers 138,000 acres, with three connecting lakes adding 30,000 acres for lake spawners. For river spawners, flood plains feeding those lakes provide extensive spawning habitat. In spring, as flows increase, the rivers reclaim old bayous filled with grass mats. These huge flowing marshes provide thousands of acres of additional spawning area.

Rather than saving spawning females, the closed season protects numbers that are concentrated and vulnerable.

"It's difficult to overexploit this stock. We've always had year-round fishing at Winnebago. Creel surveys show that 60 to 80 percent of harvested females are spawned out. They don't bite readily when they're laden with eggs. But spawning areas are only 2 to 3 feet deep, making them a target for poachers and fish hogs. Removing fish before they lay eggs and removing fish from spawning grounds have negative effects when exploitation becomes extreme."

For now, the only recommendation on the table for Winnebago is to eliminate the 15-inch size limit, Bruch says. "Since 1990, we've had average to excellent year classes, so right now we don't need a size limit. Some people feel fishing during the spawning run will damage the fishery, but we've monitored closely and have found no evidence that the spring fishery has damaged the population. If exploitation increases to the point where walleyes in Winnebago are overexploited, regulations could change."

Wisconsin maintains a closed season on most other inland waters. Mike Coshun, Woodruff area fisheries supervisor for the WDNR, says the regulation was imposed in 1881 during a period of strong conservation ethics, and it evolved traditionally to protect spawners. "It was put in place before many studies were available, but intuitions were correct," Coshun says. "Removing a female in January isn't any more damaging than taking one during the spawn. But fish concentrated shallow on small waters during the spawn are at risk."

On smaller lakes, nearly all walleyes may group in one or two spots. Rather than saving spawning females, the closed season protects numbers that are concentrated and vulnerable where fish are visible and easily found. Creel surveys indicate that Wisconsin's highest exploitation takes place from the first Saturday in May (season opener) to early June, when fish remain shallow, even though angler effort is lower than at other times. "I think exploitation would increase dramatically if we opened the season earlier," Coshun adds.

"Basically, it's a good regulation. We're trying to indirectly control angler effort with seasons, rather than issuing fishing permits or something like that. The bottom line on any closed season is that it doesn't matter when a fish is killed. What matters is how many fish are killed."

According to Carey Knight, aquatic biologist for the Ohio Division of Wildlife, "Recruitment surveys indicate that the population on Lake Erie hasn't declined. Fishing during the spawning season on the Maumee and Sandusky rivers hasn't hurt those Erie populations. We have a huge walleye population, but on systems that depend on natural recruitment without a huge population base, a big harvest in spring can produce a negative effect.

"If we could accurately predict when a year class would be good or bad, we'd be geniuses. So many variables affect successful recruitment. A high harvest during years when recruitment is down could create problems. On Lake Erie, the problem is never how many fish are laying eggs. But Erie is a special case."

Smaller inland lakes in the North sometimes tell a different story. Higher exploitation, not necessarily during the spawn, but during the year, can damage a fishery. On lakes with small but naturally reproducing stocks of walleyes that tend toward trophy size, a single season of harvest by expert fishermen during the spawn can harm the fishery.

Several such seasons can destroy a particular genetic strain. It's not necessary to kill them all—just enough to possibly bottleneck the gene pool. Closing the season at some time or another, especially during spring, when catch rates are high, protects these smaller waters.

By entering fishery data into a computer program—size of population, available spawning habitat, seasonal spawning windows, harvest rates, predation of young, forage cycles, mortality, average recruitment rates—biologists create models of existing fisheries. By altering parameters of the model—opening or closing seasons to increase or decrease harvest, changing environmental factors, mortality, and recruitment—predictions can be made about how changes may affect a population. To some extent, anglers must trust that such models are accurate. Right now, models indicate that closed seasons are necessary on some bodies of water.

"We need to consider each individual situation and focus on the objectives," McClay adds. "Some lakes in Michigan have 13-inch size limits, while others don't. On some lakes, we might consider opening the fishing year-round but only allow possession during a defined season. On some lakes, anglers and biologists might prefer managing for trophies, on others for numbers."

In other words, fisheries managers of the future will often approach each body of water individually, weighing environmental and demographic differences before addressing regulations on limits or seasons.

Deciding whether or not to allow fishing during the spawning season, therefore, depends on many variables and can't be addressed by a blanket answer for the many diverse waters across North America. Big fish, no matter when and where they're caught, remain most vulnerable to overharvest simply because in most waters so few of them exist. We continue to suggest selective harvest; that is, the release of big fish and the harvest of some smaller fish for the table.

RECORD WALLEYES TODAY: CONTROVERSY, REALITY, THE FUTURE?

The world record muskie weighed 69 pounds 15 ounces—including the sand poured into its belly. The world record smallmouth weighed 11 pounds 15 ounces—after it was stuffed full of engine parts. The world record walleye—never weighed 25 pounds, with or without stuffing.

Shaken by a rash of illegitimate records, public trust is probably at an all-time low. Not only was the world record muskie a hoax, but several line-class records for muskie have been thrown out as well. The smallmouth taken from Dale Hollow Lake by D.L. Hayes in 1955 actually weighed 8 pounds 15 ounces, according to the testimony of the man who packed three pounds of metal into the fish at the behest of his boss, a publicity-hungry resort owner.

Not surprising, then, that the blurry, overexposed photo of a walleye from Tennessee that reportedly weighed 25 pounds on a certified scale has finally been discounted. Ron Lindner doubted the veracity of the record for more than 25 years, and *In-Fisherman* ran numerous editorials that questioned Mabry Harper's "record"

Mabry Harper's record stood until recently replaced by the National Fresh Water Fishing Hall of Fame. This is the most famous of the photos of Harper's fish, said to weigh 25 pounds.

during that period. Last summer, the National Fresh Water Fishing Hall of Fame agreed with that assessment and disqualified Harper's catch.

Ted Dzialo, director of the Hall of Fame, said the decision was made by committee. "We know *In-Fisherman* had questions about the record," he said. "I remember an article you did on the subject. Our board of governors' meeting decided to disqualify the record based on measurements of Harper's hands in relation to the length and depth of the fish. We decided that Al Nelson's 22-pound 11-ounce walleye (taken from Greers Ferry in Arkansas) should be the world record."

Why the sudden demise of so many old records? "Things were a little looser in those days," he laughed. "People weren't as meticulous about records back then. Harper caught a nice fish, no question. But we feel it couldn't have weighed 25 pounds." Estimates of the true weight of Harper's fish rest in the 17- to 19-pound range, according to Dzialo.

Honest records affect all anglers. The new record establishes an attainable goal for trophy walleye hunters, true. But records are important for many other reasons. World record fish give us at least an approximate sense of the maximum size a species can attain. State and provincial records measure the potential a region has for producing fish of world-class status. Line-class records define our limitations and challenge us to redefine them.

Information about bodies of water, presentation, time of year, and other data that surround each record provides a running history of how we fish, what methods take the biggest fish, and much, much more. Records place everything relative to fishing in proper perspective. Unless, of course, the record is a hoax.

When a wildlife officer came to inspect Harper's walleye, all that remained

Are These The Biggest Walleyes Ever Caught?

Weight	Water	Angler	Date	Record
22 lbs 11 oz.	Greers Ferry, AR	Al Nelson	3/14/82	10-lb. line-class world record
22 lbs. 4 oz.	Niagara River, ON	Patrick Noon	5/26/43	Ontario provincial record
21 lbs. 9 oz.	Little Red River, AR	Ed Claibourn	1979	Former Arkansas state record
21 lbs. 8 oz.	Lake Cumberland, KY	Abe Black	1958	Kentucky state record
21 lbs. 5 oz.	Bull Shoals, MO	Gerry Partlow	1988	Missouri state record
20 lbs. 9 oz.	Greers Ferry, AR	Thomas Evans	2/10/89	20-lb. line-class world record
20 lbs. 6 oz.	Greers Ferry, AR	Neva Walters	1978	Former Arkansas state record
19 lbs. 15.3 oz.	Columbia River, OR	Arnold Berg	2/10/90	Oregon state record
19 lbs. 13 oz.	Bull Shoals, MO	Pete Gleason	2/8/91	4-lb. line-class world record
19 lbs. 12 oz.	White River, AR	Mrs. L. E. Garrison	2/12/63	Former Arkansas state record
19 lbs. 5 oz.	Greers Ferry, AR	Erma Windorff	3/2/82	6-lb. line-class world record
18 lbs. 12.16 oz.	Columbia River, WA	Mike Jones	4/9/90	Washington state record
18 lbs. 12 oz.	Ottawa River, PQ	Gordie Kingsbury	1983	Quebec provincial record
18 lbs. 8 oz.	George Lake, MB	D.L. Bigson	1954	Manitoba provincial record
18 lbs.	High Lake, WI	Tony Brothers	9/16/33	Wisconsin state record
18 lbs.	Cedar Lake, ON	Joe Edelman	5/69	Mepps record walleye

was the head and a question. Could a walleye actually weigh 25 pounds? Apparently not. We know that walleyes in the 20-pound class were caught in that region during the early 1960s. They were those "firsts" we often talk about—in this case, the first generations of walleyes reaching old age in those reservoirs. But no verified catches of a walleye over 23 pounds have ever occurred anywhere in North America, before or since, in commercial nets or in game-and-fish netting surveys. Nor has one washed up on a beach that might have approached the mythical 25 pounds.

Nelson's fish was 2 pounds 5 ounces lighter than the phony world record. That's a quantum leap to the top end of the weight a popular fish species can achieve. When individual fish begin to approach that top end, every additional ounce represents a geometric progression. Consider the next four largest walleyes ever recorded: the difference between number 2 and number 5 is 2 pounds 6 ounces—almost the same as the leap from number 2 to the phantom record.

To place this in perspective, compare these "records" to other freshwater records for extremely popular fish. The difference between the top two largemouths is about 4 ounces. The biggest two northern pike taken in North America are only 6 ounces apart.

Yet some records do make dramatic jumps. A 40-pound brown trout taken from the Little Red River in Arkansas several years ago tops the next biggest brown on record by 1 pound 7 ounces. Browns, however, were introduced fairly recently to those Arkansas rivers—just long enough ago to achieve such monstrous dimensions. A bigger brown may yet be caught there or in Lake Michigan, where the new Seeforellen strain is reaching weights approaching 25 pounds in 4 years. But no such hope exists for walleye anglers if they're chasing an impossible, bogus standard.

But what about king salmon? The largest fish on record, according to the International Game Fish Association, is a 126-pounder taken in a commercial net. The all-tackle world record, meanwhile, is 97 pounds 4 ounces. The discrepancy there

THE FORMULA FOR ...

Pike: $\dfrac{\text{Length}^3}{3500}$

Walleye: $\dfrac{\text{Length}^3}{2700}$

Bass: $\dfrac{\text{Length}^3}{1600}$

Bluegill: $\dfrac{\text{Length}^3}{1200}$

Walleye Weight Chart

$$\text{Weight (pounds)} = \frac{\text{Length (inches) x Girth (inches)}}{46}$$

	Girth				
Length	14"	16"	18"	20"	22"
28"	8-8	9-12	10-15	12-3	13-6
29"	8-13	10-1	11-6	12-10	13-14
30"	9-2	10-7	11-12	13-1	14-6
31"	9-7	10-13	12-2	13-8	14-13
32"	9-12	11-2	12-8	13-15	15-5
33"	10-1	11-8	12-15	14-6	15-13
34"	10-6	11-13	13-5	14-13	16-4
35"	10-10	12-3	13-11	15-3	16-12

With the formulas on the left, estimate the weight of walleyes or other species using just a length measurement. The formula and chart on the right provides a more accurate estimate for large walleyes when girth is also measured. Even more detailed calculations are offered in Chapter 12.

is greater than 28 pounds—but the question is, can anybody actually land a king over 100 pounds in the confines of a raging river in fall, which is where kings tend to be right after achieving maximum weight? It's possible that many fish over 100 pounds have been hooked. Landing them is another matter. This would be less true of walleyes, even if they could top 25 pounds.

Such reasoning leads to the next logical step: have giant walleyes that approach or top the new world record been caught or found through methods other than angling? Legends and myths abound, the most notable rising from Greers Ferry and the Columbia River. On the banks of Greers Ferry in Arkansas, biologists and anglers claim to have found skeletons of walleyes over 40 inches long. Those fish could have weighed over 20 pounds, but 25? The fact that the new world record walleye, Nelson's 22-pound 11-ouncer, was taken from Greers lends some credence to such tales, but hardly serves as verification.

Rumor has it that a walleye over 25 pounds found its way into a Native American's net along the banks of the Columbia. Guides say a wildlife officer saw the fish. But according to Paul Wagner, fisheries biologist for the Washington Department of Fish and Wildlife, it ain't so, Joe. "I hear that story every year, but I don't think anyone in our office has ever seen anything surpassing the Oregon or Washington state records, let alone a fish of world record proportion."

Which leads us back to where we started. Does the potential exist for walleyes to weigh 25 pounds? The world record received serious scrutiny over the past few years, and the consensus among most experts was that Harper's fish simply didn't weigh 25 pounds. Analyzed repeatedly, the photo appears legitimate to some, but the reported girth (29 inches) and length (41 inches) don't jibe statistically. According to Steve Quinn, staff fisheries biologist at In-Fisherman, "A 29-inch girth isn't physically possible for a walleye 41 inches long. Using a time-tested formula (girth² x length ÷ 800), those measurements describe a fish weighing close to 40 pounds."

An Arkansas fisheries biologist who wishes to remain nameless said, "I really

State Records

State	Record	Year	Location
Alabama	10 lbs. 14 oz.	1980	Weiss Lake
Arizona	12 lbs. 12 oz.	1989	Show Low Lake
Arkansas	22 lbs. 11 oz.	1982	Greers Ferry
Colorado	18 lbs. 13 oz.	1997	Standley Lake
Connecticut	14 lbs. 8 oz.	1941	Candlewood Lake
Georgia	11 lbs. 6 oz.	1995	Richard B. Russell Lake
Idaho	16 lbs. 2 oz.	1996	Salmon Falls Creek Reservoir
Illinois	14 lbs.	1961	Kankakee River
Indiana	14 lbs. 4 oz *	1977	Tippecanoe River
Iowa	14 lbs. 8 oz.	1986	Des Moines River
Kansas	13 lbs. 10.56 oz.	1996	Wilson Reservoir
Kentucky	21 lbs. 8 oz.	1958	Lake Cumberland
Maryland	11 lbs. 6 oz.	1993	Deep Creek Lake
Massachusetts	11 lbs.	1975	Quabbin Reservoir
Michigan	17.19 lbs.	1951	Pine River
Minnesota	17 lbs. 8 oz.	1979	Seagull River
Mississippi	9 lbs. 10 oz.	1985	Tennessee River
Missouri	21 lbs. 1 oz.	1988	Bull Shoals Lake
Montana	16.38 lbs..	1996	Cooney Dam
Nebraska	16 lbs. 2 oz.	1971	Lake McConaughy
Nevada	14 lbs. 14 oz.	1992	Rye Patch Reservoir
New Hampshire	12 lbs. 8.8 oz.	1992	Connecticut River
New Jersey	13 lbs. 9 oz.	1993	Delaware River
New Mexico	16 lbs. 9 oz.	1989	Clayton Lake
New York	16 lbs. 7 oz.	1994	Kinzua Reservoir
North Carolina	13 lbs. 8 oz.	1986	Lake Chatuge
North Dakota	15 lbs. 12 oz.	1959	Wood Lake
Ohio	15 lbs. 15 oz.	1995	Lake Erie
Oklahoma	12 lbs. 10 oz.	1995	Altus Lugert Lake
Oregon	19 lbs. 15.3 oz.	1990	Columbia River
Pennsylvania	17 lbs. 9 oz.	1980	Allegheny Reservoir
South Carolina	10 lbs.	1994	Lake Russell
South Dakota	15 lbs. 3 oz.	1979	Lake Sharpe
Tennessee	25 lbs.**	1960	Old Hickory Reservoir
Texas	11.88 lbs.	1990	Lake Meredith
Utah	15 lbs. 9 oz.	1991	Provo River
Vermont	13 lbs. 7.04 oz.	1997	Clyde River
Virginia	14 lbs. 6 oz.	1997	New River
Washington	18.76 lbs.	1990	Columbia River
West Virginia	17.22 lbs.	1990	Gauley River
Wisconsin	18 lbs.	1933	High Lake
Wyoming	17.42 lbs.	1991	Boysen Reservoir

*tied a previous record
**recently disallowed as world record by National Fresh Water Fishing Hall of Fame
(this list as of May, 1998)

doubt that a walleye could weigh 25 pounds in August. Maybe in February, but not in August." This from a man who over the years has handled many fish approaching 20 pounds during his agency's quest for eggs and milt.

The new mark of 22 pounds 11 ounces may be beaten, but probably not from any existing arena. The giants of the Tennessee Valley are ghosts of the past. Some biologists say the brontosaurus 'eyes of Greers Ferry were the result of a diet rich in trout that no longer exists to any great extent. And the Columbia River, as Wagner points out, has yet to produce a walleye much over 20 pounds, either from a net or by angling.

We've said it before—you'll win the state lottery twice before hooking a 20, and you won't land that one, either. But that doesn't mean you can't break a record. In fact, an absolute parade of mammoth fish have trooped through the outdoor pages of late, many toppling state, provincial, or line-class marks.

Oklahoma and Ohio state records were broken in 1995, the latest shots fired in the recent battle of the bulge. In all, 19 state records for walleyes have been established since 1990. Some of those records stood for a long time before falling, one of many indications that this can be the best time in history to hook a fish over 15 pounds.

We've said it before—you'll win the state lottery twice before hooking a 20, and you won't land that one, either.

Safe money would bet that the advent of catch-and-release allows more fish to attain trophy size than ever before. Certainly, better fishery management keeps more populations at optimum size, while regulations like slot limits increase the number of trophy fish. Many more walleye waters exist now than 30 years ago, with the addition of so many reservoirs and the spreading popularity of walleyes coast to coast.

Critical contributions also came from the Clean Water Act (CWA) and environmentally minded fishing groups. When the CWA was adopted by Congress in 1971, Lake Erie was dying, her native walleyes all but extinct. The Detroit River and Saginaw Bay were cesspools. Green Bay and Lake Ontario were following Erie toward a filthy demise. Each of those fisheries now ranks among the best in the world, with proven potential to produce gargantuan walleyes, following monumental cleanup efforts.

Sources are expanding, but they probably won't be enough to produce a world record anytime soon. What does it take to produce a world record walleye? Long life spans, big water (in which fish can escape pressure for many years), an efficient source of fuel (most notably shad, trout, alewives, or smelt), a long growing season, mild winters, the right genes, and incredible luck. Yet you could find all those and still not catch a 20-pounder in a lifetime of trying.

The most accessible records today are of the line-class variety. According to the National Fresh Water Fishing Hall of Fame, the 25-pound line-class record is 10 pounds 9 ounces, which can be broken with relative ease on a long list of waterways around the continent. The record for 2-pound test is around 11 pounds, which can certainly be attempted in most regions where walleyes swim. The 15- and 16-pound test marks are both in the 12-pound range, well within reach.

Most other records require a walleye over 14 pounds. That may involve travelling to top waters. The following waters deliver the best odds for bagging a walleye over 14 pounds today. Waters marked with an asterisk currently offer the best potential for producing a new world record: **Bay of Quinte**, Ontario; ***Bull Shoals**, Missouri; ***Columbia River**, Washington-Oregon; **Fort Peck**, Montana; **Fox River**, Wisconsin; ***Greers Ferry**, Arkansas; **Lake Erie**, New York-Michigan-Ohio-Ontario-Pennsylvania; **Lake Ontario**, New York-Ontario; **Saginaw Bay**, Michigan; **St. Lawrence River**, Quebec-New York-Ontario; **Tobin Lake**, Saskatchewan.

THE SECRET LURE: IS THERE A WAY TO STAY ONE STEP AHEAD OF THE CONDITIONING FACTOR?

When he was just a kid first learning to fish, he'd spend hours in the musty old basement, peering through his grandfather's timeworn fishing gear. Rusty old tackle boxes filled with huge lures, reels, and lines with strange-sounding names: Dowagiac, Creek Chub, Marathon, Ashway. The original Zara Gossa—not the newfangled version. Tubular steel True Temper rods hanging at attention next to the workbench, or stuffed high up in the rafters, either side of the single light bulb. His father's first Mitchell spinning reel, one of the first imported into the United States from France. Antique duck decoys, rusting pipes, bolts, tools, and 50 years of assorted odds and ends collecting in the basement-workshop-tackle repository of his grandparents' lakeside home.

Even Grandad changed—reluctantly—with the times.

Though they fished together mostly for bass, his grandfather often told the boy tales of fishing the northwoods when just getting there over miles of tire-puncturing gravel roads was still an adventure. Tales of muskies blasting noisy surface lures. Catching live frogs, baiting them on oversize hooks, and catching walleyes when no one else could. He never told anyone the secret, but reveled in the acclaim from other fishing camp visitors.

Reaching into the bottom of one ancient box, Grandad pulled out and fondled a weathered June Bug spinner—an odd-shaped blade that rotated on a steel shaft just ahead of a huge hook to be dressed with a minnow. A faraway look appeared in his eye, recalling glory days past. The venerable June Bug, Prescott, and Strip-On were some of his secret lures back in the '30s, but like so many traditional favorites, they fell out of style as light line refinements came into favor. Perhaps the fish became accustomed to it, or maybe they simply preferred newfangled gadgets. More likely, the aggressive walleyes susceptible to being caught on the heavy hardware were thinned out by increasing pressure. A new approach was needed to re-enact the glory days of the old secret lure.

The young fisherman's great-uncle was one of the first to jump on the wagon when the Rapala craze hit. Well, sort of: he didn't want to pay big bucks for an actual Rapala, so he bought a cheap imitation called a Raposa. The lightweight balsa lure cast pretty well on spinning gear and monofilament line, and the shivering wobble was deadly. Slower moving and more subtle than June Bug Spinners, the lure was something that fish hadn't seen before. Bass, walleyes, pike—everything liked balsa minnows.

Grandad was a bit slower to pick up on the trend, since he, like his father before him, preferred traditional Dacron line and ancient Pflueger Supreme casting reels, which couldn't cast Rapalas worth a hoot. But eventually he came around. Rapalas were the hot lure for years, and in fact, they never went out of style. But other goodies moved into the limelight, particularly for walleyes.

Snelled spinners like the Little Joe came onto the market, shifting the focus back toward spinner-livebait combos. More subtle and refined than their heavy hardware predecessors, Little Joes swept across the walleye market. All you had to do was just add a weight ahead of the spinner to get it down, tip the hook with a crawler or minnow, drift along, and hang on tight. This was big news in the '50s, just about the time the young angler was busy being born. Still works today, though often in lighter line, more refined versions.

As the young fisherman became old enough to fish for walleyes on his own, two primary tactics came to prevail in his walleye arsenal. Early forays to the Mississippi River and reading from the teachings of the venerable jigmeister Bill Binkelman proved that leadhead jigs were indisputable walleye killers. Pre-tied hair and feather jigs were the norm, but Binkelman's plain-head concept, often in fluorescent colors, was superb when tipped with a minnow, crawler, or leech.

Second, as the soon-to-be-legendary Lindner brothers were getting their fledgling Lindy Tackle company off the ground, the slipsinker livebait rig hit the walleye world. Elegant simplicity—hook, line, and sinker—presented livebait naturally on almost invisible light line. Finesse to the max, applicable to nearly any and every lake, river, or impoundment. All thoughts of using anything besides jigs or rigs for walleyes were swept away. They were the hot lures—the secret lures of the '70s—putting everything else to shame. Teamed with the introduction of depthfinders and Buck Perry's concept of structure fishing, probing the depths with rigs and jigs seemed the ultimate approach for walleyes.

They were the hot lures—the secret lures of the '70s—putting everything else to shame.

When he first moved from the big city to the northwoods, the young angler chuckled at seeing a boatload of grannies and grandpas slipbobber fishing atop a shallow reef, as if they could possibly outfish his sophisticated tactics. Lo and behold, that particular day, the oldtimers kicked butt, enlightening him once again. Right time, right place, and a tiny livebait dancing across a shallow, windswept reef was more attractive than his fancy rigging and jigging. Not that he'd abandon them; he'd simply expand his repertoire.

Jigs and rigs dominated his walleye scene throughout the '80s. Hard to imagine they'd ever go out of style—particularly in heavily fished waters demanding finesse presentations. But his travels introduced him to other tactics better tailored to certain situations. Like bottom-bouncers, spinners, and crawlers on western impoundments. Darn things crawled up and down contours without snagging, and they triggered walleyes. Tried 'em in Canada; same deal for rocky reefs, not as finesse-oriented as rigs or jigs, yet nevertheless deadly under the right conditions. Heavier versions even worked for drifting shallow basins on the Great Lakes.

Speaking of the Great Lakes, his expeditions to the Western Basin of Lake Erie made him a believer in weight-forward spinners dressed with nightcrawlers. These versatile lures performed admirably for drifting across and casting ahead of the boat for suspended walleyes. On Grandad's final walleye trip, he caught the most and the biggest walleyes by casting a weight-forward spinner—something he often reminded everyone of. He'd certainly seen changes in his lifetime—from horse and buggy days to the space shuttle, from braided black Dacron and heavy hardware to finesse tactics with light line. Never did like trolling, but casting for big walleyes was his fondest fishing pleasure.

Jigging spoons began making their mark for walleyes in the '80s, first through the ice, then on open water. Touted as the new secret lure, they really weren't—just another and more aggressive option. Cast or jigged, they showed walleyes something different from slow rigging or jigging, which almost everyone else was using for walleyes. So he popped a few in his tackle box.

Taking pride in his finesse with rigs and jigs, the young angler, now well into his 30s, was at first a bit skeptical about the new wave of crankbait trolling for 'eyes. Perhaps he'd inherited some of Grandad's preference for casting. But as hardbaits exploded on the walleye scene in the late '80s, their effectiveness became too dynamic to ignore.

Long, slender lures, with more of a shivering wiggle than a wide wobble, were taking walleyes throughout the open water season. Weighted leadcore lines and eventually snap weights that popped on and off for easy weight adjustment probed the depths with cranks or spinners. On-line planer boards spread lines to the sides of the boat, covered wider trolling swaths, and reached out to fish pushed aside by the boat's wake. Global Positioning Satellite system navigation to distant off-shore spots. Plotting trolling passes electronically. Where would it all end?

Walleye fishing had indeed become a complex science in the '90s. Taken to extremes, you could become an electronic trollin', fish-catchin' machine. Thinking back to the early basement days, he realized that he'd witnessed walleye fishing rise from humble beginnings to the computer age. And the pace was continuing to accelerate. Each new decade brought discoveries and changes . . . and a new wave of secret lures.

It's important to stay on the leading edge of technology and refinement. But . . .

In the early days, fish conditioned to certain presentations became more vulnerable to newly introduced lure styles for the first 5 or so years until those, too, became also-rans. In recent years, however, the emphasis had not been so much on new secret lures as on probing previously unexplored lake areas for suspended or basin fish and maximizing efficiency and coverage with faster-moving trolling tactics.

We've tackled drop-offs, cast the shallows, and now plumbed the mysterious depths. What new vistas are left to explore? Have we run out of options, of new secret lures? Will the fish ever become fully conditioned to our best efforts? Probably not. History has taught us that unexpected refinements surface, fueled by man's creativity and quest to catch more and bigger fish. Even if we can't visualize where the next advancement will come from, it certainly will arrive. We'll ride the first few years of the new secret lure syndrome, then likely consider what was formerly new and exciting as status quo, even old hat, and look ahead to what the future holds.

In fishing, it's possible to reach any level you wish, from the most casual outing to the most sophisticated, state-of-the-art approach. Pounds and ounces may vary, but the quest remains the same—to enjoy the outdoor experience however it suits you best. High tech or humble, a fish tugging on the end of your line is what it's all about.

And now, as he sits at the end of his own dock, watching the joy and excitement on his granddaughter's face as she catches her first panfish on a bobber rig, he realizes that the magic of the fishing experience never leaves, though the productivity of certain lures or fishing styles may wane with time. It's important to stay on the leading edge of technology and refinement. Yet it's just as important never to forget the joy of fishing.

OF WALLEYES AND WEREWOLVES: DO LUNAR INFLUENCES REALLY PLAY A PART IN FISHING?

We'll never forget the first time we failed to include Doug Hannon's "Best Fishing Times" in an issue of *In-Fisherman* magazine. Phones rang for days after readers flipped to the accustomed place for this monthly moon chart.

Readers even threatened to cancel subscriptions if such an omission occurred again. Others were more hurt than angry. "How could you do this? How can I schedule my trip to Lake Waccahaug?" Needless to say, last-minute deletions can include nearly every column in the magazine except Hannon's Moon Times.

Fans of the Moon Times and other solunar tables believe, based on experience, that the tables are guides to better fishing. Other anglers, equally confident, call it voodoo. Other folks take a reserved view, unwilling to label solunar forces fact or folly, given the diverse opinions on both sides.

The Moon's Effects—Consider that the moon exerts about 1/6 the amount of gravitational pull as planet earth and that it orbits us at a distance about 30 times the earth's diameter. This pull causes tides that can raise oceans up to 50 feet twice a day, as occurs in the Bay of Fundy. Solunar theorists propose that freshwater fish retain a primal memory of tidal effects, since their ancestors evolved in marine waters. And we know that tides strongly affect the movements and spawning of invertebrates, preyfish, and other marine species.

Full and new moons produce the strongest tides. Doug Hannon and other lunar theorists have suggested that full and new moons produce the best fishing, other factors being equal. The three days on either side of full and new moons also are assigned benefit, though it declines with each day on either side of the peak lunar period.

Hannon's examination of his own bass fishing records and analyses of record catches suggest that the day exactly between the full and new moons is a good time to fish. The brightness of a full moon can affect the nocturnal movements of plankton, zooplankton, larger invertebrates, and preyfish, all of which may trigger predators like walleyes to feed more aggressively or in different locations than during dark nights. But the full moon's apparent power goes beyond effects of light.

The In-Fisherman staff, whose combined angling research totals more than 1,000 days per year on the water, have noted many peak fishing periods that coincided with full moons, including many for walleyes. Editor In Chief Doug Stange, a skeptic of many traditional angling theories, has tracked his fall walleye fishing excursions, which tend to produce his largest fish of the year.

"I'd rate full-moon nights between 2 to 3 times as productive as nights with no lunar effect," Stange says. "More large walleyes become active in the shallow areas I fish, whether or not the moon is covered by clouds. If I plan a walleye trip, I try to fish during the four days prior to a full moon, regardless of season."

Al Lindner and James Lindner have experienced similar hot full-moon bites

Celestial Positioning

During the moon's 27.3-day revolution around the earth, it makes one complete rotation on its axis. The same side of the moon always faces the earth. Only the half facing the sun is illuminated, so we see the apparent shape of the round moon change as the sunlight moves from one side to the other.

A full moon occurs when the earth is between the sun and the moon. We see the shaded side, or new moon, when the moon is between the earth and the sun. A cycle from full moon to full moon takes an average of 29.5 days.

According to traditional solunar theorists, major activity periods occur near times when the moon is directly over (at zenith) or beneath (at nadir) each longitude. These are the traditional moon-up and moon-down times. Tidal forces are strongest then, although actual tides may be delayed by restrictions of current flow.

Minor activity periods theoretically occur at the time the moon is 90 degrees from a longitude and tidal forces are weakest.

The strength of tidal forces varies with the distance between the moon and earth, the moon's declination (its angle above or below the equator), and the relative position of the sun. Combinations of these factors affect daily and monthly tidal forces.

Some solunar theorists believe that times when tidal forces are

Monthly Lunar Cycle

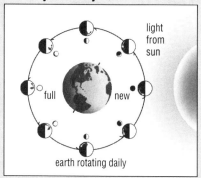

The rotation of the moon around the earth changes the moon's appearance from full to new and back to full. The outer circle of moons illustrates how the sun's light illuminates the moon. The inner circle depicts moon phases as seen from earth. The dots and small arrows on the outer circle illustrate a single rotation of the moon on its axis. This occurs over a 27.3-day period; the same side of the moon always faces the earth.

Tidal Activity

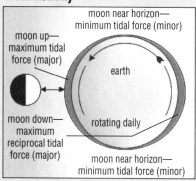

Peaks in tidal force (major activity periods) resulting in exaggerated increases in ocean depth occur as each longitude rotates under the moon. Reciprocal forces create similar peaks on the opposite side of the earth. Minimum tidal forces (minors) are found at longitudes 90 degrees from the moon. As the earth rotates, each longitude experiences two major and two minor solunar forces approximately every 24 hours and 50 minutes, with slightly more than 6 hours and 12 minutes between events.

strongest produce more activity (and thus better fishing) than times when they're weak. Ralph Manns suggests that strong solunar forces provide precise timing signals and concentrate activity within specific periods, thereby providing fast fishing for short periods. In contrast, weak nonsolunar forces spread a similar amount of activity over a longer period, making concentrated catches more difficult.

Effects of Elliptical Orbit

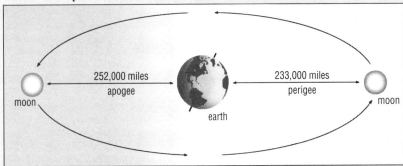

The 27.3-day orbit of the moon is elliptical, not round. At its most distant point (apogee), the moon is about 252,000 miles from the earth. At its closest (perigee), it's about 233,000 miles away. Tidal force is strongest when the moon is at perigee.

Sun-Moon Interaction

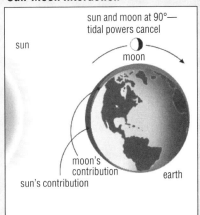

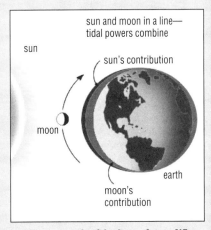

The sun creates a tidal force about 46 percent the strength of the lunar force. When the sun and moon are aligned, the two forces combine to produce highest and lowest tides. When they are at right angles, the sun's force tends to cancel the moon's, reducing tidal forces and tidal fluctuations.

The relative positions of the sun and moon, their declinations, and their distance from the earth combine to vary solunar influence. In most cases, the influence of the moon is stronger than that of the sun.

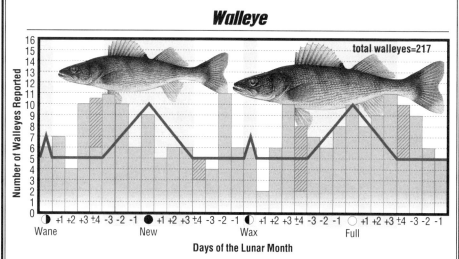

Walleye

total walleyes=217

Number of Walleyes Reported

16 15 14 13 12 11 10 9 8 7 6 5 4 3 2 1 0

◗ +1 +2 +3 ±4 -3 -2 -1 ● +1 +2 +3 ±4 -3 -2 -1 ◖ +1 +2 +3 ±4 -3 -2 -1 ○ +1 +2 +3 ±4 -3 -2 -1

Wane   New   Wax   Full

Days of the Lunar Month

The number of trophy walleyes taken on each day of the lunar month (29.5 calendar days), including partial days created by uneven lunar movement. The dark grey line shows the approximate profile when walleyes are taken according to Doug Hannon's best-day calendars. The "better" solunar days correspond to the peaks in the dark grey line. Days ±4 are partial days, and diagonal barring shows where values have been corrected to compensate for partial days.

for walleyes, particularly in fall in Canadian lakes and in bays of the Great Lakes. The first full moon in October inevitably finds James on the best trophy lake, filming a TV segment on presentations for outsize 'eyes.

A little astronomy. During its 27.3-day revolution around the earth, the moon makes one complete rotation on its axis. The same side of the moon always faces the earth. Only the half facing the sun is illuminated, so we see the apparent shape of the round moon change as sunlight moves across its face.

A full moon occurs when the earth is between the sun and the moon. We see the shaded side, or the new moon, when the moon is between the earth and the sun. According to traditional solunar theorists, major daily activity periods occur when the moon is directly overhead or beneath a particular longitude.

These are the moon-up and moon-down times or the two daily major activity periods. Tidal forces are strongest then. Two daily minor activity periods coincide with the moon's position at 90 degrees from either side of the reference longitude, which also produces the weakest tidal forces.

Many animal behaviors are linked to natural rhythms—sunrise and sunset, lunar cycles, and seasonal shifts in weather. These rhythmic adaptations affect metabolism, physiology, and behavior. Fish not only react to favorable conditions but also anticipate them.

Two theories may explain such cyclic behavior. According to the theory of *exogenous periodicity*, subtle periodic changes on the planet, such as gravitational pulls, tides, or shifts in electromagnetic fields, influence animals. These geophysical forces are thought to synchronize the organism's behavior.

The theory of endogenous periodicity argues that organisms have internal biological clocks that determine changes in physiology or behavior. Outside stimuli periodically reset the clock, so the animal stays in synch with the outside world. Scientists have suggested that lunar forces may act as a *zeitgeber*—a term for events that resynchronize the biological clocks of organisms and help them predict when bodily functions and behaviors start and stop.

Researchers have found that fish in controlled conditions in labs detect solunar forces and use them to regulate behavior like feeding and growth. The solunar forces act as *zeitgebers* to reset the biological clock, though the location and mechanics of these clocks are unknown.

Master Angler Analysis—In-Fisherman researcher Ralph Manns is one of the foremost experts on solunar effects on fish. He completed a comprehensive analysis of In-Fisherman's Master Angler Award applications from 1987 through 1990, assessing catches of walleyes over 10 pounds or 30 inches in relation to lunar days. The program requires date of catch, but not time, so effects of major and minor periods were impossible to analyze.

Manns notes that his analysis has to assume that fishing effort was equal throughout the lunar month, because it relies on total reported catch rather than catch rates. But because many anglers and our own In-Fisherman staff may fish more frequently during peak lunar periods, a bias toward larger catches during prime moon phases may be present.

The walleye graph shows traces of solunar effects. Nine of 14 peak days occurred on the better solunar days (64 percent), while only 5 peak days occurred on the remaining 13.5 poor lunar days (37 percent). Difference among these data aren't statistically significant by the strictest scientific criteria, however. Manns adds that the 3 days on either side of the middle of each moon phase show an interesting peak in production of giant walleyes.

Days on either side of the full moon produce trophy walleyes with slightly more consistency than other days. But these humps in the data could result from angler bias that favors fishing around the full moon. Eight of the 12 largest daily sauger catches fell on the 16 better solunar days (50 percent), while 4 peak days fell on the 13.5 poorer days (30 percent).

Fairly good matches occurred between peak catches and the days around the full moon and waxing and waning half moons. Walleye and sauger catches coincided more closely with lunar peaks than catches of muskie, pike, trout, or salmon, but not as closely as those for largemouth and smallmouth bass or channel catfish.

Statistical Analysis—Ralph Manns, a trained scientist, tends to be skeptical of angler beliefs, even those of noted authorities like Doug Stange and Al Lindner. "Humans are poor observers of detail," he says. "As I analyzed results of the In-Fisherman Master Angler program and my own data on bass catches, I saw that accurate records and statistical analysis are essential for determining if fishing is better during majors, minors, or full moons.

"If Stange catches one walleye every hour over a 12-hour period, he'll catch 2 during a 2-hour major, one during a 1-hour minor, and 9 during the remaining nonlunar hours. Such results reasonably lead to the conclusion that majors and minors weren't better for his fishing.

"If bites bunch up, as they often do, Doug's catch for the trip might be the same, but conclusions about solunar effects would differ. Suppose Doug catches 2 fish during each of the 2 hours of the major, 2 during the minor, and 6 during 3 of the remaining 9 hours. He's caught 6 walleyes during solunar periods for a catch rate of 2.0 per hour, and 6 during 9 nonsolunar hours, a catch rate of .67 fish per hour. Although he caught no more than 2 fish in any hour, his catch rate during solunar periods was 3 times as high as during other times.

"Suppose two less proficient walleye anglers caught 5 walleyes during a 10-hour day. If they caught a walleye during a minor (1 fish per hour) and 1 during the 2-hour major (0.5 fish per hour), the combined catch rate for solunar periods would be .67 walleyes per hour. Their nonsolunar rate would be .42 fish per hour, so the solunar periods produced 60 percent faster fishing.

"These anglers probably wouldn't realize how much the major and minor periods outperformed nonsolunar times. They caught more walleyes during nonsolunar times. But get those odds in Las Vegas, and you could retire in a hurry.

"It's hard to discern mathematical relationships when catches are small, so anglers often recall the few occasions when they made big catches during or outside solunar hours. These nontypical catches may, however, be random events."

Walleyes and other fish are simple creatures that act on genetic instincts but can adapt to changing conditions by learning conditioned responses. They live in environments where food usually is limited, so they feed whenever opportunity arises.

Whenever events like sudden cloudiness, increased current, or more wave action create a feeding opportunity, predators feed. And if many predators feed successfully, they're satiated and inactive when the next routine feeding period arrives, like sunset or a major activity period. Predators don't pass up feeding opportunities to await solunar periods.

Solunar theorists were correct when they declared a detectable solunar force that can affect fish behavior and angling catch rates. But they've apparently become so enraptured by these effects that they've become overconfident in predicting the best times to fish.

Solunar force routinely motivates only a small portion of predator populations. Its effect is erratic because the solunar cycle isn't a controlling influence. Solunar force seems to be just one of many factors that influence fish behavior. Still, it's an odds call to be on the water during major and minor activity periods.

In-Fisherman Staff Notes—John Alden Knight devised the first solunar tables in the 1920s. Many imitators and innovators have modified or expanded his basic concepts. His tables are still published.

And how do most In-Fisherman staff members use the Hannon tables?

In-Fisherman magazine and *Walleye In-Sider* publish Doug Hannon's "Best Fishing Times" in each issue. "Best Fishing Times" offers both a ranking of fishing days and best daily times. The three days on either side of full and new moons are also ranked high, plus the days of waxing and waning moons (16 days a month). The full and new moons are ranked highest, with days decreasing in fishing strength on either side.

And how do most In-Fisherman staff members use the Hannon tables? For us, the best time to go fishing remains whenever we can. And when we go, we go—on the water at dawn, quit at dark-thirty, and back the next day if possible. So most staff members tend to fish through majors, minors, and in-between times without noting them.

Most of us, though, try to schedule major fishing or filming trips, particularly for walleyes, on the days just prior to and on the days of a full moon, and secondarily of the dark moon. Does this ensure a good trip? Of course not. But after years of experience, we believe that certain aspects of angling lore hold some truth, even if they can't be proven scientifically, and even if you take the time to try.

Chapter 11

Saugeye

Sauger

Dennis McKinney

The Walleye's Close Cousins

GETTING TO KNOW THE SAUGER AND THE SAUGEYE

The sauger, found throughout much of North America, receives less attention from writers, anglers, and biologists than does its close cousin, the walleye. But sauger provide important sportfisheries in many places that don't support prominent populations of walleyes and at times of year when little else may be biting.

The sauger closely resembles the walleye but is easily distinguished by the dark saddle markings on its back. Sauger tolerate turbid water better than walleyes and are more likely to be found in flowing water. Where the two species coexist, sauger often are more numerous.

Sauger are found throughout the Mississippi River basin

and in much of Canada. They inhabit large rivers such as the Mississippi, Missouri, and Tennessee, but also occur in large lakes like Lake Erie, Lake Winnipeg, and Lake of the Woods. Most large rivers where sauger occur naturally have been impounded, but in mainstream reservoirs that are more riverinelike than lakelike, sauger often thrive. Unlike walleyes, sauger have been only sporadically introduced into lakes and rivers outside their native range.

Sauger populations reflect the health of river and reservoir ecosystems because they spawn over rocky substrates. If sediment from the watershed fills the crevices between rocks and gravel, that habitat becomes unsuitable for spawning and incubating eggs.

Successful sauger spawning requires flowing water. Unlike walleyes, lake-spawning stocks of sauger are rare or nonexistent. Female sauger, like walleyes, are incredibly fertile. A single female just 18 inches long can produce over 150,000 eggs, which she broadcasts over rocky shoals or along riprap-lined riverbanks. Depending on water temperature, sauger eggs hatch in about 2 to 3 weeks. As with many species, that critical 2 to 3 weeks of egg incubation can make or break a year class. Abrupt changes in water level or flow can have devastating effects on egg survival and subsequent recruitment of adults into the fishery.

Upon hatching, sauger fry drift downriver and into overbank areas of reservoirs, backwaters of rivers, or the main basin of lakes. They spend their first summer feeding voraciously, first on microscopic organisms and small invertebrates, then on fish. Inch-long sauger seek other fish to eat and readily prey on their own kind. Early use of fish as a food source results in rapid growth. One-year-old sauger reach 5 to 12 inches long, compared to the much smaller size of same-age walleyes in many places.

Sauger, though, aren't as long-lived as walleyes. They can survive to 10 years if fishing pressure is low. And sauger don't attain the large sizes walleyes reach—the world-record sauger is an 8-pound 12-ounce fish caught in Lake Sakakawea in 1971. A large sauger is a 4-pounder, and some sauger fisheries rely on a sustained harvest of fish weighing a pound or less.

MIGRATIONS

As young sauger complete their first year of life, they join older sauger in an annual spawning migration. Some one-year-old males may be mature, but at least 2 years are needed for most males and 3 years for most females to become sexually mature. The spawning migrations made by some sauger can be quite impressive, deserving of the name "jack salmon" that's used by many anglers.

Sauger inhabiting natural lakes sometimes move into tributary streams during winter, and those fish may not have to travel far to spawn. River-dwelling sauger, in contrast, may travel great distances and encounter at least one dam as they move upstream to suitable spawning habitat. Movements of 100 to 200 miles in just a few weeks are not uncommon, and upstream migrations of 150 miles through three dams have been documented.

Dams that sauger encounter lack fish ladders to aid upstream migration. Some sauger continue upstream by swimming into navigation locks. The number of sauger that make it through such structures depends on how water is discharged from the lock chamber and where the lock is located.

Remember that sauger prefer flowing water—if the lock is well-removed from the main channel of the river, few sauger will loiter around it long enough to enter the chamber and pass upstream. Most sauger do not move into the locks by swimming through the open doors of the chamber, as might be expected. Rather, they swim into the openings that drain water from the lock when a boat or barge passes

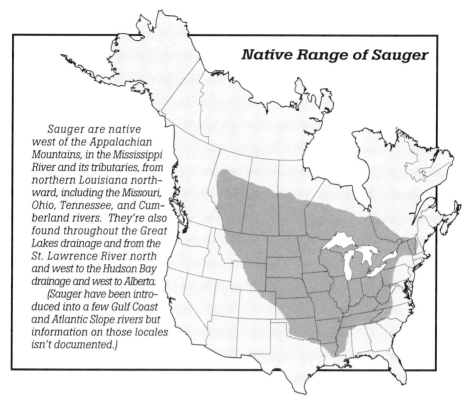

Native Range of Sauger

Sauger are native west of the Appalachian Mountains, in the Mississippi River and its tributaries, from northern Louisiana northward, including the Missouri, Ohio, Tennessee, and Cumberland rivers. They're also found throughout the Great Lakes drainage and from the St. Lawrence River north and west to the Hudson Bay drainage and west to Alberta.

(Sauger have been introduced into a few Gulf Coast and Atlantic Slope rivers but information on those locales isn't documented.)

downstream, attracted by the current caused by the lock discharge.

At many dams, the design of the locks is such that few, if any, sauger can negotiate passage through the locks and past the dam. Thus, sauger concentrations increase below dams as winter progresses. The number of sauger loitering below a dam or staging at other areas, such as the confluence of two rivers or below islands, will steadily increase throughout the winter and peak right before the spawn.

SAUGER FISHERIES

In northern rivers and reservoirs, sauger are caught incidentally throughout the year, both on ice and from open water. In the middle and lower reaches of the Mississippi River and its tributaries, sauger fisheries are decidedly seasonal, occurring during winter when fish congregate in natural staging areas or below dams.

Concentrations of sauger below dams and in other staging areas increase until the urge to spawn overtakes them. Fish holding near suitable shoals move out of deep water to spawn; those blocked by dams drop rapidly downriver, seeking riprap or any suitable substrate.

Sauger usually begin spawning by late March in Alabama and Tennessee, but not until early or mid-May in North Dakota. Once the spawn is complete, sauger disperse into the main basin of the reservoir or lake or into the middle reaches of large rivers. In many locales, this dispersion signals the end of sauger fishing for another year.

Concentrations of sauger below dams and at other staging areas provide great fishing, producing substantial benefits for local economies and freezers. But when concentrated fish are intensively pressured, the potential for overfishing exists. Recent research in Tennessee, Alabama, and Wisconsin revealed that anglers harvest 50

Heavy metal in the form of jigging spoons and bladebaits are fine baits below dams, although many other approaches work.

percent or more of all sauger in a river section during one spawning season.

Such high exploitation rates cause concern for several reasons. First, the average sauger caught will be small and many will be sexually immature. Secondly, heavily fished populations are often comprised of only one or two age classes of young fish, which poses a danger to the entire sauger population. If bad weather, suboptimal flow, or other environmental factors eliminate an entire year class in consecutive years, the fishery could collapse.

ENHANCEMENT AND PROTECTION

Although sauger populations thrive in spots like the mainstream impoundments of the Missouri River, they're imperiled in other locales. Where loss of suitable spawning habitat and overfishing have combined to reduce sauger populations, aggressive measures are underway to enhance sauger stocks. For instance, minimum size limits and reduced creel limits were recently instituted in Alabama and Tennessee. And several states have embarked on large-scale stocking programs to boost depressed stocks.

Experimental releases of water from Tennessee Valley Authority dams during spring, when egg deposition and incubation occur, are being investigated. Finally, efforts are underway in many locales to identify critical spawning habitats so they can be protected from dredging and shoreline development. If sauger have access to good spawning habitat and are protected from overfishing, they will continue to serve as a valuable addition to many sportfisheries across North America.

BEHAVIOR AND LOCATION

To catch sauger, we need to find them. In order to find them, we need to study their habits, behavior, body shape, and preferences. Understanding at least the rudiments of fish behavior is the basis of the In-Fisherman system *(Fish + Location + Presentation = Success)*.

Anglers in most regions fail to take advantage of the fact that sauger provide a four-season fishery. Sauger fuel one of our best winter fisheries—in the North through the ice in places like Fort Peck and Lake of the Woods, in the East as an open water fishery on rivers like the Mississippi and Ohio, and in tailraces all across the South. Typically, winter and spring are the only times southern fishermen target sauger, when the fish gather in huge numbers in predictable spots below dams. Legal limits tend to be high—10 or more fish per day.

Rare fisheries like Sakakawea and Fort Peck on the Missouri River system draw those few stalwart trophy hunters looking year-round for fish bigger than 8 pounds, 12 ounces. During the rest of the year, sauger fishing is an incidental affair. Most are harvested by walleye fishermen in places like Rainy Lake. If sauger were better understood, this probably wouldn't be the case.

Due to the structure of their eyes, saugers are more light-sensitive than walleyes, so they are forced deeper in most environments. Sauger also prefer murkier water than walleyes and tend to feed at slightly different times of the day. In lakes and reservoirs, the deeper areas sauger prefer offer prime light for

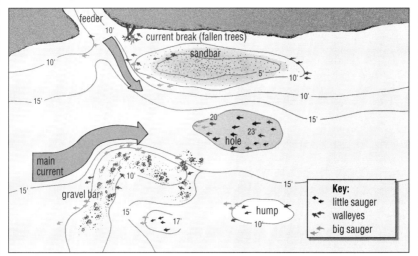

Big Sauger, Little Sauger, and Walleyes in Rivers

Big sauger in rivers don't hold with the small boys. Smaller sauger generally inhabit the deepest available pools, holes, or main river basin areas. Bigger sauger (say, over 3 pounds) cruise the same haunts that walleyes frequent, but arrive and feed on these spots early or late in the day or for more extended periods on windy, precipitous days. Look for the biggest sauger at the head of structural elements like gravel bars, sandbars, points, holes, and humps. They also hold to the current side of structural elements more than walleyes do, and they inhabit current areas that walleyes avoid.

foraging during late morning and late afternoon. Even when they're holding shallow in late spring, reservoir sauger tend to create tremendous midday opportunities. In muddy rivers, they bite all day, with midday the best. In clear rivers, sauger tend to bite early and late in the day.

After spawning, sauger move back down tributaries or back downstream away from dams to spread into summer patterns, although in southern rivers, most stay within 10 miles of a dam. In rivers, look for them near deep holes, where they can retreat during periods of inactivity. Active sauger position shallower (5 to 8 feet), usually at the head of structures like islands, humps, or shoals.

Sauger are more current-oriented than walleyes and hold to the current side of structural elements more than walleyes do. Big sauger tend to use the front face or head of a sand or gravel bar, while walleyes often use the sides, top, or tail of the bar. In summer, big sauger like to feed at the head of such elements during low-light periods early or late in the day. In most cases, walleyes and sauger use the same river segments. In fact, as a general rule, walleyes are found within

Sauger Location in Reservoirs

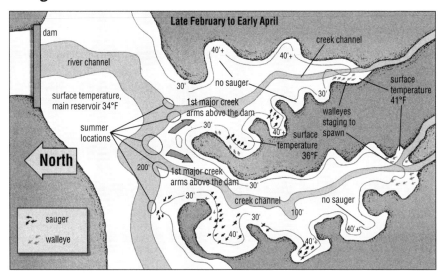

In winter, sauger collect near the mouths of major creek arms in areas where they'll eventually spawn. The illustration shows them inside the first or second primary points within these creek arms. This is classic location in February and March in western and hill-land reservoirs. In shallower midwestern reservoirs, more sauger tend to gather outside creek arms on the main lake side of points. They also concentrate more heavily in the middle third of the reservoir, as opposed to the lower third, as illustrated here.

Sauger tend to use one side of a creek arm exclusively all winter. They migrate into streams or coves at the end of creek arms to spawn, then slowly make their way back to the main lake, sometimes feeding for weeks in shallow coves along the way. By summer, they relocate to shelves and flats extending from structure in deep delta areas where creek channels meet the original river channel. In shallower reservoirs, they locate in bends of the main river channel.

---

several hundred yards of sauger during much of the year, especially winter, although walleyes will be shallower.

In deep rivers, draw an imaginary line at 15 feet. Walleyes tend to be shallower and sauger deeper, with a zone of interlap between 12 and 16 feet. Bigger sauger typically hold in that overlapping zone, especially when they're active.

In reservoirs during summer, walleye and sauger locations also tend to parallel one another. Again, sauger hold deeper. Many walleye pros observe that finding walleyes on a structural element is a strong indication that sauger will be there as well, but 10 to 30 feet deeper, if the proper habitat is available.

In reservoirs during summer, walleye and sauger locations also tend to parallel one another.

In February and March, reservoir sauger tend to group on 30- to 40-foot flats, usually between the first, second, and third secondary points inside major creek arms, and usually within a foot of bottom. Sauger are highly concentrated at this time of year. After spawning in the ends of coves, by dams, or in tributaries, sauger hold near spawning sites, often feeding on young shad or shiners in shallow coves for several weeks. Feeding frenzies in 2 to 5 feet of water are common in April and May.

Sauger then make their way out of the coves in creek arms to the lower or middle third of the main reservoir, keying on primary points just outside those major creek arms. Old deltas where creeks enter the main river channel are prime spots seldom fished in the South during summer. In clear reservoirs, sauger typically hold between 30 and 60 feet in summer, staying in or near the main river channel where it intersects major points or passes humps and other main lake structure. In cloudy or stained water, subtract 10 to 20 feet from that range.

In those key depth zones, look for flats or shelves extending away from points or humps. Sauger gather near the base where the shelf abuts structure. Those are prime locations, but don't fail to explore main channel edges during summer, when fish may move out to shelves, rockpiles, or reefs at the prime depth.

With little space for greater detail here, these keys to location are fairly universal. Yet room for thought remains on locational analysis and expanded tactics for sauger, especially in the South, where tradition dies hard.

BASIC PRESENTATION

The classic presentation for sauger is to rip a bladebait, like a Heddon Sonar, up and down within 2 to 3 feet of bottom. This method continues to be effective because sauger are so aggressive. None of this "tap, tap" stuff that walleyes are so famous for—sauger attack jigs and lures with a solid "whap."

But sauger also tend to feed right on bottom, where a few inches can make a big difference. Sauger pick baits off bottom more than walleyes do. Dragging, rolling, or moving a jig-minnow combination in place right on bottom is sometimes the most effective traditional approach. Because sauger position so deeply, heavy jigs (even 2-ounce jigs in the South) are effective.

In rivers, a jig-and-minnow combo typically outfishes the Sonar approach, even though blades work well for sauger. As mentioned, heavy 2- to 3-ounce jigs are popular in some regions, but there's generally a better way. Go to lighter line (less resistance to current or depths) and lighter jigs. Sauger can't lift heavy jigs, so they often bite the minnow in half. Try stingers, especially with heavy jigs.

In summer, try the "pop hop" approach—rest the jig on bottom while allowing some slack line between sharp upward snaps of only 6 inches. This is a vertical jigging technique, so stay directly over the area being worked. Pause at the top of the snap, then slowly lower the jig. Sauger are sometimes attracted by erratic jigging motions. But in colder water, drag a jig or Lindy rig slowly along bottom, occasionally raising it 2 feet or so for attraction.

Livebait rigs are popular in some reservoirs, especially in summer, when fish drop deep. During summer, bottom-bouncers and spinner rigs worked slowly near bottom are better options than jigs or blades for finding fish in reservoirs. During late fall and winter, switch to a Lindy rig.

Using 3-way rigs to find sauger in rivers is equally dynamic, especially in cold water. A 2- or 3-ounce bell sinker 12 to 18 inches below a 3-way swivel and a 3- to 6-foot leader to the lure is the optimum rig. The lure of choice is a 4- to 5-inch minnowbait such as a Bomber Long A, Normark Rapala, or Storm ThunderStick Jr. The key is trolling upcurrent in a lazy "S" pattern along sharp breaks in long midriver runs. This pattern works even in water temperatures of 32°F. Although seldom used in warmer water, it's equally effective.

Versatile techniques for sauger are lacking in most regions. Basically, on a reduced scale all walleye methods are applicable to sauger at one time or another. Versatility is the key to enhanced catches of sauger, and improved catches are possible by using some of these alternate methods. Knowledge of walleye techniques helps northern anglers adapt to the sauger bite. In areas of the country distant from traditional walleye fisheries, however, anglers are less able to apply the variety of techniques available as options to anglers in traditional walleye areas.

Basically, fish for sauger as you would for walleyes, but remember that sauger run deeper, prefer murkier water, and tend to feed at different times. With the proper perspective and a few keys, finding sauger can be as much fun as catching them.

The hunt leads to an aggressive quarry that schools heavily much of the year. If that's not enough to get your attention, sauger also make dynamite table fare. In areas where sauger are heavily fished and spawning areas have been compromised, consider releasing the bulk of your catch. But where these fish are overlooked and their population is dense, they offer a thrilling addition to the walleye angler's repertoire.

Sauger patrol can be as low tech or as high tech as you want it to be.

A BIT ABOUT SAUGEYE

Ever wish for a fish you could catch limits of all year long? Fish that still bite, following cold fronts in water that's barely above freezing? A fish that will hit jigs with abandon in streams with high muddy spring run-off that seem more suitable for plowing than fishing? A fish whose snow-white fillets boast culinary attributes somewhere between those of yellow perch and walleye? These wishes have been answered by state wildlife agencies that stock saugeye, hybrids created by crossing female walleyes with male sauger.

Saugeye are easy to identify most of the time: they have brown backgrounds with darker, saddle-shaped markings like sauger, and white tips on the lower margins of their tail fins like walleyes. Saugeye have a continuous black blotch on the membranes of the spinous dorsal fin, while sauger have rows of distinct black dots.

Numerous states in which past stockings of walleye fingerlings produced poor survival or inconsistent results are now stocking saugeye because they survive and grow rapidly. While this hybrid can theoretically occur in the wild from natural spawning, its occurrence is considered somewhat rare. Hybridization is almost wholly a human invention. The eggs from walleye females and the sperm from sauger males are collected from wild fish. When the fry hatch, they are placed in hatchery ponds, where they grow to fingerling size before stocking.

Some states, such as Ohio, have invested time and money into cooperative research with universities like Ohio State to improve hatchery production and fingerling survival after stocking. Two of the main areas researched were the proper amount and timing of pond fertilization for plankton production (saugeye fry feed on various zooplankton) and the timing of the gizzard shad fry hatch

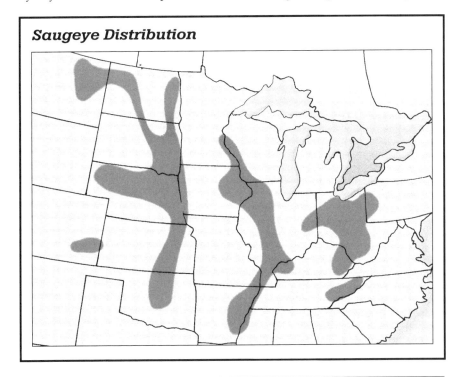

Saugeye Distribution

in reservoirs. Saugeye stocked as fingerlings require newly hatched shad fry to eat for increased survival and rapid growth.

Many states, including Ohio, North and South Dakota, Nebraska, Kansas, Oklahoma, Texas, Colorado, Iowa, and Illinois, are researching the stocking potential of saugeye. Saugeye stocking strategies are in their infancy, with most states starting at 50 fingerlings per acre of water. Ohio has reaped the benefits of successful production research and has produced as many as 11,000,000 fingerlings (not fry) in a single year. Two study lakes in Ohio receive 600 fingerlings per acre, and fish collected in fall are tagged. Fish are monitored through angler creel surveys and via electrofishing to determine their movement above and below dams. Monitoring helps calculate the population levels of young saugeye in the fishery and indicates when significant numbers are leaving the lake in which they were stocked. Lakes with high flushing rates are stocked more heavily and typically are more popular as tailwater fisheries. Reservoirs with higher flushing rates are also stocked with a greater number of fingerlings. Ohio stocks fingerlings at a rate of 100 to 300 per acre, depending on the ratio of acres of watershed to acres of reservoir.

The main area for caution in this hybrid stocking program is its potential to affect naturally reproducing stocks of walleye and sauger. The saugeye is not a sterile hybrid and is therefore capable of producing offspring with either parent stock. While the jury is still out on the extent to which such hybridizing can occur in the wild, precautions are being taken to avoid stocking reservoirs that drain into Great Lakes basins, and to avoid stocking rivers that already have naturally reproducing walleye and sauger populations. Saugeye spawning with parent species could weaken genetic integrity and reduce odds for future survival.

Myron Kibler's 15.66-pound, all-tackle record saugeye was caught through the ice at Fort Peck, Montana, in 1995.

LOCATION

Ice fishing for impoundment saugeye is catching on. Fish group tightly on the deep ends of points along old river channels, with occasional forays into shallower water and onto the ends of points and old roadbeds. The last hour of daylight seems to be the preferred time for these fish to become active during the winter Coldwater Period.

Locations that make these fish famous, however, are the tailwaters of impoundments. People line the banks all winter to catch them on jigs.

Saugeye are travelers, and therein lies the key to their location following heavy rains, generally coinciding with spring Coldwater and Prespawn periods, when fish are beginning their spawning runs. They swim upstream from a reservoir until they reach the tailwaters of the next impoundment, a lowhead dam, or occasionally all the way into the deeper pools of a headwater stream. Typically, they congregate at the dam gates, riprap, and nearby bars, although they may pass through dam gates during high flows.

Shore fishermen fish the tailwaters one or two days after high water begins. Hot fishing continues in the tailwaters until the number of fish has been reduced by fishing pressure. The longer the water remains high and the more successful the stocking program, the better the fishing becomes. Don't be scared off by the

Saugeye Location

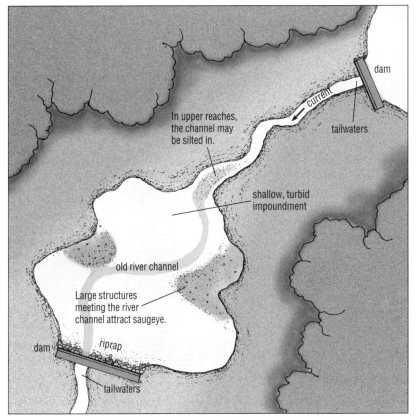

In upper reaches, the channel may be silted in.

current

dam

tailwaters

shallow, turbid impoundment

old river channel

Large structures meeting the river channel attract saugeye.

dam

riprap

tailwaters

Saugeye often run upriver in winter and spring, stacking in tailwaters below a dam. As the water warms in late spring, many disperse back downstream into shallow, turbid reservoirs. Prominent structures meeting the old river channel are key spots. Focus on the edge of the drop-off, but don't be afraid to fish shallow flats, particularly if the water is muddy. Shore fishing from riprap can be productive, too.

turbid water below dams in spring. Some of our most exciting saugeye fishing has been with black jigs in water that looked like mud.

The highest concentrations of fish in a tailwater typically hold in deeper depressions and seams along the bottom of the stream. Areas of slack water behind spillway baffles, bridge abutments, and concrete walls are guaranteed hot spots, too. Where streams resume a more natural appearance downstream from the dam, some saugeye may hold in deeper holes and along undercut banks with wood. Consider any spot that looks as if it would hold smallmouth and walleyes. If water remains high for a while, saugeye may use flooded brush and trees in calm backwater areas, too.

In lakes, the bigger the bar or point and the closer it extends to deep water in the main channel, the more attractive it is to the fish. Throw in all the classics: multiple breaklines, weedbeds, rockpiles, stumpfields, and roadbeds, and you have an area that attracts saugeye year-round. During the Coldwater Period, saugeye school tightly on the deeper breaks at the ends of bars near the old river channel. This is the most consistent pattern of the year; cold fronts seem to have a limited effect on these deep-holding fish. Fish can be caught by casting to rocky bars and along the riprap of dams at night during the peak of the spawn. In Ohio, this occurs around the end of March and the first of April as the water warms from 40°F to 50°F.

Beginning in late April as the water warms into the 60°F range, postspawn fish frequently are in the shallows. Start by fishing weedbeds, then search your way into deeper water, checking rockpiles, cuts, and turns in breaklines, tops of old roadbeds, culverts, ditches, washes, and across the tops and down the sides of bars. In extremely shallow lakes with silt-laden bottoms, fish often are attracted to current at causeway openings and along riprap shorelines, windswept points, and beaches where bottom content changes.

Once you contact fish, throw out a floating marker and triangulate a hot spot: it's worth the few extra minutes. If you use a GPS unit, you can still be off by 100 feet or more. Saugeye group tightly and can be hard to relocate without a good shore reference.

Fishing remains excellent in these areas through the Presummer and Summer Peak periods. At times, it doesn't seem to matter which bar you fish—saugeye are active across the tops of all of them.

Summer and Postsummer may be the toughest times to consistently catch limits of saugeye. Once young shad reach a size that adult saugeye can gorge on, saugeye scatter. At this time of year, fishing for suspended fish with shad-imitating crankbaits may be the best presentation.

On some lakes, saugeye fisherman often work hard to catch saugeye on jigs and crawler harnesses, while a nearby muskie fisherman hooks a decent saugeye

In-Fisherman Professional Walleye Trail touring pro Tom Bruno hoists two state record class-saugeye from John Martin Reservoir in Colorado. In lakes too warm and turbid for walleyes, where excessive siltation restricts the spawning of largemouth bass, sauger may provide an angling compromise. Stocking saugeye has revitalized numerous impoundments, often providing bank fishing along riprap or in shallow brush.

every 10 minutes by trolling large imitation shad crankbaits at 3 to 4 mph. Slowing down and switching to smaller baits often doesn't trigger fish.

Troll between points, but tick the tops of structure occasionally. During summer, many big saugeye are hooked this way. Sometimes, saugeye fisherman trolling small crankbaits like Storm ThunderSticks catch huge muskies up on the shallower areas of bars at dawn and dusk. Don't get caught in a rut. Someone you thought was doing everything wrong or who was scaring away fish with a fast trolling speed may be the only one catching fish.

Saugeye resume schooling tighter in the Postsummer and Fall Turnover Periods. During October and November, their activities parallel spring patterns, though I see increased activity in the shallows at night. Fish hold relatively deep off the ends of points during the day and are active in the shallows at night.

PRESENTATION

A basic presentation that catches saugeye all year, even through the ice, is a jig dressed with a plastic body and tipped with livebait. Use various combinations of jig weights and colors to fine-tune your approach.

The most important factor after ice-out is to keep the jig on the bottom, making frequent contact with little lateral movement. Just pretend you're ice fishing. Subtlety at this time of year can take a backseat to staying on bottom.

When high winds make holding the boat steady with your transom trolling motor difficult, however, a 3/8-ounce jig often fishes more efficiently and effectively than a faster-moving, smaller one. Keep the boat steady, your line close to vertical, and the jig on bottom. Also, thin mono line or one of the new fused superlines offers less bow in the line prior to raising the jig off bottom.

When water begins to warm during May and June, drifting jigs across the tops of points is productive. The jig should remain in contact with bottom, with slow lifts to feel for the weight of a saugeye. When fish are aggressive, you'll feel a distinct tap on your line, but half the time, all you'll notice is additional weight.

Around June, the livebait of choice switches from minnows to pieces of nightcrawler, then reverts back to minnows in late fall. Many days, adding a small stinger hook is necessary. Favorite color combinations are fluorescent orange, lime, and chartreuse. Black is worth a try in turbid water.

Nightcrawler harnesses and bottom-bouncers become effective shortly after bait preference switches to crawlers. Use a rig that resist snags but that keeps your worm close to bottom.

Saugeye seem to prefer the thumping vibration of large Colorado blades in combination with one- or two-hook tandem rigging. Use ultrasharp worm hooks, sizes 1 and 2.

Saugeye haven't seen many of those sophisticated methods often employed for walleyes.

Crankbaits can also be deadly. During spring and fall, cast rattling floating minnow imitations in tailwaters, along riprap, and across the tops of points at night. Try 3- to 6-inch lures in shad, silver, and black; firetiger and black patterns at night and in turbid water.

Trolling crankbaits with an outboard during summer is the fastest way to catch a limit of saugeye when they spread out to feed on shad. Trolling speed ranges from 2 to 4 mph. Don't be afraid to be too aggressive when you think conditions are right for active fish. At times, saugeye seem to prefer bigger shad imitations, like Bagley's 5-inch Monster Shad or Hooker Baits, trolled at 3 to 4 mph. Other popular baits include the Storm Hot 'n Tot and Wiggle Wart, ThunderSticks, Smithwick Rattlin' Rogues, Spoonplugs, and various shad imitations.

The hotter and more prolonged the summer, the more likely some saugeye will be to suspend on the thermocline. They either stick close to the ends of points or suspend between points. Troll just above the thermocline while still ticking the ends and top of the points with your lure. Determine running depths of lures by tracking line lengths needed to reach various depths. To accomplish this, count passes of your level wind across the reel, use color-coded line, or purchase a line-counter reel. A lure retriever is a must for freeing lures from snags.

Fishing for saugeye, like stocking saugeye, is relatively new, so saugeye haven't seen many of those sophisticated methods often employed for walleyes. This should put most walleye anglers steps ahead in their quest for saugeyes.

Selective
Walleye Harvest

USING OUR WALLEYE
RESOURCES WISELY

We remain strongly in favor of eating walleye. But we also remain strongly opposed to killing every walleye caught. Fish resources need to be used wisely, so anglers who want to keep some fish can do so, and those who want fine quality fishing can have it. No fundamental conflict between fishermen who want to eat fish and fishermen who want to release fish need exist. The answer is selective harvest—an idea we proposed in the mid-1980s and encourage fishermen and fishing organizations to embrace today.

Selective harvest maintains a tradition of harvesting some fish because they are nutritious, delicious, and renewable when harvested wisely. But to sustain fine quality fishing, we must also release less numerous species and size classes.

We need to move away from some traditions of the past. As we become more sophisticated in our use of tackle and technique, and subsequently more successful, stringer shots to prove fishing prowess are no longer acceptable. Keeping trophy after trophy, no matter what the species, must give way to releasing these unique fish to thrill other anglers. This is keeping fish selectively—what we call selective harvest.

Selective Harvest

Meanwhile, fishermen who want to eat fish must focus on readily expendable (renewable) species such as bluegills, crappies, perch, and bullheads. Or they must focus on more numerous size classes of larger predatory fish. In most cases, 25-inch-plus walleyes should be released because they are fewer in number and have surmounted great odds to grow so large. Instead, keep several 16-inch walleyes to eat. Usually only a few walleyes are needed as the focal point for a fine meal. This, too, is keeping fish selectively—selective harvest.

Catch-and-release, while important, should not be a knee-jerk reaction to every fishing situation, for at times catch-and-release is unnecessary and can actually do more harm than good. The object is to release the right fish to sustain good fishing while keeping more members of fish populations to eat.

It's vital to maintain a tradition of eating fish. And it's vital to encourage a new tradition of releasing the right fish. This blends an old tradition with a new focus on keeping fish selectively—selective harvest.

Catch-and-release was the watchword of the 1980s and 1990s. But the phrase and the idea are but a single component of selective harvest, that more comprehensive approach to using fish resources today. Selective harvest is a simple, sensible solution to many of the fishery resource problems that face our maturing and increasingly sophisticated fishing world, a world that faces challenges on many fronts. Not the least of these challenges is teaching the importance of using natural resources wisely in a world where antiharvest groups are becoming more vocal.

Selective harvest, then, is a concept of common sense and balance. It incorporates many ideas about handling walleyes correctly, whether they are to be released or taken home and eaten. We offer, in closing, our perspectives on handling walleyes and cleaning and caring for the catch—all important elements in selective harvest.

HANDLING WALLEYES

Gill Cover Hold—The best hold depends on size. To net or lift a walleye weighing less than about 2½ pounds, try the gill cover hold. Slide your hand forward from the rear of the fish, bringing your palm up over the dorsal fin, which usually is erect. Place your thumb and index finger over the fish's gill flaps and hold it firmly but without squeezing too hard. Place your fingers directly on the fleshy cheeks, which lie just ahead of the sharp bony plate. This pressure helps to immobilize the fish somewhat, making it easy to remove hooks and then release the fish or pop it into the livewell.

Gill Lift—If the walleye's over about 2½ pounds, slide an index finger inside the gill flap and raise the fish vertically from the net or the water. This is the lift you often see in *Walleye In-Sider* magazine and *In-Fisherman* magazine—the one Al Lindner uses to show off his lunker 'eyes on TV.

Place your right index finger inside the fish's right gill flap to show off its left side. And grasp the left gill flap with your left index finger. This isn't blind groping, mind you. Slide your finger along the bony interior wall of the gill flap, staying away from the delicate gills and their supporting tissues.

You won't damage the fish because this tissue can support lots of weight. It feels as if you're holding a triangle by its apex; your finger slides to the top, and the fish is secured. You usually don't need to pinch your thumb on the outside of the gill cover because this position seems to sedate the fish. Walleyes rarely flip violently when held this way. From the Gill Lift position, raise the tail with your other hand for a photo or to help release the fish.

Belly Lift—When you're fishing with crankbaits, keep your fingers away from all those hooks until you have complete control. Some In-Fisherman staff members prefer to net crankbait-caught fish. Others prefer not to net them because the hooks tangle in the mesh. To do a Belly Lift, first tire the walleye and bring it alongside the boat. Reach around the fish and press it lightly against the boat hull. Feel with your hand to find the fish's balance point near the center of its belly.

Then lift the walleye straight out of the water. The resulting pressure on its belly helps to quiet the fish. Once it's boated, adjust to a Gill Lift position or cradle the fish with your left hand and forearm and remove hooks with the right. The Belly Lift works best with fish over about 3 pounds. The weight creates more downward pressure and a more definitive balance point. Handling walleyes this way, though, you'll find that a fair share of them eventually end up on the boat floor.

Body Grab—The Body Grab works to take bigger walleyes from the net or to pick them off the deck, but it shouldn't be used on fish you intend to release. For this hold, move your hand backward from the fish's head, pressing down the dorsal fin. Firmly clasp the fish across the back, squeezing its ribs.

This hold works fine on walleyes from 1 to about 5 pounds, depending on the size of your hand and the strength of your grip. The problem is that the hold removes the slime coat from the gripped area and may also damage tissues under the skin. We've caught walleyes that anglers held this way and then released, and they had patches of fungus in the shape of a hand. Some of these fish succumbed to disease. This is a quick way, however, to move lots of fish from a livewell.

Other Considerations—When walleyes are netted, they often thrash wildly after they're first taken from the water. Wait a few seconds, leaving the fish in the bag of the net. When it quiets, make your move to perform a Gill Lift. Walleyes often remain nearly motionless, just curling their bodies a bit to show off their white tail.

Speaking of nets, to minimize snagged hooks, use models with large mesh coated in rubber or plastic. But the net shouldn't be so stiff that it scrapes a fish's eyes.

WEIGHING WALLEYES WITHOUT A SCALE

We're often asked about estimating walleye weight. "How much did that 33-inch weigh that I released last year?" The answer varies, based on how the fish is measured.

If you didn't measure the fish's girth (maximum circumference of the body), try this formula:

$$\text{Weight (pounds)} = \frac{\text{Length (inches)}^3}{2{,}700}$$

A 29-incher weighs 24,389 (29 x 29 x 29) divided by 2,700, or 9.0 pounds. In other words, a 33-incher weighs 13.31 pounds. This formula provides an estimate based on the average proportions of a walleye. Adjust up or down slightly for unusually fat or thin fish.

Biologists studying a fish population often calculate a length-weight relationship based on measurements of a large sample of many-size fish. They transform the lengths and weights to base-10 logarithms and calculate a regression line. Weights can be estimated from the equation:

$$\log W = \log a + b \times \log L$$

Where:
log W = base-10 logarithm of weight
log a = a population-specific intercept
b = the slope of the regression line
log L = base-10 logarithm of length

For example, the relationship for a large sample of walleyes from Lake Erie is:
log W (grams) = -6.151 + 3.43 x log L (millimeters).

For a 29-inch (737-millimeter) walleye, the equation calculates:
log W = -6.151 + 3.43 x 2.867
log W = 9.835 - 6.151 = 3.684 = 4,835 grams = 10.66 pounds.

For you mathematicians, Ed Migdalski provides the basis for the length-girth equation in his book *The Inquisitive Angler* (Lyons & Burford). First, consider a fish as two half wedges placed together in the middle. The volume of a fish is the area of a cross section at its point of maximum girth times half its length (the length of one half wedge). Squaring the circumference of a circle yields an area 16 times the circle's area (a cross section of the fish at its maximum girth). Squaring the girth and dividing by 16 thus yields the area of a cross section.

Multiply the area of this section by half its length (the length of one half wedge), and you have the cubic volume of the fish.

$$\frac{\text{Girth (inches)}^2}{16} \times \frac{\text{Length (inches)}}{2} = \text{Cubic Volume (cubic inches)}$$

The specific gravity of a fish is about 1.15, so 25 cubic inches of fish weigh 29 cubic inches of water, which weighs one pound. Divide the cubic inches in a fish by 25, and you get its weight in pounds.

$$\frac{\text{Girth (inches)}^2}{16} \times \frac{\text{Length (inches)}}{2} \times \frac{1}{25} = \text{Weight (pounds)}$$

Dr. Brian Murphy and colleagues at Texas A & M University calculated a standard equation for all walleyes based on North American average lengths and weights. They translated this into U.S. nonmetric units for easier use by anglers.

log W (pounds) = -3.642 + 3.18 x log L (inches). Using this formula, a 29-incher weighs:

log W = -3.642 + 3.18 x (log 29)

log W = -3.642 + 3.18 x 1.462

log W = 4.65 - 3.642 = 1.008 = 10.17 pounds.

You don't have to understand logarithms; just punch the log and antilog buttons on your calculator. The Gator Grip Golden Rule walleye board uses this standard equation.

If you measure length and girth, use the formula:

$$\text{Weight (pounds)} = \frac{\text{Girth (inches)}^2 \times \text{Length (Inches)}}{800}$$

A 29-incher with a 15-inch girth weighs 8.16 pounds (15 x 15 x 29, divided by 800). A 29-incher with a 16-inch girth weighs 9.28 pounds. Use of girth should make this method more accurate than the previous one.

Perhaps you'll prefer another formula, which is reported to work exclusively and accurately for walleyes:

$$\frac{\text{Length (Inches)} \times \text{Girth (inches)}}{46} = \text{Weight (pounds)}$$

We don't know the derivation but find it quite accurate for large walleyes (see table), although it tends to overestimate the weight of small fish and to underestimate the weight of huge fish. For the 29-incher with a 15-inch girth, this formula yields 9.46 pounds and 10.09 pounds for a fish with a 16-inch girth.

These formulas yield weight in decimals (tenths and hundredths of a pound). To convert to ounces, multiply the number to the right of the decimal point by 16, rounding off when necessary.

THE FORMULA FOR ...

Pike: $\dfrac{\text{Length}^3}{3500}$

Walleye: $\dfrac{\text{Length}^3}{2700}$

Bass: $\dfrac{\text{Length}^3}{1600}$

Bluegill: $\dfrac{\text{Length}^3}{1200}$

Walleye Weight Chart

$$\text{Weight (pounds)} = \frac{\text{Length (inches)} \times \text{Girth (inches)}}{46}$$

Length	Girth 14"	16"	18"	20"	22"
28"	8-8	9-12	10-15	12-3	13-6
29"	8-13	10-1	11-6	12-10	13-14
30"	9-2	10-7	11-12	13-1	14-6
31"	9-7	10-13	12-2	13-8	14-13
32"	9-12	11-2	12-8	13-15	15-5
33"	10-1	11-8	12-15	14-6	15-13
34"	10-6	11-13	13-5	14-13	16-4
35"	10-10	12-3	13-11	15-3	16-12

With the formulas on the left, estimate the weight of walleyes or other species using just a length measurement. The formula and chart on the right provides a more accurate estimate for large walleyes when girth is also measured.

CARING FOR YOUR CATCH

As we have said, walleyes are nutritious and delicious, and most walleye populations are renewable if harvested wisely. To most walleye anglers, though, conservation implies protecting habitat and releasing fish. Those are important topics. But wise use of walleyes that are kept so that they aren't wasted is also a conservation measure—not to mention plain common sense.

A fine meal is the perfect end to most fishing trips. Walleyes are delicious baked, broiled, steamed, poached, or fried. How good they taste, however, depends on how well they're cared for from the time they're caught until they're cooked.

Walleye flesh is fragile. It begins to deteriorate if the fish is roughly handled and stressed before it dies. In cold water, walleyes seem hearty because they live so long on a stringer or in a livewell. But when poorly handled, their flesh may bruise, and bruised flesh doesn't taste good.

Keeping walleyes healthy before cleaning is one step to better tasting fish. The flesh deteriorates even more quickly after the fish dies, especially if it's mishandled.

Bacterial growth is a principal enemy of fresh fish. Ensure fine table quality by retarding bacterial growth. Once walleyes die, gut them, making sure not to let their sour, bacteria-filled stomach and intestinal juices touch the flesh. Wash fish in cold water to remove bacteria. Then place them on ice to retard bacterial growth. We address this process later in this chapter. First let's pause to clean our catch.

CLEANING THE CATCH

Learning to release healthy fish successfully and keeping wounded fish for the table are a sensible approach to modern fishing. This blend of catching and releasing the healthy and keeping the injured can be a workable option for sophisticated fishermen. To be sure the fish we keep aren't wasted, here's how to clean the catch.

Tools—Tools needed to clean fish successfully depend on the cleaning method. Filleting is popular, but so are scaling and dressing and skinning and dressing.

The basis for cleaning fish rests with a fillet knife about 6 inches long and a sharpening stone and steel to keep the knife working properly. If you clean fish of many sizes, however, the addition of a knife with a 4-inch blade and one with a 9-inch blade makes cleaning fish more efficient.

One favorite method is scaling and filleting.

To enjoy baked and stuffed fish, it's necessary to know how to butterfly fish. Other baking methods call for gilled and gutted whole fish. Poaching and steaming also call for filleted or gilled and gutted whole fish, although steaked fish will work, too. Smoking usually calls for steaked, chunked, or gilled and gutted whole fish. Pan-size dressed fish or fillets work as well.

Basic tools include a fillet knife, sharpening stone and steel, fish scaler, and perhaps a fish skinner and fillet board. Or you can go a step farther and add fillet knives with different blade sizes (4-, 6-, and 9-inch blades), a protective fish cleaning glove, electric fish scaler, electric knife, and perhaps a fancy fish cleaning board.

Knives—If you're buying only one knife, a 6-inch blade is probably best. Knives with different blade sizes are helpful. Match the knife to the task. Many people prefer to use an electric knife to fillet fish, especially for a mess of bigger fish.

Stone and Steel—A stone sharpens blade edges and a steel realigns them. A good knife stays sharp for a long time, but its edge may need realigning during each cleaning session.

Sharpen a fillet knife by drawing it at a 10° to 15° angle across a fine-grade oiled honing stone. Realign edges by drawing the knife at the same angle across the steel. Use the same number and type of strokes on each side of the blade.

Scaler—A scaler can be as simple as a spoon or as advanced as an electric scaler. A spoon or even the edge of a knife works well on easy-to-scale fish like crappies. For walleyes, perch, bluegills, and the like, something with more backbone is necessary.

If you have lots of or difficult fish to scale, try a heavy-duty electric fish scaler from Bear Paw Tackle Company (4904 Aero Park Dr., Bellaire, MI 49615, 616/533-8604).

To reduce flying scales, you can scale fish while holding them under water, for example, in a water-filled sink. Of course, don't do that with an electric fish scaler. Another option is to scale fish inside a paper sack or garbage bag. After you've scaled a fish, pinch the top of the sack shut and give the bag a snap so the scales drop to the bottom of the sack.

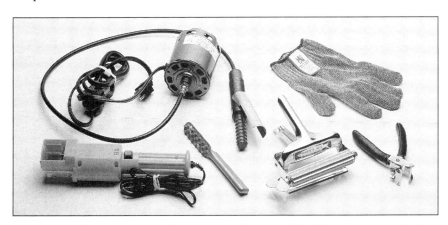

These products make fish cleaning more pleasant. The fish scalers include electric models. The Bear Paw is at the top. The hand-powered model is from Valley Ordnance. The crank skinner is from Townsend, while the pincher model (complete with sharp edge for cutting smooth-skinned fish like catfish) is from Jackson Fishing. Finally, a Kevlar glove makes cutting your hand almost impossible.

Fish Skinners—With the advent of filleting and the current preference for fillets, fish skinners may seem unnecessary. Pincher models remain the standard for skinning bullheads and catfish.

Today's models often have a sharp edge to eliminate the need for a knife. One model is the Fish Skinner with Cutter made by Jackson Fishing and Sporting (23391 Hwy. 370 W, Falkner, MS 38629, 601/837-9089). To use it, grab a walleye by the head; make a slit down the body from just behind the head to the belly on each side; skin the fish; break the neck; pull the body back and rip off the belly meat. Even if you fillet most of your fish, including bullheads and catfish, a pincher-type skinner is handy at the cleaning table. Another fine product is the ProSkinner (Sunset Sports Ltd., POB 493, Beaver Dam, WI 53916, 800/951-2416).

The old reliable Townsend Fish Skinner is an option, too. The Townsend peels a fish like an orange and leaves it neatly dressed, ready for the pan (Townsend Engineering Co., 2425 Huebell Ave., Des Moines, IA 50317, 515/265-8181).

Cleaning Glove—Made from the same material as a bulletproof vest, Kevlar gloves allow you to use a knife without cutting your hand.

Using a Knife—A knife is the centerpiece for cleaning fish. Knives are built to function like the muscles in your body. Muscular movement begins with larger muscles, then progresses to smaller muscles or muscle groups. A hook set, for example, begins with the large leg, butt, and back muscles. Then in rapid succession, smaller shoulder and upper arm muscles work and quickly pass the action to the small muscles in the lower arm and fingers.

Contaminant Concentration

The table quality of your catch is influenced by where you fish. For example, algae blooms may affect some lakes and ponds during summer. Some algae species produce chemicals that give fish a muddy taste. Use an appropriate recipe to cover this flavor. Or fish elsewhere.

Many waters harbor contaminants that transfer to fish. Some bodies of water are monitored and health advisories are posted. But many other waters aren't monitored. Use cleaning procedures that reduce the contaminant levels in fish to help them keep longer and taste better.

Many contaminants are bound into the fatty belly flaps, backstrap, and lateral line tissues. These areas taste strong and tend to turn rancid faster than leaner surrounding tissue. Remove them.

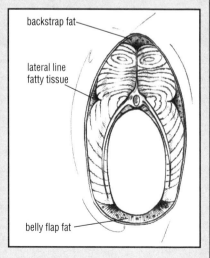

backstrap fat

lateral line fatty tissue

belly flap fat

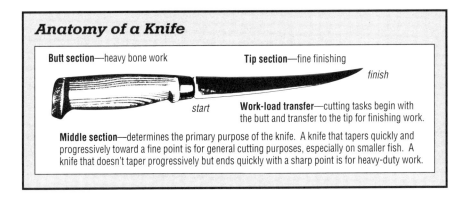

Anatomy of a Knife

Butt section—heavy bone work

Tip section—fine finishing

finish

start

Work-load transfer—cutting tasks begin with the butt and transfer to the tip for finishing work.

Middle section—determines the primary purpose of the knife. A knife that tapers quickly and progressively toward a fine point is for general cutting purposes, especially on smaller fish. A knife that doesn't taper progressively but ends quickly with a sharp point is for heavy-duty work.

Bigger muscles start work; finer muscles finish it. Larger muscles are for larger, coarser tasks; finer muscles are for smaller, finer tasks. So it is with the design and use of a knife. The heavier, thicker butt is designed to handle coarse, heavy work; the smaller, finer tip is for finishing work.

Fillet knives should have a heavy butt, tapering progressively toward a small point. Fillet knives that taper less progressively are designed for heavier fillet work.

At the Cleaning Table: General Procedure—At the cleaning table or wherever you clean your catch, cleanliness is critical. Be sure to have ice available for fish that have already been chilled and to cool fish that are still alive when they reach the cleaning table (see "Chilling Fish," p. 162).

Photo 1

Let's say you'll be filleting your catch. At the cleaning table, you'll need these:

1. Cleaning utensils, including fillet knives and sharpening tools, plus a bowl of cold water (add ice cubes) to soak fillets in briefly to remove blood and bacteria *(Photo 1)*.

2. Clean paper towels for wiping slime from fish and keeping the fillet board clean. Pat fillets dry after they've soaked if you don't plan to freeze them. (A solution of 1 teaspoon vinegar to 3 quarts water helps cut fish slime.)

3. Packing material for freezing or refrigerating fish.

Proceed—

1. If fish are alive, dispatch them with a sharp blow to the head, then bleed them *(Photo 2)*.

2. Remove the fillets, being careful not to rupture the digestive tract with your knife.

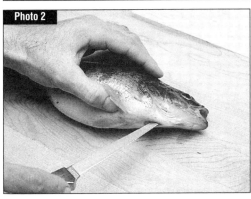

Photo 2

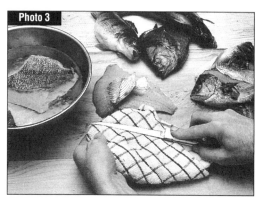

Photo 3

3. Place fillets in cold water to help remove blood and bacteria. With lean fish such as catfish, pike, or walleyes, add 1/2 teaspoon salt to help neutralize acids and draw out blood.

4. Discard the carcass, wipe the board and knife clean *(Photo 3)*, and start on another fish. Replace the water in the bowl when it begins to thicken with fish juices.

Filleting Fish—The butt of a fillet knife does the heavy work and the point, the detailed work. The first cut behind the gill covers and down to the bone of a fish on its side can be made most efficiently by using the butt and middle of the knife. Do not use the tip.

Likewise, the cut that removes the fillet from the backbone is made most efficiently with the butt of the knife laid close to the dorsal fin on one side and close to the backbone on the other side. The heavy part of the knife is used for cutting through the heaviest flesh and bones.

Now start a rib removal cut with the heavy butt of the knife, but quickly transfer the work to the middle and finally to the tip of the knife.

Fillets can be fried, broiled, poached, baked, steamed, and used in casseroles, stews, and soups. Fillets cook faster and more thoroughly than pan cuts. The result is tastier flesh, in the opinion of most experts.

Basic Filleting—Filleting is the most popular method for cleaning most fish. The steps are easy but require practice to master.

Basic Filleting

(1) Make the initial cut at an angle just behind the pectoral fin. Cut with the scales, not through them. Include as much of the loin as possible where the neck meets the back of the head. Cut down to the backbone, lift the dorsal (back) portion of the fish slightly, and turn the knife blade toward the tail of the fish.

(2) Making certain to use the butt section of the knife to cut through the rib cage, slide the knife along the backbone toward the tail. Lead with the butt of the knife, making sure to cut as close as possible to the backbone so little meat is wasted.

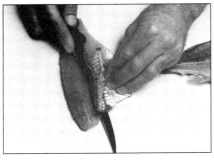

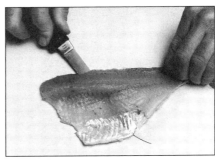

(3) Remove the rib cage by leading with the butt or middle of the knife and finishing with the middle or tip of the knife. The knife blade should slip just below the ribs, cutting through the epipleural ribs in the process.

(4) If the fish hasn't been scaled, remove the skin by sliding the blade of the knife between the skin and the fillet. Again, lead with the butt of the knife, beginning either at the head or tail end of the fillet.

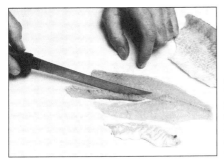

(5) For perfectly boneless fillets from bony fish except pike, trout, and salmon, remove the epipleural ribs. The epipleurals are small rib bones that lie at right angles to the main ribs, along the upper portion of the rib cage. Remove them with a V-cut. Feel for the ribs and then make as fine a cut as possible to remove only the epipleurals.

Pan Dressing

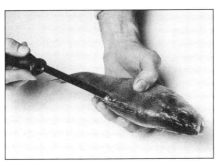

(1) Insert the knife point under the skin at the rear of one side of the dorsal fin. Slide the knife forward just under the skin beyond the front of the dorsal fin.

(2) Make a fillet cut in back of the head. Use the tip of your knife to cut along the ventral (stomach) portion of the fish, around the anal pore, and along the pelvic fin.

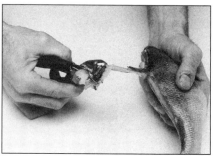

(3) Grab the pelvic fin and rip it forward. Remove the offal along with the pelvic fin, and tear the head off the fish.

(4) Remove the dorsal fin.

(5) If the fish has been scaled, it is pan ready. If you prefer to skin the fish, peal it with a Townsend skinner.

(6) The skinned, pan-ready fish.

Butterflying (Method 1)

(1) After scaling the fish, make a fillet cut along one side, taking care not to cut through the belly portion. At this point, remove the fish's intestines and stomach.

(2) Turn the fish and remove the fillet from the other side.

(3) Remove the primary ribs. The epipleurals can also be removed, but be careful not to cut through the skin.

(4) The final product. The butterfly fillet can be fried and then drizzled with your favorite white sauce.

(5) Try stuffing the fillet with your favorite stuffing (even cooked Stove-Top works) or vegetables (precooked). Bake the stuffed fillet after wrapping it with bacon strips.

Butterflying (Method 2)

(1) After scaling the fish, cut along the backbone and down to the rib cage on one side of the fish.

(2) Work your way along and around the rib cage, taking care not to cut through the skin on the side of or along the stomach of the fish.

(3) Cut along the backbone toward the tail of the fish, again being careful not to cut through the skin beneath the fillet. Repeat this procedure on the other side of the fish.

(4) The final product. Stuff and bake.

CHILLING FISH

Gutting walleyes bleeds them, and blood left in flesh speeds deterioration. After gutting fish, rinse them in cold water and then surround them with crushed ice. Don't let fish soak in water, even cold water. Crushed ice is best for chilling fish. It packs closer and cools quicker than large blocks of ice or frozen bottles of water. Crushed ice keeps fish for up to three days, although the table quality of their flesh deteriorates each day. To keep fish on ice longer, use super-chilling.

Super-chilling—Super-chilled fish can be kept on ice for up to 5 and perhaps

7 days. To super-chill, first line the bottom of an insulated cooler with several inches of crushed ice, leaving the drain open. In another container, mix coarse ice-cream salt and crushed ice at a ratio of 1 to 20. For average-size coolers, that's 1 pound of salt to 20 pounds of ice.

Wrap fillets or pan-dressed fish in plastic wrap. Layer the fish in the ice chest, making sure to surround each fish with plenty of salted ice. Super-chilling lowers the temperature to about 30°F. Replenish salted ice as it melts.

Packaging for the Refrigerator— The best way to keep fish in a refrigerator is in crushed ice. Fill a bowl with crushed ice and surround the fish with ice. Cover the bowl with cling wrap (Saran-type wrap). Drain the water occasionally so the fish doesn't sit in water. Keep the fish very cold and nearly dry.

The temperature of most refrigerators is near 40°F. To keep fish on ice in a refrigerator, you want to lower the temperature of the fish to about 34°F, which allows several additional days of storage, depending on how fresh the fish were when refrigerated.

Another method works when you don't have ice, although not as well as the

Method 1—Fill a bowl half full with ice and place the fish on the ice. Cover the fish with more ice and the bowl with cling wrap. Periodically drain the melt-water. Fish stored in crushed ice (32°F) keep longer than fish stored at the usual refrigerator temperature of 40°F.

Method 2—Remove the fillets and pat them dry with a towel. Sprinkle water droplets onto a clean dry towel so it's damp but not wet. Line a bowl with the damp towel and place the fillets on the towel. Use cling wrap to seal the bowl. The fish will keep for up to 3 days.

crushed ice method. Pat clean fillets dry with paper towels. Moisten a clean dish towel. Line the bottom of a bowl with the towel and spread the fillets on top. Cover the bowl with cling wrap. This keeps the fillets cold and moist but not sloppy wet. Never keep fish in a plastic bag, soaking in water containing their juices.

FREEZING FISH

Too many fishermen use the wrong type of packaging, keep fish in the freezer too long, and store them at the wrong temperature. Properly frozen fish keep well and hold their flavor for months, although the quality of fish flesh deteriorates the longer it's frozen.

Fish flesh deteriorates in the freezer through dehydration and oxidation. "Freezer burn" (whitish, leather-tough flesh) is an advanced stage of dehydration. Freezer burn results from using the wrong wrap or wrapping improperly. When the wrap doesn't seal in moisture effectively, fish flesh loses its moisture and turns tough.

Oxidation is also caused by poor packaging. Using the wrong wrap or failing to remove air from the package before freezing causes oxygen to combine with polyunsaturated fats and oils in the flesh. These fats turn rancid in the presence of oxygen.

Packaging Materials—Seal packaged fish to hold in moisture and lock out oxygen. Be sure to remove any air surrounding the flesh.

Some popular materials do a poor job. Polyethylene, the material used in bread wrappers, fails the test. Waxed paper and cellophane are other popular wraps that don't measure up. Each is too porous.

Aluminum foil works, although it punctures easily. It's best used as a final wrap on top of cling wrap. Polyvinylidene chloride, from which cling wraps such as Saran Wrap are made, forms good barriers and clings to fish, eliminating air pockets. It's the best initial wrap. Wrap fish in cling wrap, making sure to remove the air from the wrap, then follow with another layer of cling wrap, and finally a layer of wax-coated freezer wrap.

Bags sold as "freezer bags" are good, too, especially as outer bags. They form barriers against the transmission of air or moisture. They're harder to wrap tightly around fillets, however, so air pockets are more likely to result from their use. To minimize that, plunge the

Packaging materials for freezing divided into those that work and those that don't. Those that work when used correctly include polyvinylidene chloride cling wraps, aluminum foil, Tupperware-type containers, polyester freezer bags, and wax-coated freezer paper. Wax paper and polyethylene plastic bags (like bread bags) don't lock water vapor in and oxygen out.

One of the best ways to freeze fish is to tightly wrap it in cling wrap or aluminum foil. Follow with a secondary wrapping of freezer wrap. Write the contents and date of packaging on the outside.

filled bags in water to force air out. Seal the bags underwater. Leaving a little water in the bags is better than leaving air.

Finally, wax-coated freezer wrap prevents oxygen and water vapor from passing through to the fish. This material is difficult to make airtight and waterproof, however, so use it as a final wrap on top of initial wraps with cling wrap. Write date frozen, fish type, size, and other information on the outside of the package.

Freezing in Water—Commercially frozen fish is often glazed with a coating of ice to protect the flavor and table quality. The temperature of home freezers can't be set low enough to accomplish this. But you can seal your fish in water.

Place fish into a polyester freezer bag and submerge the bag in water to squeeze out the air, or add a small amount of water to the bag to help force out the air. Seal the bag.

Pack the fish tightly in plastic containers (such as Tupperware) and fill the containers almost to the brim with water. Use enough water to cover the fish, but don't leave large empty spaces for water, because water (1) draws nutrients from the fish and causes the fish to freeze more slowly; and (2) crushes the fish when the water freezes. Pack the container with as much fish as possible, minimizing empty spaces. Then seal remaining spaces with water. If fish portions protrude from the ice after freezing, add a little more water and refreeze.

Fat Content and Storage Life

SPECIES	STORAGE TIME
lake trout, rainbow trout, whitefish, carp, catfish, ciscoes, smelt, pike	3 to 5 months
suckers, chinook salmon, coho salmon, white bass	5 to 8 months
walleyes, yellow perch, bass, burbot, crappies, bluegills	8 to 12 months

Source: *Fixin' Fish*, University of Minnesota Press.

Fish with high fat content generally become rancid quicker than lean fish when frozen. Exceptions include ciscoes, smelt, and pike, which may not withstand frozen storage as well as other fish of similar fat content. On the other hand, king and coho salmon, with their relatively high fat content, store better than fish with less fat. Always keep your freezer as cold as possible.

Freezing Tips
- Divide cleaned fish into serving-size portions to eliminate leftover thawed fish.
- The faster fish freezes, the better. Place packages in the coldest part of your freezer and don't overload it. Keep the temperature at 0°F, if possible.
- Thawing fish at room temperature allows thawed parts to deteriorate while frozen parts thaw. Instead, thaw frozen fish in the refrigerator, allowing 24 hours for a 1-pound package. Or place frozen fish in cold water until it's thawed while keeping it in its vapor-proof wrapping.
- Refreezing thawed fish causes a big loss in table quality. Freezing breaks cell walls, which is why frozen fish is less firm than fresh fish. The flesh turns to mush when refrozen.
- Fish like walleye, with low fat content, may hold its flavor well when frozen for as long as 6 months. Be sure, however, to remove fatty areas and to package the fish properly.

FIT FOR THE TABLE

Look at pictures of fish on stringers. Do they look colorful, alive, and kicking? Those fish on a stringer probably shouldn't be released, but they're fit for the table. Or are their eyes set and sunken, skin discolored, scales loose, and gills white and slimy? Those fish have spoiled.

Times have changed. Just as we now know more about catching fish, we also know more about keeping them properly.

Spoiling Fast!

This early 1970s photo shows Al Lindner and friends with a full stringer, the old way of holding fish. But they die quickly and start to spoil. It's best to keep fish alive until just before they're cleaned. Immediately gut and gill, wash, and transfer them to ice. Other options for keeping fish include livewells, fish baskets (panfish), and nylon or burlap keep sacks.

Nutrient Value

Fish	Calories	Percent Protein	Percent Fat	Sodium (mg)
Burbot (Eelpout, Lawyer)	80	17	0.9	—
Carp	125	17	5.9	44
Catfish	119	18	5.2	60
Clams	63	11	1.7	190
Cod	74	17	0.5	67
Flounder	88	18	1.4	54
Freshwater Drum (Sheepshead)	—	17	5.5	—
Haddock	77	18	0.5	98
Halibut (Pacific)	119	19	4.3	71
Herring (Lake)	—	19	3.3	—
Lake Trout	169	17	11.1	43
Northern Pike	—	19	1.2	52
Oysters (Eastern)	68	8	1.8	160
Perch (Yellow)	85	19	1.1	63
Rainbow Trout	154	21	6.8	43
Salmon (Chinook)	182	18	11.6	42
Salmon (Coho)	148	21	6.6	—
Shrimp	86	20	0.4	155
Smelt	86	17	3.9	80
Suckers	—	21	1.8	53
Tuna	122	24	2.2	76
Walleye	89	19	1.5	—
Whitefish	121	19	5.2	52
Other Common Foods				
Beef Steak	266	17	26.0	61
Beef Liver	141	22	5.0	33
Pork	298	17	24.7	60
Chicken	127	23	7.0	—
Lamb	186	15	13.5	52
Cheddar Cheese (1 oz.)	113	7.1	9.1	198
Egg (1)	80	6	6.0	70
Whole Milk (1 cup)	159	8	8.5	122

Source: Adapted from information supplied by the National Marine Fisheries Service, U.S. Department of Agriculture, *Nutritive Value of American Foods in Common Units* (Agriculture Handbook No. 456, 1975) and Jeff Gunderson, *Fixin' Fish* (University of Minnesota Press). The calculations are for 3½-ounce portions.

This chart shows the nutritional value of a select portion of your catch. Fish—walleyes in particular—are nutritious: high in vitamins, minerals, and protein, low in calories and fat.

Of course, no such chart exists that purports to measure deliciousness. Walleyes are close to 9.9 on a 10-point scale.

A Pound of Walleye

Dr. Dave Willis, professor of fisheries at South Dakota State University, Brookings, and fisheries student Brian Van Zee determined that the fillet weights for a range of walleye lengths can help anglers decide what size of fish to keep. They also were curious about walleye anglers' size preferences because these had implications for management. The walleyes used in their tests were caught in natural lakes in eastern South Dakota. Fillets without rib bones were weighed. Weights obtained at a given length varied a bit because of differences in filleting techniques and fish plumpness.

They found that a 14-inch walleye weighing close to 1 pound produces only about 0.3 pounds of fillet. Fillet weights climb quickly as fish length increases. A 22-inch walleye produces about 1.5 pounds of fillet. Dress-out weight (fillet weight divided by total fish weight) averaged 33.8 percent for the fish we filleted.

Surprisingly, the dress-out weight percentage increased only slightly with fish length. For walleyes measuring 12 to 16 inches, dress-out weight averaged 32.4 percent, while dress-out weight increased to 35 percent for fish 17 inches or longer.

This fillet weight information relates to length limits in two ways. Consider an angler who likes to eat walleyes and isn't supportive of length limits. If that angler harvests two 13-inch walleyes, their four fillets will weigh approximately 0.44 pounds. One 16-inch walleyes produces more fillet weight than two 13-inch fish. One 19-incher produces as much fillet

weight as four 13-inch fish. Anglers who consider walleyes a food fish may therefore decide to support moderate length limits if the regulation will improve the sizes of walleyes.

Secondly, consider an angler who enjoys catching walleyes, even if they must be released, but who also likes to eat a few fish now and then. Perhaps that angler fishes a body of water with a limited number of larger walleyes and an abundance of smaller fish. The angler would like to keep fish for a meal but doesn't want to harvest larger fish. In this case, the angler may want to keep four 13-inch walleyes for a meal and release that 19-incher that's so rare in this population.

Glossary

Action: Measure of rod performance that describes the elapsed time between flexion and return to straight configuration; ranges from slow to fast; also refers to gearing of reels.

Algae: Simple plant organisms.

Alkalinity: Measure of the amount of acid neutralizing bases.

Anal Fin: Fin located on the ventral side of most fish between the urogenital pore and caudal fin.

Aggregation: Group of one species of fish within a limited area.

Backwater: Shallow area off a river.

Bag Limit: Restriction on the number of fish that an angler may harvest in a day.

Baitfish: Small fish often eaten by predators.

Bar: Long ridge in a body of water.

Bay: Major indentation in the shoreline of a lake or reservoir.

Bell Sinker: Pear-shaped sinker with brass eye on top.

Blank: Fishing rod without grip, guides, or finish.

Break: Distinct variation in otherwise constant stretches of cover, structure, or bottom type.

Breakline: Area of abrupt change in depth, bottom type, or water quality.

Cabbage: Any of several species of submerged weeds of the genus Potamogeton.

Canal: Manmade waterway for navigation.

Internal Anatomical Features Of A Walleye

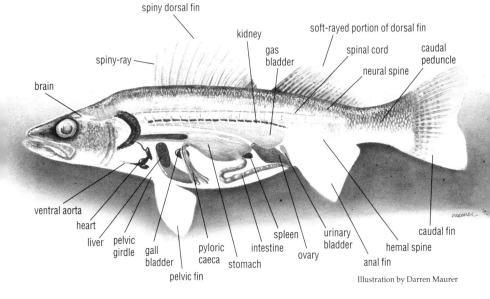

Illustration by Darren Maurer

Carrying Capacity: Maximum density of organisms that a body of water can sustain.

Catchability: Measure of the willingness of fish to bite lures or bait.

Caudal Fin: Fish's tail.

Channel: The bed of a stream or river.

Cline: Vertical or horizontal section of a body of water where water characteristics change abruptly.

Community: Group of interacting organisms within an area.

Coontail: Submerged aquatic plant of the hornwort family typically found in hard water; characterized by stiff, forked leaves.

Cove: An indentation along the shoreline of a lake or reservoir.

Cover: Natural or manmade objects on the bottom of lakes, rivers, or impoundments, especially those that influence fish behavior.

Crankbait: Lipped diving lure.

Creel Limit: The number of fish of a species or species group that an angler can retain or harvest in a day.

Crustacean: Hard-shelled, typically aquatic invertebrate.

Current: Water moving in one direction.

Dam: Manmade barrier to water flow.

Dark-Bottom Bay: Shallow, protected bay with a layer of dark organic material on the bottom that warms quickly in spring.

Dissolved Oxygen: Oxygen molecules dispersed in water.

Diurnal: Occurring within a 24-hour daily period.

Dorsal Fin: Fin located on center of fish's back.

Downfishing: Level of fishing pressure that reduces fishing quality and abundance of large fish.

Drag: System for allowing fish to pull line from reel while antireverse switch is engaged.

Drainage: The area drained by a river and all its tributaries.

Drop-Off: An area of substantial increase in depth.

Eddy: Area of slack water or reversed current in a stream or river.

Egg Sinker: Tapered, oblong sinker with a hole from end to end.

Epilimnion: Warm surface layer of a stratified lake or reservoir.

Eutrophic: Highly fertile waters characterized by warm, shallow basins.

Fecundity: Number of eggs produced by a female in a season.

Feeder Creek: Tributary to a stream.

Feeding Strategy: Set of behaviors used for capture and metabolism of prey.

Fertility: Degree of productivity of plants and animals.

Fingerling: Juvenile fish, usually from 1 to 3 inches long.

Fish Culture: Production of fish in hatcheries.

Fished Down: Fish population adversely affected by fishing pressure.

Fishery: Group of fish that support fishing.

Fishery Biologist: Person who studies interaction of fishermen and fisheries.

Fishing Pressure: Amount of angling on a body of water in a period of time, usually measured in hours per acre per year; its effects on fish populations.

Flat: Area of lake, reservoir or river characterized by little change in depth.

Float: Buoyant device for suspending bait.

Float Stop: Adjustable rubber bead or thread, set on line above float to determine fishing depth.

Fluorescent: Emits radiation when exposed to sunlight.

Forage: Something eaten; the act of eating.

Freeze-Out Lake: Shallow northern lake subject to fish kills in late winter due to oxygen depletion.

Freeze-Up: Short period when ice first covers the surface of a body of water.

Front: Weather system that causes changes in temperature, cloud cover, precipitation, wind, and barometric pressure.

Fry: Recently hatched fish; cooking method using heated oil.

Gamefish: Fish species pursued by anglers.

Gear Ratio: Measure of a reel's retrieve speed; the number of times the spool revolves for each complete turn of the handle.

Genetics: The study of mechanisms of heredity.

Gradient: Degree of slope in a stream or riverbed.

Habitat: Type of environment in which an organism usually lives.

Harvest: Remove fish with intent to eat.

Hole: Deep section of a stream or river.

Home Range (Area): Defined area occupied by an animal for most activities over an extended time period.

Hybrid: Offspring of two species or subspecies.

Hypolimnion: Deep, cool zone below the thermocline in a stratified lake or impoundment.

Ice-Out: Short period during which ice on a body of water completely melts.

Impoundment: Body of water formed by damming running water.

Invertebrate: Animal without a backbone.

Jig: Lure composed of leadhead with rigid hook, often with hair, plastic, rubber, or other dressings.

Lake: Confined area where water accumulates naturally.

Larva: Immature form of an organism.

Lateral Line: Sensory system of fish that detects low frequency vibrations in water.

Ledge: Sharp contour break in a river or reservoir.

Length Limit: Regulation that prohibits harvest of fish below, above, or within specified lengths.

Livebait: Any living animal used to entice fish to bite.

Livewell: Compartment in boat designed to keep fish alive.

Location: Where fish position themselves in response to the environment.

Management: Manipulation of biological system to produce a fishery goal.

Mesotrophic: Waters of intermediate fertility between eutrophic and oligotrophic.

Metalimnion: Term for thermocline.

Migration: Directed movement by large number of animals of one species.

Minnow Bait: Long, thin, minnow-shape wood or plastic lure designed to be fished on or near the surface.

Monofilament: Fishing line made from a single strand of synthetic fiber.

Mottled: Blotchy coloration.

Nares: Nostrils of fish or other aquatic vertebrates.

Native: Naturally present in an area.

Niche: The role of an organism in an ecological community.

Nymph: Larval form of an insect.

Olfaction: Sense of smell.

Oligotrophic: Infertile waters; geologically young; characterized by deep, cool, clear oxygenated waters and rocky basins.

Omnivore: Organism that eats a wide variety of items.

Opportunistic: Feeding strategy in which items are eaten according to availability.

Overharvest: A level of fish harvest from a body of water that substantially reduces abundance of catchable fish, particularly large fish.

Overwintering Area: Area where fish hold during winter, particularly in cold climates.

Panfish: Group of about 30 small warm-water sportfish; not including bullheads or catfish.

Pattern: A defined set of location and presentation factors that consistently produce fish.

Pectoral Fin: Paired fin usually located on fish's side behind the head.

Pelagic: Living in open, offshore waters.

Pelvic Fin: Paired fin usually located on lower body.

pH: A measure of hydrogen in concentration.

Phosphorescent: Ability to glow in the dark after exposure to a light source.

Photoperiod: Interval during a day when sunlight is present.

Photosynthesis: Process in which green plants convert carbon dioxide and water into sugar and oxygen in the presence of sunlight.

Phytoplankton: Tiny plants suspended in water.

Pitch: Sound determined by the frequency of sound waves.

Plankton: Organisms drifting in a body of water.

Plug: Solid-bodied wood or plastic lure.

Point: Projection of land into a body of water.

Polarized: Capability of breaking up sunlight into directional components.

Pool: Deep section of a stream or river.

Population: Group of animals of the same species within a geographical area that freely interbreed; level of abundance.

Postspawn: Period immediately after spawning; In-Fisherman calendar period between Spawn and Presummer.

Pound Test: System for measuring the strength of fishing line; the amount of pressure that will break a line.

Predator: Fish that often feed on other fish.

Presentation: Combination of bait or lure, rig, tackle, and technique used to catch fish.

Prespawn: Period prior to spawning; In-Fisherman calendar period between Winter and Spawn.

Prey: Fish often eaten by other fish species.

Quick-Strike Rig: European-style system for hooking live or dead baits; includes 2 hooks and allows hooks to be set immediately following a strike.

Radio Tag (Transmitter): Device emitting high-frequency radio signals which when attached to an animal indicates its location.

Range: Area over which a species is distributed.

Rattlebait: Hollow-bodied, sinking, lipless crankbaits that rattle loudly due to shot and slugs in the body cavity.

Ray: Bony segment supporting a fin.

Reservoir: Large manmade body of water.

Recruitment: Process by which fish hatch and grow to catchable size.

Reeds: Any of several species of tall, emergent aquatic weeds that grow in shallow zones of lakes and reservoirs.

Reef: Rocky hump in a body of water.

Resting Spot: Location used by fish not actively feeding.

Riffle: Shallow, fast flowing section of a stream or river.

Rig: Arrangement of components for bait fishing, including hooks, leader, sinker, swivel, beads.

Riprap: Large rocks placed along a bank.

Riverine: Having characteristics of a river.

Run: Straight, moderate-depth section of a stream or river with little depth change.

School: Group of fish of one species that move in unison.

Seiche: Oscillation of water level in a large lake or reservoir caused by strong directional winds.

Selective Harvest: Deciding to release or harvest fish, based on species, size, and relative abundance.

Sensory Organ: Biological system involved in sight, hearing, taste, smell, touch, or lateral line sense.

Set Rig: Rig that's cast or drifted into position on the bottom to await a strike.

Shot: Small, round sinkers pinched onto fishing line.

Silt: Fine sediment on the bottom of a body of water.

Sinkers: Variously shaped pieces of lead used to sink bait or lures.

Slip Float: Float with a hole from top to bottom for sliding freely on line.

Slip Sinker: Sinker with a hole for sliding freely on line.

Slot Limit: Type of regulation that prohibits harvesting fish within a specified length range.

Snag: Brush or tree in a stream or river.

Sonar: Electronic fishing aid that emits sound waves underwater and interprets them to depict underwater objects.

Spawn: Reproduction of fish; In-Fisherman calendar period associated with that activity.

Species: Group of potentially interbreeding organisms.

Spine: Stiff, sharp segment of fin.

Spoon: Any of a wide variety of metal, plastic, or wood lures with a generally spoonlike shape and a single hook.

Sportfish: Fish species pursued by anglers.

Stock: Place fish in a body of water; population of animals.

Stress: State of physiological imbalance caused by disturbing environmental factors.

Strike: Biting motion of a fish.

Strike Window (Zone): Conceptual area in front of a fish within which it will strike food items or lures.

Structure: Changes in the shape of the bottom of lakes, rivers, or impoundments, especially those that influence fish behavior.

Substrate: Type of bottom in a body of water.

Suspended Fish: Fish in open water hovering considerably above bottom.

Swim (Gas) Bladder: Organ of most bony fish that holds a volume of gas to make them neutrally buoyant at variable depths.

Tailwater: Area immediately downstream from a dam.

Temperature Tolerant: Able to function in a wide range of temperatures.

Terminal Tackle: Components of bait fishing system including hooks, sinkers, swivels, leaders.

Thermocline: Layer of water with abrupt change in temperature, occurring between warm surface layer (epilimnion) and cold bottom layer (hypolimnion).

Tracking: Following radio-tagged or sonic-tagged animals.

Trailer: A plastic skirt, grub, pork rind, live bait, or other attractor attached to a lure to entice fish.

Trailer Hook: An extra hook attached to the rear hook of a lure to catch fish that strike behind the lure.

Transducer: Electronic part of a sonar unit that emits and receives sound impulses and converts them to visual images.

Tributary: Stream or river flowing into a larger river.

Trigger: Characteristics of a lure or bait presentation that elicit a biting response in fish.

Trolling: Fishing method in which lures or baits are pulled by a boat.

Trolling Motor: Electric motor positioned on the bow or transom to push or pull a boat.

Trophic: Relating to the fertility of a body of water.

Turbid: Murky water discolored by suspended sediment.

Ultraviolet (UV) Light: Radiation with wavelengths shorter than 4,000 angstroms; beyond violet in the color spectrum.

Watershed: The region draining runoff into a body of water.

Weed: Aquatic plant.

Weedline (Weededge): Abrupt edge of a weedbed caused by a change in depth, bottom type, or other factor.

Wing Dam: Manmade earth or rock ridge to deflect current.

Winterkill: Fish mortality due to oxygen depletion under ice in late winter.

Year Class: Fish of one species hatched in a single year.

Zooplankton: Tiny animals suspended in water.

Index